Pelican Books
A Portrait of E

Ann Dummett was born in London in 1930, the daughter of Arthur Chesney, the character actor. She was educated in London and graduated from Somerville College, Oxford, where she was president of the University Liberal Club, a performer of comic songs for the E.T.C., and the first woman undergraduate to be invited to speak in the Oxford Union's Eights Week debate. She then married Michael Dummett, a philosopher and Fellow of All Souls, and they have three sons and two daughters. After fourteen years mainly devoted to the children at home with occasional articles contributed to the *Guardian*, she became Oxford's first full-time Community Relations Officer, but resigned in 1969, disillusioned with the Government's race policies. Since then she has taught black and white pupils in a College of Further Education and is doing research on race and history teaching for the Institute of Race Relations. Ann Dummett's other publications include numerous articles on race and a chapter (written jointly with Michael Dummett) on 'The Role of Government in Britain's Racial Crisis' in *Justice First* (ed. Donnelly).

Ann Dummett

A Portrait of English Racism

Penguin Books

Penguin Books Ltd, Harmondsworth,
Middlesex, England
Penguin Books Inc., 7110 Ambassador Road,
Baltimore, Maryland 21207, U.S.A.
Penguin Books Australia Ltd, Ringwood,
Victoria, Australia

First published 1973

Made and printed in Great Britain by
Richard Clay (The Chaucer Press) Ltd
Bungay, Suffolk
Set in Linotype Times

To my mother Kit Chesney
and to the memory of
my father Arthur Chesney

Contents

Introduction

I have not attempted to construct a theory or a system of race relations in England. I dislike and distrust the term 'race relations', though frequently forced to use it. It is one of those names like 'the Dark Ages' or 'Prehistoric Man' whose existence as a generally accepted description makes it impossible to see clearly, and therefore obviously impossible to evaluate, what is being described. It seems funny to me now that, as a child, I pictured the Dark Ages as a long, uneventful period when there was twilight all day long: lethargic peasants – a bit round-shouldered, like the figures adapted to the medallions in stained-glass windows – worked laboriously in the mud; monks spent all day copying things out in dimly lit monasteries; and everyone thought, spoke and behaved in mindless slow-motion. The Renaissance, on the other hand, looked like a time when the film camera speeded up: all over Italy, in particular, people were painting, chiselling, quarrelling, poisoning, loving and laughing in a blaze of sunlit Technicolor. It seems funny – and yet I have a strong suspicion that many people of considerable scholarship and sophistication allow their attitudes to the people of the past to be distorted by this kind of *naïveté*. Indeed, in the case of Prehistoric Man it is demonstrably true that highly intelligent and well-informed people were so completely deceived by their own theories about the past that they refused to accept physical evidence that conflicted with these theories; when cave paintings at Altamira were discovered in 1879, Cartailhac, the professor of prehistory at the University of Toulouse, denounced them as a fraud without even bothering to go and look at them, and Dr Jesus Carballo condemned them with the words, 'Primitive man was little more than a gorilla, incapable of conceiving arts and sciences.' Not until after the death of the discoverer of Altamira and further discoveries of paintings in Perigord was scepticism overcome, and eventually, in 1902, Cartailhac published a handsome refutation of his former views. But pride, and prejudice, are not unique to nineteenth-century prehistorians: we all suffer from them to some extent in forming our judgements. The important thing is to be aware of the possibility that they exist in us, and to be able to reassess our own opinions about other people, past and present, according to the evidence. The modern term 'race relations' implies that there are different races of man, and that they are sufficiently separate for sets of relationships between them to deserve study. Yet once we even introduce the word 'race' into a discussion of human relationships in political and social terms, instead of leaving it to the widely differing definitions under which it is used by biologists, ethnologists, anthropologists and historians, we are on dangerous ground. Race. in any discussion of social and political matters, is a term that means different things in different countries, and different things to individuals and groups within those countries. Race is a word in the language of racists; to the opponents of racism, it is not a word but a cloak of darkness, obscuring real distinctions and muffling the truth.

This, then, is not a book about race relations but about English people: the way they think about themselves, the values on the basis of which they make their judgements, and hence the way they think and act towards the human beings they do not regard as English. The problem of relationships between people of different physical appearance and diverse ancestry is, in this country, a problem of English attitudes and actions. It is the problem of racism; the doctrine that mankind is not one, but two, the naturally superior and the naturally deprived, divided by an arbitrary man-made rule which condemns children yet unborn to inferior status. Racism in England is little understood. Even now, there are many who deny its existence at all, since they are uneasily aware that it is something evil and they cannot face the possibility of its presence close at hand. But ignoring the facts in front of us, preferring the old beliefs in which we grew up even when the facts contradict them, is a sure way to be made fools of. It is also a sure way, in our present situation, of ensuring that injustice and unhappiness in this country are going to increase.

In the autumn of 1958 Lord Justice Salmon sentenced nine youths convicted of assault in the Notting Hill riots, with the words,

> You are a minute and insignificant section of the population who have brought shame on the district in which you lived, and have filled the whole nation with horror, indignation and disgust. Everyone, irrespective of the colour of their skin, is entitled to walk through our streets with heads erect and free from fear. This is a right which these courts will always unfailingly uphold.

In the spring of 1970 gangs of youths were reported to be systematically attacking Pakistanis and their homes in another part of London, Tower Hamlets. One Pakistani was murdered by having his throat cut. Fifty youths marched down Brick Lane a week or two later, smashing windows and beating people up. There has been no report of court proceedings. Independent Television, however, invited a group of youths to appear in a programme, in which they described how they went out 'Paki-bashing'. A report on the situation by four social workers, quoted in the *Sunday Times* of 19 April, remarked that not all skinheads indulged in Paki-bashing. Although the average young person might be prejudiced against the Pakistanis, he was unlikely to attack them. However, he might lose this restraint if he joined a gang. 'What is disturbing', adds the report (evidently having accepted the state of affairs reported so far as normal rather than 'disturbing'), 'is that some parents do not disguise their prejudices and are encouraging their children to show contempt towards Pakistanis.

The tensions this causes have been reflected in the local secondary school, and we suspect that some Pakistani children are afraid to go to school.'

A very great change has occurred in England between 1958 and 1970. The right 'to walk through our streets with heads erect and free from fear' has vanished for a considerable part of the population. It was no new right that Lord Justice Salmon was upholding; the idea of the King's Peace is basic to the laws of England. The sharp increase that has occurred, in a decade, of willingness to accept racist practices, and the violence and fear which they produce, can be confirmed from a steady series of violent incidents that have taken place, by no means all in areas that are thought of as 'tough'. It is a long time since West Indians in England felt confidence in the willingness of the police to protect them, and Pakistanis interviewed in the East End after the first reports of Paki-bashing stated that it was of no use for them to call the police to their aid; they said that the police, when called, were slow to arrive and frequently seized upon Pakistanis who had been attacked rather than upon their attackers. It was for this reason that the Pakistanis were discussing 'self-defence' organizations.

Self-defence organizations are not a new idea: Indians in Leamington Spa bought themselves guns after a wave of hostility towards them in 1966, during which one Indian had a burning cross pushed through the letter-box of his home. This move to self-defence was a successful one; evidently the attackers had the sense to realize that an angry Sikh with a gun is not an advisable target.

The most striking change that has occurred is not in the kind of violent incident that is reported in the press, but in the tone of public and official reaction to such incidents. Whether Lord Justice Salmon was right or wrong in claiming that the hooligans of Notting Hill had 'filled the whole nation with horror, indignation and disgust', the fact that he used such terms in court indicates a mood very different from that in which the following report can appear without any public reaction of surprise or indignation:

Bradford, 17 April 1970

A British citizen was recommended for deportation by Bradford magistrates today in what is thought to be the first case of its kind in the country.

Tanweer Akhtar Khan, aged 22, machinist, of Cecil Avenue, Bradford, faced the possibility of being shuttled round the world, Mr Thomas Lister, his solicitor, said. 'He is a British citizen, but not a citizen of the United Kingdom. He is one of an estimated 35,000 second-class citizens who are stateless ... The notice of deportation causes considerable concern. This man has no right to remain in this country, but he has no right to go anywhere else. He is not a citizen of Pakistan. He is a British subject, not a Kenyan, so he cannot go to Kenya. If you think this is a case where you must recommend deportation, to where should he be deported?'

He added that Mr Khan had been employed ever since his arrival in Britain. After being granted an extension to his original one-month's stay friends told him that he had no need to apply for a further extension.

Mr Clifford Norton, for the prosecution, said that Mr Khan landed at Dover in November, 1968. He was allowed to stay for a month and was later given a two-month extension by the Home Office. He was arrested in Bradford on April 1 and had been in custody ever since.

(*Guardian*, 18 April 1970)

Mr Khan, in short, had so far spent over two weeks in jail for the offence of contravening the immigration regulations by residing in the country of his citizenship, earning his living there, and committing no crime. He had had no free choice to go anywhere but Britain, once even temporarily admitted by the Home Office, since he had no citizenship other than the one he had, ironically, wanted to choose – British: so that the punishment already dealt him (sixteen days in prison) and the punishment threatened (deportation) were for actions to which he had no legal or physically possible alternative.

When this can happen, while Paki-bashers remain free, is it surprising if many dark-skinned people in England look upon it as a racist country?

There are, of course, some vocal and comparatively well-known people in Britain who are loud in the praise of all things British, who blame, sternly, other people of their own colour for causing problems, and who keep very quiet about injustice. It is no surprise that they should take this attitude. They are among the tiny minority of dark-coloured people who have established a toehold in the English social system, who have jobs with status, homes in 'nice' areas, and a strong desire to keep hold of their own privileges and be 'accepted'. This minority includes others with a very different way of looking at things, who are ready to use the status they have gained to speak on behalf of those who are denied not merely privileges but basic rights.

Their difficulty is to find anyone outside the black community who is willing to listen to them. English people are used to thinking of racism as a Bad Thing, but they are convinced that it is always happening somewhere else. It may go on in parts of Africa, and in the United States, but it is not an English phenomenon. Even those who concede that it occurs in England at all always know of another town where you can find it, never their own. It is, moreover, generally agreed that even if there is any manifestation in England of racism, the situation in this country is so different from that in any other country you care to name that we have nothing to learn from the history of other countries, or from the most immediately contemporary happenings in them.

If English racism is something so different from the phenomenon we all accept as real in other nations, we had better at least find out what it is. If we have to find our own solutions, starting from scratch and on the basis of our own experience, we have no time to lose in collecting information about it, and this information will not be of the kind that the newspapers so often place under a 'race' heading; that is, information about 'immigrants', or people of dark colour. It will be information about English people.

This book is a personal account that provides some of this information. I want first to explain how I use some of the descriptive words in it, for the use of words between people with a common language is often a cause of deep misunderstandings. 'Pig', for example, was a joyful word to Stanley Baldwin, who liked to play the trustworthy rustic off duty; it means something very nasty, however, to a Black Panther.

England and English

Throughout this book, I have used 'England' and 'English' rather than 'Britain' and 'British' to describe the state of affairs in this country. I have several reasons for doing this. One is that 'Britain' includes countries of which I know hardly anything first-hand. Whether any of what I have to say applies to Wales, Scotland or Northern Ireland, readers better informed than myself about those countries will be able to judge for themselves. Secondly, Scotland, Wales and Ireland have themselves been at different times colonized by England, and what I have to say about English people's ideas of their own national identity clearly does not apply to them. Thirdly, I happen to be English myself, and so feel able to speak with some confidence, which I should not feel in generalizing about Britain.

Racism

I have used this word in preference to racialism; it means the same thing but it is shorter and, I think, more expressive.

Names, places and people

My personal qualification for writing about racism in England is that I was engaged voluntarily from November 1964 to May 1965, and professionally for just over three years after that, in working on behalf of equal rights for racial minorities, for cooperation between organizations, and for better understanding between the local white population and dark minorities, in one city of 109,000 people: Oxford. For the purposes of this work the important thing about Oxford was that it was a small industrial city in the South Midlands, short of housing but happily free of slums; cosmopolitan and unconventional in its central square mile but very like other industrial towns in the rest of it; cursed with a certain amount of complacency about its own excellence (in contrast to a place like Swindon, which wants to improve its own image) but blessed with a very good local daily newspaper. Oxford embraces great human variety, partly because it has some of the character of a West Country cathedral town as well as of an industrial centre, and partly because its two major factories, its large hospital group, and its service industries have between them drawn Welsh, Polish, Irish, Pakistani, West Indian, Indian, Italian and Spanish immigrants to the city over the last forty years.

It is a very different place from Liverpool, and different again from Nottingham, Gloucester and Gravesend, to name a handful of other towns with a mixed population. My practical experience is based largely on work in Oxford, and has this limitation. On the other hand, I was accustomed to being asked to help in cases which took me outside Oxford, to see an English employer in the East Midlands, for example, or a Pakistani family in Reading, because there were often appeals from the relatives or friends of Oxford citizens, who might live far away. There are now over fifty people in England doing the kind of job I had (they are called Community Relations Officers, but when I took the post, it was generally called Liaison Officer); but when I was appointed in May 1966 there were less than twenty of us, and in many important boroughs there was no such worker to appeal to. So the few of us there were, were occasionally called upon from outside our own areas. Moreover, Liaison Officers met regularly for formal meetings, and were frequently in contact with each other over individual problems, such as finding a man a job, getting a place in a training college or dealing with an immigration difficulty. Many organizations that had to be approached were concerned with areas that crossed borough boundaries: trade-union officials, for instance, and immigrant organizations. It was therefore possible to learn in the most practical way about the situation outside one city. At the same time, the job had all the strength of a limited, local task, in which it is possible to get to know people and situations intimately and continuously.

The work involved getting to know a cross-section of the whole population. A typical day might start with arriving at the office, to find a Pakistani outside who had been waiting since eight in the morning to ask for help because his son was being held in the police cells at London Airport; proceed with a visit from a local midwife wanting to learn Punjabi so that she could communicate better with some of her patients; a call from the Police Liaison Officer to discuss talks to police cadets; an interview with an English teacher who had spent thirty years in India and wanted to help teach the children of immigrants locally; a request from a Scotswoman who had lived in Zambia to know if you had any part-time secretarial work; a call from a Jamaican inviting you to a christening party the next Sunday; and a student arriving to help with leaflets about the Housing Association. Outside calls later in the day might take you to a kindly person offering some furniture for a family in need; to a West Indian family living in one room, with hardly any space to squeeze between the double bed and the two cots; to an official at the Town Hall; and to a mechanic's wife in a smart suburban street who was complaining about the Indian neighbours. The phone calls at the office ranged from Government departments compiling statistics to a member of the Congregationalist church down the road wanting to know what kind of present to take to a Nigerian wedding. Evenings were often taken up – sometimes ten times in a month – by speaking at meetings. A meeting could mean four people in a sitting-room, ten in a Nissen hut, or two hundred in a school hall, but it meant a gathering entirely, or almost entirely, of English people who, looking for some means of filling up their organization's programme, and having already tried Great Country Houses or Drug Addiction Today, came to the end of the line and had Race Relations. Some of these meetings were exciting, some encouraging, some violently heated, and some, I must admit, deeply depressing. Many were in Oxford itself, of political groups, church groups, social clubs and students; many more took me far outside Oxford, even up to two hundred miles away. They were occasions on which I met a cross-section different in approach from those I met in the rest of the working day; these were people usually without much direct involvement or interest in race relations; it was just one item on a programme for them, whereas those I met at or around the office were either people with a hostile complaint – officials with some professional involvement, immigrants complaining of discrimination – or people with a positive desire to give practical help.

When I first thought of writing an account of what I had learnt in this job, I was faced with a dilemma. On the one hand, I had the kind of everyday knowledge of how racism affects the life of a community that only a few white people have been lucky enough to gain. A Liaison Officer does not meet with only one kind of problem, but hundreds; and, apart from the great variety of people one meets, from Government ministers to Health visitors, from rich to poor, white, brown and black, there is the opportunity to follow the story of individuals from one week, and one year, to another.

On the other hand, I could not easily describe in the sort of personal detail that is essential for true understanding the real people I had met, and whose trust I had often been given, and resort to calling them 'Mr X' and 'Miss A', resident in Blankshire. To do so is both heartless and ineffective, I think: heartless because one has no right to use real people as raw material, and ineffective precisely because to do so is dehumanizing. It is very hard to care tuppence about all the As, Bs and Cs of sociological and official reports. They become single elements in a system, presented for analysis so that the system itself can be analysed and changed, often by some elephantine administrative measure that remedies some of the old evils while it creates new ones. True, the aim of such reports is eventually to help the As, Bs and Cs to a happier personal fate, but the technique of treating human beings as 'cases' has always seemed to me a very dangerous one. To describe one person's case at a particular time is to tell very little of the truth about that person. Imagine, for instance, how differently we would react to the following case-history before and after learning the names involved. A social worker reports on a visit to an elderly man, nearing retiring age and about to lose his home. She observes on the home visit how affectionately the two elder daughters, A and B, treat him, and how well he responds to their obvious affection. The youngest girl, C, is rather withdrawn, an uncommunicative girl, who causes her father to lose his temper with her. The worker recommends that the offer of a home with the two elder girls, in turn, be accepted; they are materially well off, and seem to have balanced and successful married lives.

The names of the family are Lear, Goneril, Regan and Cordelia.

The tragedy of Lear was the tragedy not only of a king but of Man. It is possible to write a flat report about him – 'mental condition degenerating', and what not – but such a report does not lessen the anguish and the tempest for him. When human events appear readily classifiable and commonplace, it is the observer, not the observed, that makes them so. And when our compassion is not engaged for the victims of injustice, we have nothing to offer them.

I have to apologize for the inadequacy of my own attempt to convey what the tempest is like. What I have done in this book is to use fictitious names for characters composed from a number of real people, and to use dialogue I have actually heard, but not from the lips of any one recognizable real individual. I hope the result is both more true to life and more comprehensible than descriptions in more scientific reports. I am not a social scientist, and if I were to use apparently scientific techniques I should produce something phoney. There are plenty of first-rate works of reference now on the race situation in England, notably the encyclopedic Rose Report, *Colour and Citizenship*, published by the Institute of Race Relations. Mine is a personal account of the truth as I see it. In the places where I *have* referred to real individuals, I have made this clear.

Part One

Every man in his humour
BEN JONSON

1. Man in the Street
2. Man with a Restaurant
3. People at a Meeting: the Club
4. Englishness and Whiteness
5. What's in an Attitude?

1. Man in the Street

Standing on the corner of the street is a man. Broad-shouldered, five foot ten in smart new shoes, he is dressed for a summer day: pink shirt, polished cotton trousers from a multiple store, and a thick knitted jacket with bone buttons. There's a pub on the corner: an old brown English town pub, with clouded windows marked in whirligig lettering; the brickwork, streaked in grime, has weathered into its undistinguished surroundings. Next door, a row of brick terrace houses runs for fifty yards towards a brash new furniture store, blazoning its mottled carpets and expensive three-piece suites across a plate-glass window. Two children are playing hopscotch. Across the road, a Peugeot pulls up at the small filling-station incongruously stuck between more houses, whose milk-bottles, on every step, proclaim them occupied.

The man is waiting for someone. People pass by him every few seconds, for the corner is at one end of a shopping street, where Tesco's, Radio Rentals, Mr Flaherty's Bargain Shop (Washing Machines! Radios!!) and Marjorie's Hairdressing of Paris offer a consumer's paradise for the not-so-rich. To everyone who passes, he is someone different. Many fail to notice him at all. A few register his presence as a black man, hanging round a street corner. A middle-aged lady of straitened means, going by neatly hatted and gloved to Tesco's where the meat is cheaper, pays him a longer glance with a romantic eye. How beautiful the pink shirt looks against the brown, blue-shadowed skin. Like the Gauguin reproductions she learnt to admire in her youth. To her, the romance of the noble savage illuminates this prosaic and completely unsavage individual. But something about him – the knitted jacket, perhaps? – does not quite fit the aloof dignity a brown man should, in her view, possess. She passes on to the supermarket – where the Jamaican girl on the checking-out desk (who happens to be the cousin of the man on the corner) arouses in her no thought of Gauguin or noble savagery at all. She is just another cashier in an overall, ringing up the lowest grocery bill in town.

Two blond youths, eighteen and nineteen, builder's labourers, walk past the man next. He's a blackie to them, the sort who always whines when he's given the heavy jobs. They had one of his sort on the last site they worked on. They called him Sambo. Sullen, he was. Complained to the foreman that he was always left to lift pipes, when they were up on the scaffolding. They fixed him. They put Bill's wallet into his donkey-jacket pocket. That got him fired. The foreman had been fed up with him anyway. They're all the same, think they own the bloody country.

The Peugeot has driven away from the filling-station, and a Triumph Herald draws up. The driver, a girl in sun-glasses, pulls in to fill up before zooming down the motorway to tea in rural Berkshire. She hasn't long to get to the shadowed drawing-room, twenty miles and a generation away, where the view through the window is across a soft lawn to the quiet and expensive Thames. She sees the man on the corner, and watches him idly as the filling-station attendant attends to the petrol. Why, she wonders, do all coloured people hang round the street corners? She has nothing against coloured people. Actually, of course, she doesn't know any, except a few like that Dr Ram she met at some awful garden fête, but of course he wasn't like a coloured person really; he was educated, which is different. Incurious, and seeing nothing in the man across the road, she drives away, her mind tightly closed to the world around her, encased in the steel and glass of the car, passing unaffected through the shopping crowds.

The next passer-by, an elderly lady dressed in the kind of

fashion the *Daily Telegraph* Women's page was advocating ten years ago, sees the man on the corner and, rather uncertainly, smiles at him in case he is Nigerian. Her elder brother, Robert, whom she has adored since childhood, spent years in Nigeria; he loved the people there and they simply adored him, of course. She is not *quite* sure that this man could possibly be Nigerian, because his clothes don't look quite right; all the same, she never misses a chance to make one of them feel at home in England, for Robert's sake. Poor dears, they must feel so cold when they come here. Really, it might be kinder not to let them come at all, very often. Such happy, simple people, just like children and so lovable, but of course a lot of them get very unhappy over here, and sometimes it's their own fault, they seem to expect everything done for them; and poor Mrs Marriott who, being a real Christian woman, actually let her house to a Nigerian family when she went to Canada for six months, came back and found it in a simply filthy state. She'd thought they were such a charming couple, but of course they'd been used to lots of servants at home, and had no idea how to run a house properly on their own. The loose covers were ruined, and Mrs Marriott had to redecorate throughout. Well, no wonder people don't want to let their house to anyone coloured. How can you blame them, when that sort of thing happens? The wife *was* charming in a way, but of course bone-lazy, like so many of them, and it was quite beneath her dignity to scrub a floor!

'Hullo Bert!' calls an English bus conductor, walking past the corner to reach the bus garage. 'Hullo there,' answers the man on the corner. So his name is Bert. As a matter of fact, his full name is Horatio Herbert Fraser, but his English mates call him Bert. He is a bus conductor, now off duty and waiting to meet his wife so that they can go shopping together. The friend who has just hailed him in a cheery way is Fred Walton, who lives a few doors away from him. Fred, walking past the corner of the street, has recognized in him not an anonymous 'coloured man', but one of his mates. Fred likes the Jamaican music that Bert plays on his record-player. They are both keen gardeners. When Bert put in six dozen new plants a few months back and somebody came in the night and pulled them all out of the earth where they had been so carefully set, it was Fred who sought out the neighbour who had done it and gave him a clip round the ear.

A bus swings round into the street. The driver sees Bert, and gives him a nod as he passes, but he doesn't like Bert or want anything to do with him. A few years ago, when some of the West Indians thought they could just walk into the bus company social club, this driver made it clear to them that they needn't think they could behave as if the place were their own. Let them have their own social club, if they wanted it. He had nothing against that. But once they started thinking they could mix, there'd be trouble. The management had made a bit of a fuss recently, trying to encourage the Paks and the West Indians to 'make use of social club facilities'; and all the Paks and the West Indians had said they didn't want to come. *They* knew when they weren't wanted. So the management had decided none of the coloured employees wanted to mix. And now you only see white faces at the busmen's social club.

And the passengers look idly out of the bus windows and see, for a brief moment, Bert standing on the corner waiting. And all of them see a black man, but none of them sees Bert.

Well, what does *he* see? That's one question nobody is likely to ask. For everyone, he is standing on the corner as a kind of object, not as an ordinary, off-duty bus conductor with thoughts and feelings of his own. Some of those who pass him by see him favourably, but what about him? Perhaps some keen young sociologist may approach him with a questionnaire, and ask him where he lives, where he was born, how many children he has, whether he owns his house, whether he votes, whether he's ever been refused a job because of his colour and so on, but to the keen young sociologist he is of interest not because of his own personal qualities and experiences but because he is a member of a group – black people. Bert is just as likely to feel bitter as grateful for this kind of interest; as far as he's concerned, the sociologist is just using him and his friends to advance his own career and be a specialist on 'the race problem'. Bert can be mistaken as much as the next man, but he's no fool. He knows, as he stands waiting, that he is *vulnerable*. His neck prickles uncomfortably as the builder's labourers go by; he tenses his muscles, just in case one of them decides to bump into him, accidentally-on-purpose, and then pick a quarrel. He doesn't want trouble.

What about Fred? Fred himself is a very decent man, and is sincerely certain that there is no consciousness of colour between him and Bert: they get on well; they laugh together; they do things for each other. But does Bert feel exactly the same about him? No: a tiny incident that Fred has completely forgotten about soured things. Another West Indian on the buses once lost his temper in an argument with an English driver, and bloodied the driver's nose. The driver was a popular man, twenty years with the firm, and Fred had said of the West Indian, 'That's the sort of behaviour that gives coloured people a bad name. If they were all like you Bert, we'd have no problem.' In other words, Fred was willing to accept and tolerate Bert because he wasn't what 'coloured people' are expected to be like. In one way, Fred can see Bert as an individual, but in other ways he sees Bert as one of a group; Bert is a good sort *in spite of* being a black man. But Bert does not ask to be accepted *in spite of* his colour; the expectation which Fred's attitude implied was of some kind of disloyalty to all those others of the same colour with whom he is unwillingly or willingly associated. Acceptance of this kind is a social probation order; any violation of it throws you back into the condemnation of being not a person but a 'coloured' person.

Fred could never have guessed the effect of this remark on his friend. He would be really indignant to be told that he had any colour-consciousness at all. And indeed, as English people go, he is remarkably free of prejudice and unkindness. Yet he is not completely free – what English person *can* be completely free? – of attitudes and ideas that have been dinned into him since his earliest childhood about 'white' men and 'black' men, about Englishness and foreign-ness. He has rejected or modified a lot of these attitudes and ideas in the light of his own experience, and because he is both sensible and good-hearted, but at moments of stress they flow back into his mind.

The education of English people has for a long time been strongly imbued with racism. This education is derived from many different sources; newspapers, popular fiction, comics, school text-books, the conversation of adults including conventional anecdotes and jokes, and at a more intellectual level from serious works on science and history, from carefully prepared speeches by leading politicians, from ponderous leading articles, and, most insidiously, from well-meant but ill-considered demands for liberalism, tolerance and niceness to our coloured friends. All these sources of racism are influential from childhood through to maturity. Their influence may be greater or lesser; the tragic fact is that even the least tinge of racism, generally not recognized at all for what it is by English people, is glaringly obvious to the people at the receiving end of it – the Berts, Toms, Dicks, Harrys, Mohammeds and Kofis – that form the overwhelming majority of the world's population and the overwhelmed minority in England.

Mutatis mutandis – if only one could change a lot of other factors in England, and in the rest of the world, the implied racism in our society would not matter very much, and might gradually disappear. If Bert had felt himself in every way secure and equal as a member of English society, he would have been able to laugh to himself at Fred's notion that all other 'coloured people' ought to be like him – just as Fred would be able to laugh if someone made a similar remark to him in Jamaica, as a white man or as an Englishman. But Bert does not feel secure, or equal. He sees himself referred to every week, on television or in the newspapers, as a 'problem'. He knows that the chance of getting his relatives to this country is very much less than the chance an Italian has of doing the same thing – and for no other reason than that he is black and the Italian is white. He knows that when his little girl reaches school-leaving age, she is going to be faced with rebuffs if she applies for the kind of job thought unsuitable for 'coloured people'; if she wants to be a secretary or work in a bank, she is going to have to face humiliation and disappointment. He hopes she'll want to be a nurse, because black girls are accepted as nurses. But supposing she wants to be a secretary, how is he going to explain to her what the difficulties are? She'll ask, but why? but why? – and there is no answer to give her that makes any sense, except that people despise her because of the colour she was born with.

And Bert knows too, from television and newspapers, what is happening in other parts of the world to people who share his colour. Because they face the same problem as he does, to a greater or lesser degree, he has a fellow-feeling with them, though he may never have seen them, and may understand very little about them. Bert could not tell you who Dean Rusk or Spiro T. Agnew are, but he knew who Robert Kennedy was; he knows who Stokely Carmichael is, and when a white American killed Dr Martin Luther King, he knew that a man on his side had been killed by the other side, and that this was important to *him* – not just to Americans.

None of us can speak or act towards other people of a different colour as though there were no America, no South Africa, no Wolverhampton, no history of slavery. All these things are present in every encounter, whether we want them to be there or not.

Bert is just one individual. Some of his thoughts and feelings are shared by others he knows, infinitely varied but all falling into the same category of 'coloured people' as far as English people are concerned. Others are not. His wife, even more than he does, wants to avoid 'trouble'. She turns the television down so low that you can hardly hear it because the neighbours on the left are always complaining about noise. The week after Enoch Powell's April 1968 speech (in which he seemed to see the River Tiber foaming with blood), the wife next door shrieked a lot of abuse over the fence at Bert's wife when she was hanging out the washing. Bert's wife didn't answer back; she went indoors and cried. But her sister Gloria is a different sort of character. Gloria, a tall, handsome Jamaican girl with a strong mind of her own, went into the garden and shouted back; she used some homely Jamaican swear-words, which the English neighbour did not understand; however, it was quite clear that Gloria's remarks were not complimentary, and after that the neighbouring wife confined herself to muttered remarks.

Bert's wife wants to go home to Jamaica, but Bert doesn't agree with her. They are buying their house on mortgage, after years of saving enough for the extra-large deposit that the building society asked of a Jamaican. He does his job as well as the next man; his daughter is doing quite well in school. Why should he go back? What job could he get there paying anything like as well as his present job, which brings in twenty-five pounds a week, including overtime? He has put a lot of work into the house and garden in his free time; he pays his income tax and insurance stamp; he saves through a credit club run by West Indians; he plays in the bus company cricket team; he has a favourite local pub; this is his *home*. He first came from Jamaica to England because he knew there were jobs going; he saw jobs in England advertised in a Jamaican newspaper back in 1956, and so he came. His wife works part-time at the local old people's hospital, where three quarters of the staff are from Commonwealth countries and Ireland. If Bert and his family left for Jamaica, as several of their friends have in fact done over the last ten years, they would leave a gap that other new arrivals from *somewhere* would have to fill, or their jobs would not be done at all. Twenty miles away is a hospital in a small town that has closed two wards for lack of staff. There is not a great pool of labour waiting eagerly for the jobs done by Bert and his wife and their friends; they would never have come to England at all if they had not seen advertisements begging for workers – because there were not English people available wanting these jobs. So why should he leave? His wife is worried about the future. She is convinced that things are going to get worse for 'coloured' people in England. English people don't want us, she feels, and in many ways she is more exposed to hostility than her husband is. When he is out at work, and she has to put up with the unpleasantness from her neighbour; when she takes the little girl to school and hears the English parents saying loudly that they want to move their children to a different school because there are 'too many coloured children' at this one; when she avoids the big store, with a dress she likes in the window, because she is fearful of what the shop assistant's attitude to her will be, she is on her own, and miserable. She does not belong to any clubs. She had an invitation to go to the community centre family party last Christmas, but she did not go because she knew most of the people there would be English, and she was afraid of how they would behave to her. She puts a lot of energy into her house. Careful saving and hire purchase have enabled her to have a sitting-room with wall-to-wall carpet, a three-piece suite, highly polished tables with frilly mats that she has sewn herself, and a handsome television set, above which – the only sign to distinguish this room from other sitting-rooms all along the street – is a framed wedding photograph, colour-tinted, of herself and Bert in the brilliant sunshine of Jamaica. The furniture shines with polish; the carpet is hoovered daily. Nobody can say that *her* house is dirty.

Yet they do. Other women in the street, who have never set foot inside Bert's home, are quite ready to describe 'coloureds' as dirty people, though they have to admit that the little girl is 'very nicely kept'. And indeed, few English children appear daily in such a dazzle of defiant cleanliness; whiter than white socks, crisply pressed hair-ribbons, clothes without a spot. Bert's wife takes a pride in the little girl's appearance anyway, but there is more to it than that; those clean, smart clothes are an assertion of equality and respectability to the world. There is a Pakistani family, fifty yards along the road on the other side, and Bert's wife resents the way in which the children play outside, dressed in a muddle of clothes: crumpled satin, gold-embroidered, covered with a chunky cardigan or a second-hand sweater with holes in it. She resents their presence, because she knows that to the English people in the street she and the Pakistani wife are both 'coloured women', and anything that can be disapproved of in the Pakistani household will be blamed upon her equally because she shares this 'coloured' description. She has never talked to the Pakistani wife, though she has smiled at her once or twice going by, and has received a big smile back; the Pakistani wife speaks not a word of English, and Bert's wife speaks nothing but English. And Bert's wife now feels herself so much part of this respectable street and its ways that, without realizing it herself, she behaves towards the Pakistani women in a thoroughly English way. She complains to Bert about the character of the street, and about how bad it is to let those little children play out in front. Neither accepted in the street herself, nor accepting one of those whom the local English residents would class with her indiscriminately, she is, apart from her Jamaican friends living farther off, alone.

2. Man with a Restaurant

The restaurant walls are papered with a very English wallpaper: deep red damask with a traditional design, originally borrowed, as it happens, from a design on Indian textiles when Indian cotton technology was first copied and adapted during the Industrial Revolution. The carpet, a patterned Axminster, would be at home in any comfortable English sitting-room. The plate-glass windows are covered by green plastic venetian blinds, and in one corner a large-leaved green plant has been trained over trellis work. The people sitting at the white-clothed tables, eating their various curries, kebabs, biryanis and pilaos, are extraordinarily varied. The oldest are a gentle-looking couple dressed in timelessly respectable fashion: he is a healthy-looking man with a greying moustache, in a well-preserved suit with a waistcoat; she has a 'good dress' from Marshall and Snelgrove, and a discreet little brooch with seed pearls set in sterling silver. They are talking, not loudly, but with the penetrating quality of voice of those who have been accustomed to command, agreeing with each other that they've not had such good food since the old days of the Maratha Railway.

At the other end of the restaurant are four young men from the opposite end of the social scale, conventional too in their way, for they all have hair cut short back and sides, and clothes in muted browns and blues. The manager has his eye on them, though to all appearances he is standing at the service-door end, taking little notice of what is going on. This group is very likely to try to leave the restaurant without paying, as a large number do each week, especially on Friday and Saturday nights. The only question is, which technique will they try? Will they go into the gents and climb out of the window into the alley? Will they walk out brazenly, giving a shove to the small waiter who tries to intercept them? Will they pretend they want credit, making a heavy-handed joke of it?

There are students at other tables, long-haired and colourful. One very pale young man with waving blond hair is wearing an Indian shirt and beads, in contrast to the manager, a dark-skinned Bengali, who is in a dinner-jacket. A married couple at another table eat without apparent pleasure or displeasure; they address hardly a word to each other. She has had her hair set for the weekend and has a new Crimplene suit; he is taking her out for an inexpensive treat, for there is no other restaurant in town where the surroundings are as elegant with the prices so low. Although this couple would nod their heads to any accusation that immigrant neighbours are undesirable because of their cooking smells, they like Indian food, and the wife sometimes makes curry at home from a recipe she cut out of a women's weekly paper.

The manager, Mr Gani, is on the whole a happy man. It is a real pride to him to stand presiding in his restaurant; he has built up his own business by years of hard work and saving, and now he is a man of high standing. When he first came to England, he worked long hours in an iron foundry; the work was hot and exhausting and the pay low. There was no trade union, but the managing director liked to look after his employees with a personal touch, and would present each of them with a Christmas pudding every December. Mr Gani never really liked Christmas pudding, but he appreciated the fact that the job was a secure one; very few English people wanted to work in the foundry, and most of the workers were Pakistanis, like himself, or West Indians. The wages were low, but so were his expenses. He had lived at first in one room of a house belonging to his uncle; all the members of the family had shared resources, and the kind of food they liked to eat was not expensive. So he had saved steadily, several pounds a week. With the consent of his uncle, who was head of the household, he had eventually got enough together for a deposit on a house of his own. By letting rooms in this house to two cousins, he had not had too much to pay for the mortgage, and in another two years he felt he could afford to send home for his wife. Long delays in getting a passport followed, but at last she arrived; the lodgers left and he was a householder. More work, more overtime, more saving, and at last he was ready for the next stage. First he had to own his house. Next he must have his own business. All the time, of course, he had scrupulously given 2½% of his income to charity, as his religion demanded. He had been active in working for the building of a mosque in the town. He had lent money to others less lucky than himself, to help them with their first deposit on a house. Being fluent in English, and quick to learn all the complications of income tax, industrial benefits and so on, he had given much of his free time to helping other Pakistanis fill in forms. All the local people from East Pakistan knew him. By the time he had his own restaurant, he was a respected figure among the entire Pakistani community. He was not a friend of Mr Ali, the owner of the local Pakistani shop; Mr Ali was from West Pakistan, which Mr Gani resented as bitterly as a Welsh nationalist resents England. But they were polite to each other, and able to cooperate in raising funds for the mosque. Islam was of far, far greater importance than any political disagreement, and it was essential for the children now growing up in England that they should not lose their religion; the mosque was of paramount importance.

One day he was going to go home to a rich retirement. But that day was still far off. He had several members of his family to provide for in Pakistan; his father was elderly and past work, so Mr Gani's mother must be supported. Mr Gani was the eldest son of his parents, and the responsibility for their last years was entirely his. His sister's son, a clever boy, had to have his education paid for, and the sister's husband earned very little. All these continuing expenses, and the instalments to be paid off for the restaurant and its furnishings, wages and S.E.T., reduced the possibility of saving. Still, one day he would return home, welcomed as a man of substance in the place of his birth.

Mr Gani is a lucky man. He is intelligent and adaptable, and backed by enough education to be able to realize his ambitions. Being a man to whom his religion is the first consideration in life – something very difficult for most English people, even if they are churchgoers, to comprehend – he has combined his ambitions to be a self-made man with an unself-conscious willingness, at every stage, to turn aside from his own ambition and help people lower down the ladder. He has escaped from the foundry now, but he is concerned about the number of people from Pakistan, working there in acutely uncomfortable and tiring jobs, who have little prospect of escaping it. Many of them, after years in England, still speak no English, and neither do their wives. It is the children who have to do the interpreting if a social worker turns up on the doorstep to make inquiries, or if a mortgage has to be arranged. They have adapted from their former village life to an astonishing degree; the wives go out, unveiled, into the street without any shyness now, though of course they found this very difficult at first. Noor Rashid's wife even learnt English and has a part-time job at the plastics factory. A lot of husbands would not allow such a thing, but many women envy Noor Rashid's wife, because she does not spend all day in the house alone – and it can be very lonely with no other women in the household; so strange after life at home, and so difficult if you feel ill. Some of the English neighbours are quite friendly, but all they can do is smile and smile; there are no words in common. Others are not so friendly; they come into the back garden and shout over the fence, looking very angry, and pointing sometimes at the children, or at the washing on the line, but it is impossible to tell what they are so angry about.

Two new customers walk into the restaurant: an English local government official with a turbaned Sikh, Mr Gill, who works for the local authority too. Mr Gill is not in fact from

India; he has never even set foot in India, but was born in Kenya and regards himself as Kenyan. He has got used now to the fact that everyone English he meets refers to him as either Indian or, in spite of the turban, Pakistani – used to it, though still irritated. He is the only employee of the local authority to wear a turban; indeed he is one of only two non-Europeans out of hundreds in the local authority offices, but he is frequently referred to by the Mayor, Town Clerk and others as evidence of the excellent racial integration achieved by the Borough Council. The fact is, he is so exceptionally good at his job, and the English applicants at the time when he applied were so very obviously inferior in qualification, that he had been taken on without a second thought. That, of course, was back in 1962, when 'race relations' was a phrase used about countries outside England, and the wearing of a turban not instantly taken to be a difficulty. It helped, of course, that the Mayor at the time was an old Army officer with a warm regard for the Sikhs as fighting men and a large fund of reminiscences on the subject. Although the Mayor had nothing to do directly with the appointment of course, his loud public affection for the Punjab was not completely irrelevant to the readiness with which Mr Gill, to whom the Punjab was a foreign land, was accepted.

Mr Gill is the only non-European in the restaurant; it runs, in fact, on English custom. The English local government man feels rather embarrassed when Mr Gill remarks, quite loudly enough for Mr Gani to hear, that it would have been better to eat at home: the cooking oil here is not of the first quality and the spices are not fresh. Mr Gani hears, of course – little that happens in his restaurant escapes him – but he is untroubled by this conventional remark from a host to his guest. He smiles, and exchanges a word or two with the local government man and Mr Gill with the same cordiality that he shows to the elderly couple in the corner when they congratulate him on the delightful meal they have had, and tell him how many years it is since they were in India.

Lucky Mr Gani. He does not know that, this very evening,

when he is walking to a friend's house only two hundred yards away, three young men who don't know him, but who see in him a small, slightly-built wog, are going to knock him down and kick his face, breaking his nose. For the next few days, he will not be presiding over the restaurant, but will be in a hospital bed. The police are going to advise him to bring a civil action for assault, and explain there is nothing they can do, though there are witnesses to what has happened. The policeman whom Mr Gani is destined to see is a man who knows what Pakistanis are like: they come over here illiterate and never do a hand's turn; they're too cunning at living off the social services.

3. People at a Meeting: the Club

The Get Together Club consists mostly of women. But three men are visible in the audience of fifteen, sitting around in the rather too brightly lit church hall where I arrive at eight p.m. The Chairman, a plump and genial lady, fusses kindly over the important question of whether I want to sit in front of the table or behind it. Perhaps I would prefer in front? That's more informal.

'I'm so sorry there aren't many here this week. We had such a lot last week for Japanese flower-arranging. But of course, your talk is the sort of thing that frightens some people off, isn't it? I'm afraid you'll find one or two people here with *very strong views.* I'm not like that myself: I always say it doesn't matter whether a person's green, yellow or sky-blue-pink.' She laughs cheerfully, and calls the meeting to order. She is a nice person; no malice in her, and I do not mind when she announces me as the officer of the Oxford Committee for Racial Discrimination, though I am a bit disturbed that none of the audience seems to notice anything wrong with this description.

I give my talk. Every time I face a new audience, I wonder which things to say and what to emphasize, and often make mistakes; it is impossible to tell in advance how any group is going to react. Two different groups of churchgoing women may look very similar to one another; yet while one set thinks all Indians are 'tribesmen' living in mud huts in a state of brutalized ignorance and speaking a language called Indian, the other will be perfectly familiar with Indian families living in the same street, and even express a wish to learn Punjabi, 'because the poor things must be so lonely'. This time, I sketch a history of migration from Commonwealth countries into Britain since 1945, emphasize that there are two so-called 'white' immigrants for every non-white because of the volume of Irish and European workers coming here to settle, describe the immigration restrictions and the effect these have had and try to analyse what colour prejudice is and how it has far-reaching effects upon people's lives.

The audience applauds: a few warmly, most with energetic politeness, and one not at all; a grey-haired man with a nut-cracker face, who keeps his arms folded. The Chairman announces that I have kindly agreed to answer questions, and she is sure that after that interesting talk there will be lots of questions.

There is dead silence.

After a sticky pause, a lady at the end of the front row says that she has some West Indian neighbours who are very nice people, and quiet, and they keep the children beautifully; really she wishes all white people would turn out their children so clean and smart, but the one thing that worries her is the Pakistanis; they will wear their national dress when they come over here, and she thinks that if these people are going to come over here, they ought to adapt to our ways. She doesn't think the Pakistanis want to integrate, really.

Would she wear a tunic and shalwars if she went to live in West Pakistan? No, she wouldn't. (However, it is clear that she does not think of this in the same category at all as people wearing their own familiar clothes when in England. English dress is *normal.* Other kinds of clothes are odd.) What about the West Indian neighbours? Has she ever spoken to them? Oh no, they might not like it. She believes in keeping herself to herself. I am about to ask her whether it is all right, in her view, for Pakistanis to keep themselves to themselves, when a lady in the next row chips in with a question. She doesn't agree at all with the first questioner; she likes to see those beautiful saris on the Indian women, but she's never felt the same since she had a very upsetting thing happen with a coloured bus conductor; he'd refused to have her push-chair on the bus, and had been most rude about it, and since then she's felt all uncomfortable every time there's a coloured conductor on the bus. Before I can reply, her neighbour starts to argue that *she's* always found the coloured conductors much nicer than the white ones, and another member of the audience then claims that the Pakistani and Indian conductors are very gentlemanly, but some of the West Indians are very rough types and she has heard one of them using dreadful language, which she couldn't possibly repeat, to quite an old man just because he had no money smaller than a pound note.

It looks like bus conductors for the rest of the evening, when the man with the nutcracker face stands up and speaks in a loud voice which cuts through the excited argument in which six women have now joined, and several are talking simultaneously. 'I'm prejudiced', he says, 'and I don't mind saying so.' There is a flutter of shock; the Get Together Club is not used to this sort of plain speaking, and the conductor argument falls silent. 'I'm prejudiced because I know what these people are like. I work with them. There's no getting away from it; they have lower intelligence than white people.'

'Where do you work?' I ask, as he draws breath.

'In hospital administration. And what I say is this. There's shocking conditions in some of our hospitals. Hardly a white face to be seen among the doctors. And what I say is this; they should be stopped from coming over here, and we'd soon find enough British doctors.'

'How would we do that, when no new medical school has been opened in England since the end of the last war? When our own population has risen sharply, and a lot of English-trained doctors are emigrating?'

'Ah,' says the man triumphantly, 'and *why* are they emigrating? Because of all the blacks coming in, that's why. The cream of our race is leaving these shores – the cream of our race – and a lot of black riff-raff's coming in as sweated labour.'

The Chairman, rather upset, intervenes: 'Mr Partridge, I don't know how you can talk like that. I think the coloured doctors are wonderful. I know when I had my operation in June, I had an Indian doctor who couldn't have been nicer, and the nurses –'

'The nurses are doing a good job,' concedes Mr Partridge. 'We seem to get quite a good type coming as nurses. Though, there again, what are they doing? Keeping wages low, that's what they're doing. If we stopped them coming in, we'd find English nurses from somewhere.'

'If it's possible to find English nurses somewhere, why are there hospital wards closed down for lack of nurses already?' I ask. 'And what's the point of getting rid of good nurses because you don't like the colour they are? And what are you doing to the girls themselves, telling them you don't want them to look after people here just because of their colour? Do you call that right?'

'I call it right not to have any more of these people here,' says Mr Partridge firmly. 'The humane thing would be to ship the lot of them home on the next banana-boat to where they came from. They're not wanted here, and they'd be better off in their own countries.'

I'm just about to say something pretty strong to Mr Partridge when the Chairman, who is very flustered by all this unpleasantness, intervenes again in a rather shrill voice to say that she thinks someone else ought to have a chance to ask questions as she sees Mrs Lowe and Miss Sampson have just got the coffee ready, and – she goes on breathlessly in case Mr Partridge or I start again – she's got a question of her own she has been wanting to ask: what can be done to help the West Indians and the Pakistanis to speak English, as she knows a lot of them do find it difficult.

Oh dear, the Chairman is so nice and well-meaning that I must find a tactful way to explain that English is the mother-tongue of people in the former British West Indies. Thank Heaven there are no West Indians present to be enraged by her mistake. Still, of course, if there were any, they would have been too angry with Mr Partridge by now to have taken too much notice. It's one of those meetings where I don't know whether to laugh or cry or lose my temper. But national character tells: I keep a stiff upper lip and explain, in a manner that suggests the Chairman was really asking about Pakistanis and Indians, all about the different languages of the Indian sub-continent; about adult classes in English; about what schools are doing in different parts of England to teach English to so-called immigrant children; and finally, as if by an afterthought, talk about English in the Caribbean and the different structure it has in some ways from the English of Southern England, and, again, from the English of Yorkshire and Lancashire. I'm going on too long; all eyes are swivelling to the table at the side where Mrs Lowe and Miss Sampson are pouring out milky coffee, and so I come to an end in the middle of a rather dull bit. I'm angry with myself for not standing up and letting them all know fairly and squarely that there isn't one of them that can see a person with a dark skin with clear vision, undistorted by racist myth; yet at the same time I'm in despair of being able to say anything at all that can break through the thick layers of misunderstanding they have acquired over the years. Mr Partridge is different; he is a man of bad will towards others; he is full of a hate which will feed on any piece of information, true or untrue, to justify itself and flourish, but the others are not bad people. They have learnt from television and the newspapers to talk about 'coloured' people, and to lump together the most varied human beings as 'coloured' and so all alike, regardless of different culture, language, religion, and even colour itself, from a brown lighter than a Margate tan to ebony black. They are unaware of how potty it is to think that because one man from Pakistan was rude to someone last month, all Jamaicans, Barbadians, Trinidadians, Ghanaians, Arabs and Indians are likely to be rude next Tuesday. They are even unaware that it is just as ridiculous to talk about all the coloured conductors being nice as about all the coloured conductors being nasty. I remember the boy called Surinder, who arrived ten days before at London Airport, to join his father, an Indian hospital porter. Surinder has been moved from the police cells to Goldhawk Road Remand Home, while the Home Office reviews his case. The Home Office is saying Surinder is not really Mr Singh's son, because when the immigration officer interrogated the boy immediately on his arrival, and before he was allowed to see his father, he gave answers about members of the family contradictory to the answers his father gave. So, at least, his interrogator said. The interrogator had done a course in Urdu, but, not surprisingly, was not familiar with the particular Punjabi dialect the boy spoke, and no doubt the interrogator's accent had been very difficult to follow for a boy just arrived after a long flight – the first time he'd ever been on a plane, and indeed the first time he'd been far from his own village. I should have told the meeting about Surinder. He's in the remand home while his case is 'under consideration'. He can't understand what's going on around him; no one speaks his language; the food is strange and he has difficulty eating it; it's like a nightmare, not allowed to go with his father, not knowing what is going to happen next.

But would they have believed me if I'd told them about Surinder? They might have thought it impossible for such things to happen in England. Would they have connected the way Surinder got treated – and many more boys like him, every week – with the general attitude in England that 'coloured' people were different?

Miss Sampson brings me a cup of coffee, and says with great enthusiasm that she did enjoy my talk; it's good for them all to learn about these things, and the Get Together Club is really a wonderful way to learn a bit more about the world; it's so easy to get narrow, isn't it? with the same old household routine every day. She hopes I didn't mind Mr Partridge too much, and he's not a bad person really; he's done a lot for boys' clubs.

Effusive goodbyes from the Chairman and several other

ladies. I thank them for inviting me. They thank me for coming.

Next week they'll be having Miss Stubbs from the Gas Board on Getting the Most out of your Cooker.

4. Englishness and Whiteness

What is it to be English? Many popular works have been written on this subject: some ponderous, some facetious, and all firmly based in the bedrock of self-satisfaction. But however sweeping and however silly, the generalizations that are made about the English national character have an enormous effect upon the lives of members of English society. Whether these generalizations have much or little truth in them is unimportant. The important thing is that they represent not the truth about English people themselves but the truth about their aspirations, their standards of good or bad, their measuring-rod for judging individuals. Whether King Alfred ever burnt the cakes or not is, as a matter of historical fact, quite unimportant. But it is very important indeed that King Alfred burning the cakes is a familiar piece of English folklore, known to most people whether they have the foggiest idea or not of when Alfred lived and what else he did. The widespread English belief that experts are not practical people, and that the great and dignified deserve to be debunked every now and again, lives in this story. Alfred went on from burning the cakes to win a battle. The English happily believe, regardless of the evidence from any war in history, that they lose every battle except the last. And here again is a belief of binding social importance. The virtues of such a state of affairs must be: a state of unwillingness and unreadiness for war; slowness to react and to organize; but then a dogged endurance and determination not to be beaten that can succeed in defeating the most militaristic and highly-organized enemy.

English society admires a muddle, and admires obstinacy; it admires the endurance of the weak, and distrusts the values of military glory. English discoverers and inventors are not admired for competence and expertise, but on the contrary for succeeding by indolence and accident. Sir Isaac Newton is known to very few for working out the calculus, but he is known to the multitude for having an apple fall on his head while snoozing in the warmth of late summer in an orchard. And whatever thought and method Watt applied to the building of a steam engine are quite unimportant to the English public. To them he is the boy who watched a kettle boil, and saw the lid bouncing up and down.

Our national popular mythology tells us all we need to know about the conventions and beliefs by which our society has been formed. The incidents and stories that are a matter for common everyday allusion bind us together, not because of the information, true or false, that they contain, but because of the morals they illustrate, the beliefs about ourselves and our fellows around us that they inculcate, and the values they uphold.

This genuinely popular mythology can be shared equally by children growing up in such completely different environments as suburban Surrey and the Liverpool docks. It needs to be very clearly distinguished from the completely separate system of values that has been cultivated and advertised as 'English' by the English upper middle class. This powerful, cohesive social group exists not by heredity but by a rigid set of conventions and rituals; adherence to these is essential for membership. Asked what he values about England, a member of the class will produce illustrations which for him are powerful symbols, but which would be meaningless to a very large part of the population. For his are the values of a class within a country, not of the country as a whole. Tea in the afternoon means, to the middle class, a leisured and unnecessary refreshment between lunch and dinner. You take it around four o'clock; the bread and butter will be cut thin, and you will not, except for a children's tea party, eat it in a dining-room or kitchen, but in a drawing-room or on a grassy lawn. Whatever the everyday reality, this is the English middle-class mystique of tea. But tea to the majority of the population is the meal of the evening, eaten about five-thirty when father gets back from work and has had time to wash and change his clothes. You sit round a table and have egg and chips or baked beans, and 'something nice' for tea is not a plate of langue-de-chat biscuits but a thoroughly filling tin of grade I salmon or a piece of steak.

Tea-time is one trivial but revealing example of how what is accepted both here and abroad as something characteristically English means, in fact, quite different things to different groups of people in England.

When politicians speak of England and what it means, they may strike a hundred different notes in the course of a speech; their hearers are attuned to different pitches, and some will respond to some of these notes, some to others. Politicians who have led particularly sheltered lives can jangle badly; the sentimental reference by Lord Butler (when still Mr Butler, and still a runner for the Conservative Party leadership) to over-ripe pheasant and port as part of the nation's birthright was not a success. The really skilled politician, on the other hand, who understands that for most people facts are less important in themselves than the deeper things they signify, can play a whole symphony of evocative sounds in a few sentences, and affect his audience powerfully. Who has not heard those painstaking and sincere candidates at political meetings who can marshal columns of irrefutable facts, build a powerful argument on them, and leave their audience completely cold? Enoch Powell, on the other hand, by referring to England's green and pleasant land as under threat, can rouse feelings instantly.

For the home of the new Jerusalem to be under threat from without strikes the fear of the devil into the least Christian of men. Powell did not mean to describe present-day England as a green and pleasant land in any literal sense, nor was he taken to mean that. If that had been the case, he could have been made to look rather foolish by a comparison of present-day

Belgravia, where he lives, or Wolverhampton, which he represents, with Jerusalem old or new. The mere outward look of things had nothing to do with what he said, nor with how he was heard. The reaction was all the more powerful because no politician since Churchill has had any gift at all for uttering in the voice of a prophet, and speaking in images that have power independent of their superficial reference. The prophetic voice is one that can be understood by a person of any class, of any level of education, because it reaches a level of understanding that is shared by all the members of a society.

Of course, varying sets of values, and different pictures of the world around one, cannot co-exist in a society without influencing each other. And in this country, a long history of emigration and conquest in other parts of the world has conferred on every Englishman some of the more unattractive values of the English ruling class. In 1945 Britain still ruled over six hundred million people. The awareness of this situation was explicit among the upper and middle class whose sons could very reasonably expect to be put in administrative charge of substantial territories, containing thousands of inhabitants, provided they could pass the right examinations. The sons of market gardeners and tool-grinders had no such direct rule to look forward to, but their awareness of the Empire, through the popular press, and the text-books written by scions of the governing class, was firmly defined: England had a destiny to rule other people less favoured and less competent than Englishmen.

Yet although different sets of values may infiltrate each other, they still remain distinct and incorporate important differences. English popular institutions and attitudes are hostile to competitiveness, expertise and boasting. Yet these are the values on which the English ruling class – the politicians, bureaucrats and business men of the twentieth century – has come to thrive: naturally, for positions of power can now be maintained only by acceptance of such values. The history of our former Empire has been very adeptly presented to the public at large in terms which a popular view finds acceptable. The

Empire grew by accident, Elizabethan adventurers took the King of Spain down a peg. Independent-minded Englishmen went away to set up colonies where they could do things the way they wanted, and keep themselves to themselves. Sailors and explorers stumbled on new places. People who couldn't manage to rule themselves asked us to help and protect them. And so the British Empire came about. The real truth about the history of the Empire is not palatable to English people, for two very understandable reasons. The facts conflict with what they have learnt, not only formally, in history lessons at school, but in every assumption underlying popular fiction, children's comics, picture books, newspaper columns and radio and television comedy programmes; and secondly, it conflicts with the basic standards of good behaviour and British decency that they have also learnt in growing up. Together, these two reasons make it almost impossible for English people to accept or understand the truth about their country's past. They know that England abolished the slave trade; they do not know that England first grew rich enough to capitalize the world's first industrial revolution on the profits of slavery that had accrued over two centuries. To accept and understand the ugliness of the truth, of which the slave trade (from which Gladstone's father made the money that sent his son to Christ Church and on to a distinguished political career as a Liberal) is only one part, would, for many, tear apart their sense of personal and national identity.

A minority, of whom many are very young, *are* torn apart by the realization that the values they have been taught to respect as characteristically English, Christian and fair, have been systematically disregarded by the very people who claim to uphold them. The same conflict is much more readily visible in America, where the issues are more sharply-edged, the language on both sides more uninhibited, and the clash more violent. The war in South-East Asia and the race conflict are the two issues that have, in recent years, forced Americans into clear opposition, one to another. The American situation has the clarity of a cartoon in black and white; the English is more reminiscent of Turner's *Rain, Steam and Speed.* Uneasiness and revolt are as confused and muted as the verbose statements of leading politicians in both major parties. But it is clear that many young people dislike the society they are living in, whether they react by studying sociology and joining protest marches, or by smashing telephone boxes and beating up queers and Paks.

Awareness of one's own identity is formulated in terms of one's relationships with the surrounding world, and most of all in terms of one's relationships with other people. Attitudes, measurements of good and bad, conventions of behaviour, are learnt by the individual growing up; he learns to fit his own pattern of behaviour towards other people, and to understand his own position in relation to them, in terms of a body of knowledge and ideas shared by the people nearest to him. And much of what he learns is in terms of appearance and symbols. The child in Hoxton may learn, on seeing a policeman, to nip smartly round the corner; the child in Kensington will learn to go up to a policeman and ask him the way to the station. For the Hoxton child, a police uniform means 'enemy'; for the Kensington child, 'friendly menial'. But not all relationships are as fixed as these are likely to remain; however complex a society may be, a growing child can learn to adapt to it. But when the rate of change in the nature of a society is very rapid, as with us in England now, and categories change like a kaleidoscope's patterns, those who have already matured and adapted to one particular kind of complex pattern find themselves faced constantly with problems. If they see the problems for what they really are, they may struggle to understand them and to readjust; but if they do not, if they try to fit new experiences into their own familiar pattern, they lose sight completely of things as they really are and live their real lives as if in a fantasy world half the time. Take the kind of solidly middle-class, middle-aged person who has been brought up as a Christian gentleman, decent to inferiors, taking on responsibilities for the public good, perhaps as a J.P. or a magistrate, caring about good table manners, honest craftsmanship, the team spirit, kindness to dogs and horses, clean and sober clothes and a respect for old buildings: this gentleman is confronted by a young man, perhaps his nephew, who apparently shares with him not a single idol. He is not decent to inferiors, because socially speaking he does not reckon he has inferiors, and is angry at the very thought of such an attitude, which he regards as hypocritical and patronizing. He takes on no public offices; he either hates them, as actually harmful, or jeers at them as ridiculous. He has the manners, his uncle thinks disparagingly, of a lorry-driver (shocking). If he cares about craftsmanship, it is because he wants to make something to express himself, not because he expects an artisan class to make things efficiently for the employing class. He abominates the team spirit as a tool for destroying individuality; he laughs at it. He is indifferent to dogs and horses; he grows his hair long, and wears brilliantly coloured clothes, and old buildings leave him cold. The older man simply cannot fit the younger man into his categories except as a thoroughly unpleasant and undesirable character. For the older man, long hair and coloured clothes mean exhibitionist vanity, homosexuality, extravagance, wild and anti-social bohemianism – because these are the things he learnt to associate this general kind of flamboyant appearance with when he was growing up himself. He simply cannot shift himself into a position where these rules no longer hold. To the young man, a dark suit, with neat collar and tie and a short haircut stand for what is anti-social and sinister; they stand for bureaucracy, dehumanization, hypocrisy, violence against the weak, manhood corrupted and dried up. The older man is angry if a CND demonstrator kicks a police horse, but is quite unmoved by a farmer branding sheep or ill-treating calves. The younger man may be angered by just these latter things, and unmoved by a blow at a policeman's horse – or even pleased about it. Is either of them really concerned with the treatment of animals as such? Perhaps to some extent – but much more important is what these different animals represent in their patterns of the world: the police horse is a creature tamed and trained to work for authority, and to strike fear into a dissident crowd; the sheep and the calf are disposable objects in commercial farming operations. To the old man and the young alike, the horse is on the side of authority while the farm animals are used by authority and at its mercy. The symbols mean more than the facts; what the symbols stand for, though, are fundamentally important characteristics of society and the people in it. Quarrels about surface inconsistencies sometimes seem absurd, but they may be about real things. When we come down to the *real* issues between the older man and the younger, we find them living in two completely different kinds of conventional societies; their values and standards are quite dissimilar, yet they may belong to the same household, the same town, the same country. Physically they are neighbours, but mentally aliens, like the men at the Tower of Babel who were suddenly confounded by being unable to understand each other any more.

People develop ideas of their own identity in many different terms, according to the groups they feel they belong to; as members of a class, or a caste, or a nation, or a family, or a religion. But these are identities that can be adapted or renounced. I can change my name and leave home or be converted to a different way of life. But ideas about identity in terms of colour are of a completely different kind. There are people who see themselves as part of a group that is 'white', an enormous group that includes very different nationalities, languages and styles of living. And another group has come to see itself as 'black', again including many people of many nationalities, languages and styles of living. The 'white' man in England sees himself as 'white', not in relation to other 'white' men, but in relation to 'black' ones. He has learnt to associate the superficial appearance of skin-whiteness with certain admirable qualities, and skin-blackness with bad or ridiculous ones. In Sapper's novels, which both reflected and perpetuated one kind of widespread attitude, the hero was sometimes referred to simply, in an exclamation of admiration, as 'a white man'. And the reader saw in this description not an albino, but a brave, honourable, physically strong and commanding character. 'He was white through and through' meant not that his flesh and blood were curiously bleached, but that his character was frank, straightforward, trustworthy and strong. 'White', in these novels, was both a colour word and a character word. This is obvious not only from the way in which 'white' is used but also from the fact that the undesirable characters, such as Wogs and Dagoes, or even the occasional English-born rotter, although mostly people whose skin pigmentation is of the usual European kind, are described as physically different: Greeks and Spaniards were Dagoes to Sapper – greasy and 'olive skinned' as well as untrustworthy, shifty, cowardly characters. The famous saying, 'Niggers begin at Calais', was not uttered in ignorance of the fact that Continental Europeans are the same colour as Englishmen; it was uttered to convey the meaning that all who are not English are shifty, greasy, untrustworthy characters. Whiteness stood for the goodies. Nigs and Wogs were baddies. In this general kind of racist literature and set of attitudes, it is perfectly possible to find an occasional lovable and decent non-European; the faithful African servant, the noble Redskin guide, and so on. Despite their pigmentation, they will not be wogs or nig-nogs. But neither will they be 'white' men. The most heroic African servant is barred from this category. The best he can hope for is to be something like a white *child*. He may occasionally be honest, truthful and good, but he can never be allowed, in racist literature, to be in a position of strength or command. He can have no authority; he may not deserve equal respect. His speech is reported in words that would be more suitable from a toddler than from a man; he is never, never allowed to speak correct English, even if he is spared the indignity of being reported as speaking of himself, like a baby, in the third person: 'Massa, Mbongo see bad man coming', the faithful fellow will report, even if he has supposedly had the advantages of a sound missionary education.

For although 'white' stands for good in popular racist fiction, rather than for actual colour, it cannot be used indifferently of *any* person's character, regardless of that person's colour. Symbol and fact have become intertwined, in the racist myth, in a very special way. That middle-aged Englishman in a dark suit *chose* his suit, and his haircut, to express something about his own character that was important to him and that he wanted others to recognize. His young nephew grew his hair and put on an embroidered Kashmir jacket for the same reason. But each of them *could* choose differently. The uncle could become a devotee of some obscure cult, and dress up like a Druid, with a long white beard. The nephew could decide to go and work in the City, and have his hair cut and buy a bowler hat. These changes would signify real changes of character or behaviour. But neither of them could change the colour of his skin, or the nature of his hair, and look like an African because he wanted to be thought of as that kind of man. People cannot choose to belong to a particular physical division of mankind; they are stuck with the bodies they were born with. A man can make a gesture in the way he dresses: in wearing African clothes, some black Africans have chosen to announce in their appearance as they walk down the street that they have rejected the values of 'white' society, whereas a black American who wants to build his career inside the American business world or political structure will get a Brooks Brothers suit and smooth his hair down to show that he accepts these values. But the skin cannot be changed. And therefore those observers who associate 'whiteness' with the good and 'blackness' with the bad, and judge people they come across by allotting them a character according to their skin-colour, are judging them not by what those people have chosen to be, but by what the observer chooses they shall be. If the sin of pride were looking for a contemporary name, it would have to choose racism. 'You may not be what you will: *I* shall say what you are,' says the racist, and in saying this he tries to make himself God. If Lucifer were looking for a contemporary description, 'white through and through' would supply the *mot juste*.

The very model, and extreme example, of racism in action was performed by the European slave-traders, shipping men like freight from Africa to the Americas, when they took from the enslaved not only their wives, their children, their homes, their freedom of action, their right to life, their right to justice, but *their names*. All the rest was a story of horror familiar in the annals of human brutality, though on a scale seldom surpassed, and with a systematic organization that only twentieth-century genocide and mass deportation can compare with. But to take away people's very names, and to force them to go by the names of the slave-masters who had already taken everything physically possible from them, was more than a denial of rights; it was a denial of identity itself. 'You may not be what you will. I shall say what you are. You are not Kwamena or Oladipo, a man known by his name; you are Williams or Brewster of Jones, marked by our names to show you are our property, made into what you are by us.' This is what the slave-masters meant, and the children of slaves were called by slavery names too; they knew no ancestry but slavery, no history but the history of life on the plantation or in the servants' quarters, no family but the master's family – for slave mothers, fathers and children were deliberately separated and sold into separate households, to prevent the growth of solidarity and rebellion. A new identity of faceless servitude was moulded, into which black people had to fit.

Malcolm X, in calling himself Malcolm X, did something very significant. He was refusing to use the name of a slave-master, and was telling the world that his name had been taken from him and his true identity denied him. 'Black Muslims', members of the American Nation of Islam, have in general chosen new names in religion to proclaim their new identity and religious conversion: Elijah Mohammed and Mohammed Ali (formerly Cassius Clay) are the two best-known examples. But Malcolm X did something different again from them. It was not enough for him to proclaim a new, self-chosen identity. His choice of a name that was not a name – X, the sign of anonymity – was a statement and an accusation. He was, in effect, giving to white racism at last the only valid answer: 'You shall not say what I am. *I* shall tell you what I am.'

This is the statement that Black Power makes: I shall tell you what I am. Black Power can mean a hundred different things, but it is always supported by this basic significance. When a black person asserts his own identity, he is not being a racist or, as some people are fond of saying, 'an inverted racist'. If he were a racist, he would be saying to white people what they have for so long said to him, 'You may not be what you will; I shall say what you are.' But that is a statement that can be made only from a position of superior power. Certainly there are black people whose hatred of white people in general is virulent, and hatred is not a pretty quality – but there is a difference between hatred and contempt. Hatred pays some acknowledgement to its object; contempt gives none. Racism is essentially a mystique created by Europeans as a definition of their *own* identity as being greater and stronger than anyone else – a race of rulers. Racist doctrines tell us no truths about black people at all; but they tell us much that is true and important about white people's picture of themselves. 'Blacks are like children' is patent nonsense as a statement about black adults. But it tells us that the man who utters this sentiment is convinced of his own right to command and dispose of other human beings, and of their lack of right to command him.

The notion of what it is to be English, and of what it is to be a white man are distinct notions, although in many ways closely intertwined. The Englishman may regard all foreigners as somehow odd or comic, but he bases his serious policy decisions towards foreigners on the basis of some rational estimation. Frenchmen may be to him excitable jabberers who eat snails, but a French salesman entering an English inquiry office will be treated seriously as a salesman. The girl at the desk may laugh at his funny accent after he has gone, but she would not dream of telling him, on her own initiative, that the manager would not be able to see him. The Pakistani salesman entering such an office is likely to be greeted immediately with the assumption that he has come there looking for a job on the factory floor, and told there aren't any vacancies and so it's no good asking for the manager. The difference between 'Englishness' towards foreigners and 'whiteness' towards black people illustrates something very important about the nature of prejudice and ignorance towards others. What a person *thinks* and *says* are only important in so far as his *actions* are likely to be consistent with what he thinks and says. Even the most insane prejudices held by Englishmen towards foreigners make only a very slight difference to the actual *behaviour* of any one English person towards any one foreigner and are generally modified in practice by reactions towards an individual in a particular situation.

This has, of course, not always been so: sixty years ago English behaviour towards foreigners was frequently more irrational and influenced by prejudice than it is now. But the change that has occurred is not a change in actual acquaintance between English and non-English people. The change has been one in the self-conscious wealth, power and political importance of the Englishman. The sort of person who would, sixty years ago, have accused all Frenchmen of cheating him, would have been someone who travelled in France and had met at least as many Frenchmen as the modern tourist – probably more, since he was less walled in by the apparatus of coach tours and mass bookings. But the modern tourist goes to European countries that are demonstrably cleaner, less shabby and more rapidly developing than England, and if he is inclined to complain he will restrict himself to some defensible comment on the deplorable weakness of the tea; he may perhaps still feel innately superior to the entire class of foreigners, but he will not be able to express his superiority in his actions. His prejudices are therefore not very important, even to himself, for circumstances prevent him enjoying the luxury of self-deception very often; his prejudices come out of him not as bullying, but as jokes shared with his fellow-nationals.

It is sometimes pointed out by those eager to prove that the English are not so much racist as suspicious of all foreigners, that there has been hostility as great towards Italian miners and Polish workers as there has towards West Indians and Asians in Britain. Certainly there have been plenty of superficial similarities in reactions. The immigrant workers concerned, whether black or white, have met resentment expressed in familiar generalized condemnations: 'they' come to take our jobs away from us; they'll work for less money; they breed like rabbits; they overcrowd their houses; they have dirty personal habits, and so on. But similar accusations have been made in the past by rich English people towards poor English people; if you dislike or resent a particular group to begin with, you will pick upon some characteristics about them to dislike, after your dislike is already present in you, and pretend that these characteristics cause your dislike, or you will invent characteristics for them and then claim these as giving good reason for dislike. The same kind of behaviour can be seen in relationships between single individuals. A young man in love with a girl may watch her eating an apple and making a loud scrunching noise as she eats it, and remain enchanted. If his great-aunt eats an apple, he wishes she'd make less noise. But two people eating an apple make much the same sound; it is not the noise he finds irritating, but the person responsible for it.

Plenty of prosperous middle-class English people have dirty personal habits, like picking their noses; there are peers of the realm and business executives with large numbers of children, and for many years genteel English people have lived in one or two rooms in large houses, letting out the rest as lodgings – referred to nicely as 'rooms' – so as to make a living from their only assets: an inherited house and their own unskilled labour. Nobody objects. The manner in which a person's way of life is described tells us the attitude of the speaker towards the people he is describing, not towards the people's characteristics and activities. If someone said that Queen Victoria bred like a rabbit, we should know the speaker disliked Queen Victoria, or perhaps disliked royalty, or disliked the House of Windsor. If he had no objection to Queen Victoria and her kind, he would simply say that she had a large family. There may be two identical middle-income houses in one street, in one of which an English family live, with their married daughter, her husband and children, in rather cramped conditions, while in the other a Jamaican family live in identical circumstances. The usual way to refer to the two households is that the Jamaican house is overcrowded ('once they're in they bring all their relations in and turn it into a slum'), while at the other house the Robinsons have had to take in their daughter's family because they can't get a house. One is overcrowded, one mysteriously is not; yet both have the same number of people for the same reason. But the descriptions would have been the same of any two households where the speaker approved of one kind of family and not of the other; one might have been Scottish (they've had to take their daughter in) and one Irish (overcrowded).

To say, then, that English attitudes towards all foreigners and towards black people are the same, because some of the symptoms of these attitudes are the same, really tells us nothing at all. For the same symptoms are evident in all kinds of human relationships, many of them being between different groups of people of the same nationality and colour. We are forced back again upon the main question: what is the nature of the dislike itself – of English racism? How is it different from the random selection of more or less harmful prejudices that we all carry about with us? And why is it an issue of such bitterness, rousing fierce tempers and moving otherwise gentle and rational people to make statements that would be unthinkable for them in any other context?

A theory can be defined in general terms, but what human beings actually think, say and do can never be reduced to a generalization in terms that are invariably true. When talking of people's attitudes we have to begin from particulars, and from imponderables. To find out what racism in England is, and what its importance is, requires a complicated and subtle inquiry, looking for not one answer, but for many. I believe there is such a thing as English racism, sharing many of the qualities of racism in other countries yet distinct, and it is important for us to understand the nature of our own home-grown variety if we are to be able to solve the problems it raises for us.

5. What's in an Attitude?

The trouble with talking about racism in England is that everyone defines it differently, and nobody stops to think what it means. Race prejudice, colour prejudice, racialism, racism – everyone knows that the attitude to life these terms describe is publicly disapproved by respectable people. It may even be deemed libellous to call someone a racialist. Bishops disapprove of racialism. Mr Harold Wilson has said that he would not sit down at the same table as a racialist. The men at the top of major trade unions have issued statements condemning racial discrimination, and Lord Hailsham deplores it. On the surface, it appears that racism is generally held in this country to be evil, and that the holders of power and influence are united in condemning it.

If one accepts this superficial appearance as the truth about England, it does seem as though a few hysterical people are making a fuss about nothing when they claim that black people in England are deprived of their rights and of equal opportunities. There is a widespread reaction to such complaints: 'Oh, I'm sick of hearing about race. If they don't like it here, why don't they go home? The trouble is, they see prejudice everywhere. You can't be rude to a black person, or he'll say it's just because he's black. Why, English people fall over backwards to be nice to them. If only the newspapers and television would stop harping on it all, the whole problem would disappear. All it needs is time.'

If a general definition could be given of the English idea of racisim, it would be: a position to the right of whoever is giving the definition. Only a very tiny minority indeed would accept the description 'racist' of themselves. Yet there are some who would say coloured people are less intelligent, less civilized, more lecherous, and less honest than white people, and still deny themselves to be racist. Others would point to *this* group as racist, and absolve themselves from the description, while still saying there were important differences between 'white' and 'coloured' people. Others would agree *that* position to be racist, and put the whole matter in terms of cultural difference – a difference in which the superiority of European culture to all other cultures is assumed to be self-evident. More subtle than this, one can defend the segregation of races on the grounds that all cultures should be respected and so kept separate. (The trick with using this argument is to use the terms 'race' and 'culture' as interchangeable, without defining either, and hope your hearers won't notice – and they usually don't.)

In short, everyone is agreed that some other people are racists, but they all differ as to who those other people are. One wonders if Mr Harold Wilson remained standing throughout the *Tiger* talks, or whether, if he sat down at a table at any point, Ian Smith had to get up? If Ian Smith is not a racialist, it seems a little hard of Mr Wilson to have described Peter Griffiths, M.P., as a parliamentary leper when he entered the House of Commons to represent Smethwick in 1964. After all, Mr Griffiths has actually spoken since then against Mr Wilson's own Immigration Act of 1968 as going too far in restricting immigration. It is all very confusing. One can, I am afraid, make sense of events like these only by remembering that people say different things to different audiences. When Mr Wilson said he would not sit down at table with a racialist, he was addressing the Commonwealth Prime Ministers' conference – a mostly black audience. If we want to know the truth about anyone's opinions on race, whether we are looking at a prime minister or at any private citizen, the only way we can judge is to study their words on all occasions, and, furthermore, their actions. And it is here that the superficial appearance of an anti-racist Britain breaks down.

A practical study of words and actions was made very efficiently in 1967 by P.E.P. (Political and Economic Planning). P.E.P. is a research organization which makes investigations when paid and commissioned to do so, generally by large firms or Government departments. It was charged with investigating racial discrimination in Britain by the Race Relations Board and the National Committee for Commonwealth Immigrants jointly, and the results it produced actually surprised both these commissioning bodies because discrimination was found to be more widespread and virulent than either had suspected. What is more, it found discrimination to be more widespread than coloured people themselves believed it to be.[1]

Away from impressive public statements, many remarks made by English people in the towns under survey are refreshingly unhypocritical, and match their actions towards the coloured population a good deal more accurately than top peoples' public statements do. A manufacturer in one town stated to P.E.P. 'The Managing Director is prejudiced and so am I. If one came here for a job, we'd just say there was no vacancy.' And a local authority officer remarked, 'We're very lucky here we've managed to keep the buses white.'[2] When P.E.P. interviewed the senior head-office representatives of twenty-five major national employers, responsible between them for the employment of nearly 3 per cent of the total work force in this country,

> all informants were anxious to point out that the policy of their organisation rejected any form of discrimination based on colour, race or nationality and that this policy operated at all levels of employment and in all branches and divisions of the organisation. There was, in addition, total agreement on the bases of staff recruitment: the criteria were ability, potential and qualification, and 'colour has nothing to do with it'.[3]

This sounds just like the statements we are so used to from bishops, cabinet ministers and so on. It comes from the same kind of top level. Even at this level, however, further questioning about how many coloured people were *actually* employed and in what type of job, brought answers not quite consistent with the general statements made at the beginning.

Informants indicated that, from experience, they knew 'what to expect' from coloured applicants writing speculatively for executive employment and it was stated that it was 'not worthwhile seeing them'.

We send them back the usual 'Thank you, but . . .' letter.
There is nothing else to do![4]

And out of the twenty-five firms, seventeen had *no* coloured employees at the executive or senior administrative level, while the remaining eight companies employed no more than fifteen immigrants at this level between them.[5]

Inconsistencies, and the frequency of downright lying, on the part of employers, is evident from the results of interviews with coloured applicants themselves. Some employers said truthfully what they thought:

Informant applied to tyre manufacturing company for any kind of work and was told, 'No black bastards wanted.'

Applicant to foundry for vacancy as labourer was told: 'No vacancy, and why don't you go back to your own country.'

Application by informant, with diploma in civil engineering, Punjab, for general factory work was told: 'We don't want any more Indians.'

These are all frank enough. Something close to frankness, the bare-faced lie that you cannot be expected to believe, is exemplified in this application to a steel company for any kind of work:

'It was six of us. I was the only coloured. Three of them came before me. The man called me first, and before I could even talk he told me there were no jobs. So I went outside and a little while after three of the men came out with jobs. I didn't wait for the others.'

A little more subtle was the reaction to an application for a labouring job:

'I was told that if I was twenty-six I could get a job but as I was thirty-three I couldn't. Applied under a different name stating my age as twenty-eight. Told no vacancies. Just after that they gave two white chaps labouring jobs.'[6]

This sort of lie does not always command belief – but it has the effect of prolonging the suspense for the applicant anxious for a job. If he is told, 'No black bastards wanted', at least he knows where he stands. There are many more subtle gradations of refusal, besides those quoted here from the P.E.P. report. Some employers will explain to an applicant, in the kindest possible way, that it would really be unfair to him to be given a job, because he might find white people nasty to him in the course of his work. This is to kill with kindness, and it is not surprising if the applicant, who wants to make his own decision and take his own risks just as long as he is given the chance to work, is more bitter about this kind of fatherly refusal than about being told he's a black bastard. The fact is that discriminatory refusal can take place at every level in employment: it is the language in which it is expressed that is different. And differences in language do not affect the stark fact that at the end of the day the applicant is still without a job. That fact matters to him a good deal more than the personal mannerisms of the various people he asks for work.

If we use the P.E.P. report as a yardstick, it is clear that racism is in practice very deeply embedded in this country in jobs, insurance and credit facilities. The report does not touch on many other important matters where racism might be looked for, such as education. But it did quite enough to show that racial discrimination was the normal practice rather than the exception. The survey was made with great scrupulousness, to ensure that the factor of colour and nationality was isolated. Because there are so often, for instance, arguments against employing 'coloured immigrants' based on those immigrants' lack of English or their unknown overseas qualifications, or their lack of familiarity with English life, P.E.P. used test applications in hundreds of instances from a West Indian, a Hungarian, a Cypriot and an Englishman. Every time, the West Indian met massive discrimination, and the Hungarian and Cypriot very little, in comparison with the Englishman. The report revealed, indeed that *more* discrimination was experienced by those coloured applicants whose English was good, and whose qualifications were acquired in this country, than by those who lacked such advantages. Seventy per cent of the group with English school-leaving qualifications or English trade qualifications said they had been refused jobs solely because of their race or colour, and were able to produce evidence for this. One example was a West Indian aged twenty-nine who had come to Britain in 1961, and had a City and Guilds diploma in electronics and was a member of the Institute of Radio Engineers. He applied to the area manager of a national radio and television manufacturer who told him, quite positively, 'that it was not the company's policy to employ coloured people.' This firm was then 'tested' by P.E.P. testers. The English and Hungarian applicants were told that there were jobs if they wished to apply. The West Indian, applying for exactly the same kind of work, was told that no personnel were employed in the type of work he was seeking. Another lie – but this time a lie that might have been believed by a West Indian, if he had not known of the other two testers' experience. Another example was a Pakistani who had served a gas fitter's apprenticeship in this country, and on applying for a job as a gas fitter was told that he couldn't have the job because he was a Pakistani, and coloured people couldn't go to work in white British homes.[7]

There is an analogy between the gradation of different styles of racial discrimination in employment all leading to the same refusal of a job and the gradation of different styles of racism in other departments of English life all leading to some form of rejection. No doubt most people would recognize as a stark statement of racism a wall-sticker that I remember seeing around Paddington in 1955: 'Communist Jews finance black immigration to Britain.' But even the National Front has got more subtle in its propaganda in recent years. Their line at the moment (early 1970) is to say that black people must not be blamed for having come here; the fault lies with the English politicians who have encouraged them to come. Leaflets with this message are carefully worded so that they cannot infringe Section I of the 1965 Race Relations Act, which prohibits the publication of words bringing people into hatred or contempt solely because of their race, colour, national or ethnic origin. But the message is none the less plain to the reader: it's a bad thing to have black people in this country, and anyone who encourages their presence is betraying Britain. A lady at a club meeting I addressed in 1966 sat muttering throughout my talk, 'I hate them. I hate them, I do.' This statement was unambiguous.

Still, the number of English people prepared to say outright, 'I hate them', or 'We don't want any niggers here' is a minority. It is a very sizeable minority. A detailed survey by the Institute of Race Relations, documented in the Rose Report of August 1969, puts the 'prejudiced' at ten per cent of the adult population – about four million people. Mr Mark Bonham Carter, while Chairman of the Race Relations Board, frequently referred in speeches to this same ten per cent of extremists, or openly prejudiced people. But if the 'prejudiced' are such a minority, why is racial discrimination as widespread as the P.E.P. report demonstrated it to be? Is the difference between the man who says, 'I hate them' and the man who says, 'I've nothing against them: some of them are good chaps, but –' a difference in substance or a difference in style?

There has been a good deal of serious academic work on the subject of racial prejudice. Some explanations of the phenomenon of prejudice interpret it in terms of individual psychology, linking prejudice with the 'authoritarian' kind of personality that sees social problems as the creation of a few misfits (or outsiders or troublemakers) and wants to solve social problems by the suppression of these dangerous characters. Such an attitude, on this theory, may stem from a prejudiced individual's relationship with his own parents. There are also psychological explanations of prejudice in terms of in-groups and out-groups. The Rose Report compares two very different sociological interpretations of prejudice with one another: Michael Banton's *White and Coloured*, in 1959, 'found a widely-diffused norm of tolerance, and explained such discrimination as occurred in terms of the uncertainty generated by the arrival of the immigrants.' Eleven years later, John Rex and Robert Moore, in *Race, Community and Conflict* were concerned to explain the behaviour not of a minority but of the majority of the host community. 'We therefore thought it necessary to explain this prejudice not in terms of the personality system, but in terms of the social system, that is, in terms of a structure of social relations.'

A psychiatrist distinguished in this field, Dr Farrukh Hashmi, believes racial prejudice to be a kind of mental disorder: in its extreme form, a dangerous madness in the clinical, rather than the rhetorical sense. A classic Marxist explanation of racism is that it is used as a tool by capitalists to create division and dissension among the working class. The *Morning Star* has been consistently anti-racist, on the ground that people who are deceived into believing in the inferiority of black people are playing into the hands of the bosses, who like nothing better than to see workers disunited.

There are also historical explanations of racism, which see it as a function of imperialism, an inferiority myth invented to justify the exploitation and conquest of other peoples, or as an extension to the idea of a Christian Europe, which saw the Moors as a Muslim threat, and dismissed the noblest achievements of Indian and Chinese civilization as the work of the superstitious Hindoo and heathen Chinee.

But before we ask which of these explanations is correct, we need to ask whether or not they are all explanations of the same thing. What *is* racism? What is racial prejudice? The different explanations of their existence, whether scholarly or popular, are often assuming different definitions: they may refer to an individual attitude, a function of social institutions and relationships, or a political tool. My own definition is this: racism is a description of two things, a doctrine and a social reality. The doctrine has many variations, but it always classifies human beings into groups according to a definition that supposes either visible physical characteristics, or the nationality of a person and of his ancestors, to be the criterion of a significant division between the groups. It then says that any member of one such group, having the power to do so, has the right to treat members of the other groups differently from members of his own. That is the doctrine of racism, of which 'Keep our schools white' or 'Expel the Jews' or 'No coloureds or Irish' are specific expressions. So are '*They* should not be allowed to come here' and '*They* ought to know *they* can't expect to get a house in this kind of neighbourhood.'

Racism as a social reality is a characteristic of a whole society. A racist society has institutions which effectively maintain inequality between members of different groups, in such a way that the open expression of racist doctrine is unnecessary or, where it occurs, superfluous. Racist institutions, even if operated partly by individuals who are not themselves racists in their beliefs, still have the effect of making and perpetuating inequalities.

In any case, racism is about power. Nothing shows this more clearly than the widely different definitions of race itself. Racial difference is the criterion used to divide groups into the more and the less desirable, but what *is* racial difference? In the United States, anyone with any Negro ancestry is classified as a Negro, even if his skin is exactly the same light shade as his 'white' neighbour's. In South Africa, you have to be all black or all white, by descent, to be classified as Black or White; if you have mixed ancestry, you are Coloured. In the former Dutch East Indies, anyone with even one Dutch ancestor was Dutch – never mind if the person's appearance, birthplace, culture and language all belonged to Indonesia. In India, under the British Raj, the word for people with one Indian parent and one English parent was Anglo-Indian, and the Anglo-Indians were a separate group, thinking of themselves as English, even talking about England as 'home' when they had never seen it, but not regarded as English by English people. I remember a social worker telephoning me one day and complaining about an Anglo-Indian mother who had lived in England twenty years and whose father came from Glasgow, 'She doesn't seem to *realize* she's an *immigrant*.' In the schools of Washington, D.C., native American black children are classified as black, and the black children of African diplomats are classified as white. Think that one over.

Biologists and anthropologists do not all agree on one definition of race. If there is any single, broadly acceptable statement, it is something of this kind: all men are a mixture of a number of physically differentiated groups; all definitions of race are useful as very broad descriptions only, and become blurred at the edges; the rare examples of physically very similar groups that have lived in isolation from others for many generations are all diminishing in number because of the physical health hazards of inbreeding. General terms like 'Negro' in fact include a number of markedly different physical types, which in any case have mingled with one another to some extent. If scientific definitions of race vary now, they have varied much more in the past. Sir Arthur Keith, a Professor of Anatomy, writing in the 1920s on *Racial Spirit as a Formative Force in History*, claimed to 'look at Race Spirit not with the eye of a politician but with that of a student of evolutionary processes'. He goes on to conclude that 'patriotism is the force which builds and maintains national frontiers, and patriotism, we shall find, gives birth in the course of time to that larger manifestation of human feelings – Race.' This sounds pretty political to me. He goes on to speak with great approval of the Saxon Spirit: the Saxon

> was strongly built, independent and courageous in spirit; he could labour as well as fight. His instincts were democratic; all the members of a tribal community claimed a share in the management of its affairs. They had a power of self-discipline and of subjecting their own interests to those of their tribe; but the interest of their own tribe they regarded as paramount. They would never admit that tribes of an alien people who stood in their way had any rights more than the sword gave them. Thus we see the tribal spirit working in its primeval way.

He goes on to compare the Spanish and the Saxon (*sic*) colonization of the American continent; states, quite incorrectly, that whereas the Spaniards yielded to sexual temptation in a new land, the Saxon retained 'his purity of blood'; comments on the situation in the United States, South Africa and Australia, where the Race Spirit of the North Sea stock (called this rather than Saxon, since the Dutch got in on the act in South Africa) refuses equality to coloured people; and then states that our feelings towards races which differ from us markedly in a physical sense are feelings which proceed from some intuition which goes deep into the grain of our mentality. My favourite bit in this display of scholarly scientific detachment is the sentence describing the Saxon race expansion in the American hemisphere: 'They set out to establish new homes in a continent already inhabited by an alien race from Atlantic to Pacific.' I do think I have ever seen more economically stated the doctrine that white people are the right people. To Sir Arthur Keith the inhabitants of the Americas, people who had developed over generations a rich and varied civilization, including for example a sophisticated mathematics using the zero and a science of medicine and anaesthetics from which European medicine has copied the use of cocaine and quinine, were *aliens*. The invaders from Spain looted, destroyed and killed across the centre and south of the American hemisphere: according to Sir Arthur they were men of stamina and resource, but the reason for his condemnation of these non-Saxon types is not that they were cruel, destructive and blind to the hideousness of the crimes they were committing, but that their movement was not a true race movement; they took wives and concubines from the native population and so produced no more than a vast experiment in hybridism. So much for Latin America. The 'Saxons' in the northern part, who seized land from its owners, murdered men under flags of truce, broke treaty after treaty and reduced the remainder of the American Indians to a destitution and humiliation which has persisted to this day, are described by Sir Arthur thus: 'they were an eminently moral people with a tender conscience for all that concerned their own public and private welfare; they never regarded themselves as intruders; they dispossessed the natives of their lands just as their forefathers had done in England.' Well, I suppose that makes it all right.

Sir Arthur Keith was not a wild figure on the lunatic fringe of science; his article, published in a Universal History of the World which included contributions from the most distinguished figures, such as Harold Laski, Leonard Woolley, J. L. Myres, F. M. Stenton, Elie Halévy and Harold Nicolson, expressed a widely held and orthodox belief in the evolution of humanity from the most primitive to the most successful and excellent: the Nordic. Scientific knowledge has, it is true, advanced since he wrote, but the reason why no respectable scientist would write in such terms now is not because of an increase in factual knowledge but because of a change in the evaluation of facts which have long been available. The nature of the evaluation is something outside scientific method in the strictest sense, for it derives from changes which can only be described as political. We can see clearly through the absurdity of Sir Arthur Keith's claim that he is not looking with the eye of a politician; it may be less easy for us to disentangle from the statements of our contemporaries what is scientific and what is not.

It seems that the only safe way to define race is to say that race is whatever the people in positions of power say it is. There is no other definition that can satisfy the ludicrous contradictions between varying descriptions of what racial differences are.

Racial prejudice is an indvidual attitude, an individual form of belief in racist doctrine. Of course, when I use the word doctrine I do not mean one known dogma that anyone can look up in a dictionary; what I have called the doctrine of racism is a particular way of looking at other people, and my definition of it is a general description that, I think, holds true for all sets of racist beliefs. Racial prejudice is a term used to describe the attitudes and beliefs of some specific racist individual. Because racism is so inconsistent and illogical, and because individuals vary so greatly, it is hard to find two people in whom racial prejudice manifests itself in just the same form. We all have quirks and superstitions of our own, and our own personalities modify our individual brands of racism. The people who think Indians are perfect gentlemen and West Indians rather rough, the people who think West Indians are thoroughly English while the Indians are sinister, devious Orientals, and the people who think both are just coloured people and all the same, are all racially prejudiced: they all postulate basic racial divisions among men which determine character and personality.

It is difficult to separate different degrees of prejudice from different styles. People whose normal conversation has at least one four-letter word to every sentence will often use four-letter words in talking about racial groups, and are therefore often thought to be the most prejudiced people around. Yet they use the same familiarity with the f-ing foreman, a f-ing spanner and the f-ing blacks. Such a man may abuse the black man on the assembly line one day and be quite friendly to him the next. A well-brought-up lady in a cathedral town, on the other hand, whose harshest condemnation is 'not a very nice kind of person', uttered with venom but without verbal crudity, may not sound very prejudiced to anyone when she declares it would be much kinder to the coloured people to send them back to their homes in the sunshine; poor souls, they can't really like it here. She works diligently for a political candidate who wants to ban black immigration completely, remove the vote from Commonwealth citizens in Britain, and zone residential areas so as to encourage separate development. The lady has enough know-how to defend these policies as Christian kindness, and can sound quite liberal in her insistence that people should not, after all, force themselves on each other. But who is my neighbour then?

Descriptions and analyses of racial prejudice have to be looked at very carefully, and never compared with one another unless we are sure that the different descriptions are describing the same thing every time. Newspapers, reacting to opinion polls and surveys on race, generally fall into the trap of supposing a particular poll or survey to be testing what the reader thinks of as racial prejudice and not what the person conducting the questions was thinking of.

The Rose Report, *Colour and Citizenship*, includes in its section on 'Attitudes of the British Public' the report of a survey by Dr Mark Abrams, which was conducted in 1966. The terms of reference for the five social scientists conducting this survey were 'to measure the incidence of colour prejudice in the white population, the demographic characteristics of those who could be described as highly prejudiced, and the social circumstances and the psychological traits which differentiate prejudiced from non-prejudiced people.'

The most publicized findings of this survey depend on the answers people gave to four 'key' questions.[8] Points were also allotted to the total prejudice scores of people replying, on the basis of ten other questions, scattered through the questionnaire, in answer to which an unfavourable attitude to coloured people could be expressed. On the basis of the final scores, those answering were classified under four headings: tolerant, tolerant-inclined, prejudiced-inclined and prejudiced.

The four key questions were:

If you had any choice would you particularly avoid having neighbours from any of the following places – West Indies, India, Pakistan?

Do you think the authorities should let or refuse to let a council house or flat to a family born in the West Indies, India or Pakistan?

Do you think a private landlord should let or refuse to let accommodation to a family born in the West Indies, India or Pakistan?

Do you think the majority of coloured people in Britain are superior, equal or inferior to you?[9]

In the case of each of these four, the interviewer ensured by asking supplementary questions whether a hostile reply was unconditional, or whether, in certain circumstances, certain coloured people might be exempt from refusal. Those whose replies were unconditionally hostile were given a prejudice score of fifteen.

The average pattern of responses in the five boroughs surveyed (Lambeth, Ealing, Wolverhampton, Nottingham and Bradford) produced 'tolerant' scores for 30–40% of respondents. These were the ones who answered all four key questions in what is described as a non-hostile manner. The tolerant-inclined were those who gave only one hostile answer; the prejudiced-inclined gave two and the prejudiced either three or four.

What Dr Abrams was testing here was a means of measuring broad trends in attitudes by plotting a numerical scale. Such measurement may satisfy his own needs and those of other sociologists; it may, indeed, in their own terms, be a precision instrument, and it certainly enables him to draw a number of comparisons on the scale between particular groups. He finds that women are slightly more tolerant than men, for instance, and that people whose full-time education extended beyond the age of fifteen are less prejudiced than those who left school at the first opportunity. The authors of this report were not, surely, seeking to establish fixed results about attitudes of the population at large, but to establish a fixed scale for the making of comparisons.

The terminology of 'prejudiced-inclined', etc., may be altered, and has indeed been altered in the Panther paperback abridged edition of the Rose Report, in which stronger terms are used. None the less, the basic objection to the use of the survey still remains: that people who give both hostile and non-hostile replies are more likely to be muddle-headed than to be lacking in prejudice, that the tolerant are so classified because of favourable answers to what are usually hypothetical questions, and that we do not learn from this survey the answers to the really vital questions: how much discrimination against coloured people would the respondents actually tolerate, whether or not they positively approved it, and how many of them would stand out in opposition to other white people when the rights of the coloured population were threatened?

My own working experience makes me very sceptical about what lies behind the replies such a survey elicits. Those who compile questionnaires are, of course, aware of the fallacies that may creep in: people replying to them may not be frank, may misunderstand the question, or may have volatile attitudes subject to frequent change. Questions, and the analysis of the answers, try to allow for these considerations. But the analysis of results relates them to factors that may or may not be relevant to the attitudes being studied. Let us imagine a lady who votes Conservative, works in a bank, lives in a suburban house with a nice garden, and who comes out highly prejudiced in a survey result. Is she prejudiced because of what her father said about India? because her nanny told her black men would come and eat her up if she was naughty? because of what her school-friends said? because she read G. A. Henty when she was thirteen? because she is a Conservative? because she lives in a desirable residential area? Which is cause and which effect, which irrelevant and which factor has greater or lesser importance? 'Respondents' are not an anonymous bloc, but real people, whose attitudes are shaped by the absurd as well as by the predictable.

Accepting that those who come out of the survey as highly prejudiced are people I would think highly prejudiced too, I do not find the next category (prejudiced-inclined in the 1969 report) a very encouraging lot. For example, an accountant in his owner-occupied house in a nice part of town might well have said he wouldn't want a coloured neighbour, while having no objection to coloured people getting council houses – after all, a lot of riff-raff live on council estates anyway, in his view. Such a man could have said he thought coloured people inferior, but not have demurred at the idea of a private landlord letting to them: actually, he is drawing rent from a flat his aunt bequeathed to him in West London that is let to three students, one of them a Pakistani, who is paying through the nose, since he comes from a very rich family in Pakistan. Such a man, with two hostile and two non-hostile replies, would not come out on the most prejudiced end of the scale. But surely, he is just as much a racist as the people in the 'prejudiced' group; his only reason that he has no objection to council tenancies for coloured people is that he is prejudiced against council tenants too! And his only reason for allowing private lettings to them is that he is a landlord with an interest in the matter, of a profit-making kind. Had he been a landlord with only white tenants, he might have replied differently to this one, and come out as 'prejudiced' on the survey scale. But his reason for letting to the rich Pakistani is not bonhomie; this boy can pay a much larger rent than most English students.

The 'tolerant-inclined' gave only one hostile reply to the four questions. Presumably many of these must have been among the two thirds of all the people interviewed who said they regard British people as superior to those who lived in Asia and Africa! (Page 566, Rose Report.) An inclination towards tolerance which would give a hostile reply to any one of the four questions can hardly be called leaning over backwards in the right direction. Indeed, any state of mind which could answer these questions three-one is likely to be a confused one, and the value of its inclination therefore questionable. An English mother, who has spent years living with her in-laws and suffering from quarrels about how she brings up her children, how she cooks meat that is too expensive for her husband's income and so on, who is on the council waiting-list for a house and can think of nothing but the blissful day she gets away to a home of her own, might well answer as follows: she wouldn't mind having coloured neighbours (*any* neighbours, if only she could get away from Bob's mum); she doesn't mind private landlords letting to coloured people, so long as they're clean and respectable: that's their business, isn't it? – and people have to live somewhere; she doesn't think coloured people are inferior, though you've got to admit the country's overcrowded and she doesn't think any more of them should be let in, and it's not fair to them to let them come; but she doesn't think they should be given council houses. After all, she's lived in this town all her life, and so have her Mum and Dad, and why should a coloured person come along and walk straight into a council house? Down at the Council, they'll give anyone a house if he's got a black face. Why, she was told by Mrs Parsons about a family that got a house last week, West Indian they were, and driving a big flashy car: how do they get the money, then? No, she doesn't think they're inferior: a lot of them are cunning; they're never short of money; her midwife was Indian and ever so nice, but she's different from a lot of them. No, she wouldn't mind one as a neighbour; after all, you don't have to talk to your neighbours, do you? When she gets her own house, she'll have too much to do getting it really nice to be bothered with neighbours anyway.

Of course there are hundreds of other possible variations of attitude consistent with a three-one set of answers that would score as 'tolerant-inclined'. A highly-prejudiced, insecure and unconfident middle-aged man in a dead-end clerical job and living in a small villa in a slightly decaying but still genteel suburb might reply to questions in the way he thought the interviewer would expect a nice type of person to reply; this sort of character is familiar to all canvassers for political parties as the man who will tell all comers he is voting for them. Made rather nervous by a lot of questions, however, such a respondent can easily slip up and say the wrong thing, letting his real opinion come through. And attitude tests are carefully designed, so as to obtain more of the truth than such a person would wittingly divulge. Yet in any survey seeking opinions, the answers, as sociologists would often admit, may give only part of the truth about attitudes, simply because the questions are framed in terms decided by the questioner, and these terms may not be related to what the respondent sees as reality. The individuals I have described here are imaginary people, though saying things, and having personal backgrounds, based on my own observation of many real persons. A true story about prejudice, however, illustrates very well how extraordinarily inconsistent people's attitudes can be, and with what practical results. An Oxford landlady had been horrified to hear about events in Little Rock at the time when the National Guard had to be sent in to ensure the physical safety of the few black children who attempted to take up their legally guaranteed places in public school. This landlady had two young white American students as lodgers. She went for them vehemently, calling them racialists, telling them how ashamed of themselves they ought to be and addressing them as though they were henchmen of Governor Faubus and personally responsible for the ugly events in Little Rock. The students, who were both from the North of the United States, and who had both moreover, at some physical risk to themselves, taken part in demonstrations in the South on behalf of integration, were very taken aback by her attack. Before they could get a word out, however, to dissociate themselves from the policies of Governor Faubus, the landlady went on, 'Mind you, I wouldn't have a black person in my house.'

Maybe this landlady was 'tolerant-inclined'. Maybe 'prejudiced-inclined'. Who knows what she might have replied to Dr Abrams' key questions? One thing, however is clear: she would have refused a lodger on grounds of his colour, so that, however one describes her inclinations, her words and actions in that department of life where she had some social power – the disposal of accommodation in a situation of general shortage of accommodation – were straightforwardly racist.

Well, perhaps at least we can be encouraged by the number of 'tolerant' characters who answered all four key questions in the survey in a 'non-hostile' manner. And, of course, there are crazy but encouraging instances of action being non-discriminatory although attitudes are not: the Rose Report's editorial commentary on the Abrams Survey quotes a study by Kutner, Wilkind and Yarner, in the *Journal of Abnormal and Social Psychology* (July 1952), in which 'restaurant owners who declined to make reservations for racially mixed couples had in fact already served them.' The trouble is, racial prejudice being such an irrational and inconsistent set of attitudes, an assessment of its different degrees, as in the Abrams survey, really tells us very little about how people in general are likely to speak and behave in different circumstances: most important of all, such a survey cannot tell us to what degree people in general are going to acquiesce in an increasing amount of injustice towards the people who are the objects of racial prejudice. I am sure that if anyone had thought to conduct a survey in Germany in 1930 on attitudes to the Jews, and had included the question, 'Should they be systematically exterminated by the Government?', only a tiny and evidently lunatic minority would have answered 'Yes'. Yet extermination, and the many measures removing the rights of Jews that preceded it from 1933 onwards, remained unopposed by large numbers of kind-hearted and ordinary people, some of whom still refuse to believe that the whole business ever happened, and explain the pictures of the concentration camps as Anglo-American propaganda. For all those who would have opposed Nazi policy towards the Jews but for physical fear of the consequence to themselves and their families, there were many more who allowed themselves to be persuaded that it was the Jews who had ruined Germany and that they were aliens in the Germans' land.

If an inclination towards prejudice means anything, it is presumably this state of mind, willing to accept false information about these groups. An inclination towards tolerance presumably is a state of mind not quite free of prejudices and yet open enough to be able to drop these prejudices in a generally favourable climate of opinion and a secure position. But what is it worth to be 'tolerant'? And is tolerance a suitable or adequate response to our present situation in Britain? Or is tolerance in fact little better than an inclination towards tolerance? How many people classifiable in this survey as tolerant would actually resist prejudice and discrimination on the part of others? How many, like the Germans, would keep quiet?

I do not wish to appear to complain of Dr Abrams' survey on the ground that it is not the survey I should want to have made. It is in many ways a valuable and informative piece of work, and it does not set out, after all, to provide information outside its own strictly-defined range and terms of reference. What worries me is the kind of importance that non-sociologist readers of his report, and non-sociologist readers of newspaper articles, and auditors of speeches, referring to his findings, are likely to make of it. Taking a handful of its conclusions, and putting their own construction on the significance of terms like 'prejudiced' and 'tolerant' used in it, some journalists and politicians have already claimed that this section of the Rose Report is very encouraging, showing that most British people are tolerant, very few prejudiced, and so we have not much to worry about. This kind of misuse of a serious study of attitudes is highly dangerous, for it encourages complacency and blunts the will to action. There is plenty in the Rose Report to alarm in the section on 'Attitudes of the British Public'. For instance, 96% of respondents to a Gallup Poll just after Enoch Powell's speech of April 1968 had heard of the speech, and *three quarters* of the sample agreed with it.[10] In answer to the question, 'Do you think that on the whole this country has been benefited or harmed through immigrants coming to settle here from the Commonwealth?' 61% said 'harmed', only 16% 'benefited', 14% thought it had made no difference and 9% didn't know. How do we match these results with the much more encouraging replies received at the same time: 58% being in favour of legislation against racial discrimination, only 19% wanting unconditionally to move away if coloured people came to live next door to them, and 80% having no objection to there being coloured children in the same class as their own children at school?[11]

It would be forgivable for anyone to lapse into complete bewilderment in the face of such apparent confusion, to withdraw into the comforting thought that statistics are lies anyway, or at best to despair of being able to discover a clear and rational account of the degree of racial prejudice in the English population. What we need to hold on to, I think, is the realization that all assessments of the kind and degree of prejudice in England are likely to be confused and inconsistent, simply because racial prejudice itself, as we have seen, is infinitely variable, riddled with logical inconsistencies, and arbitrary in its expression and its effect on other people's lives. If an old woman living alone, with no rooms to let, no jobs to offer and no social contact with black people, believes that all black people have long tails and live in trees, her opinion has no bearing on the quality of life in England in general. But the much less ignorant and prejudiced businessman, who sits down to dinner with Asian customers and pays the bill, but turns down immigrant applicants for jobs in his office because of a niggling fear in his mind that the office-girls' mothers might object, has a considerable adverse influence on the achievement of racial equality. And when contradictory attitudes exist side by side in one person, as with the Oxford landlady with her two American students, who can guess which attitude will be the most important? The answer depends on the circumstances in which a response is called for, not on guessing which feeling is subjectively stronger at one particular moment in the person concerned. 'Prejudice' is not a unit, but a protean superstition, rapidly changing form. Is tolerance, then, or absence of openly expressed prejudice a clearer and more hopeful state of mind?

'Mrs Weybridge isn't prejudiced. But she couldn't bear actually to touch a black person. And that's natural, isn't it?'

This remark was made to me, with perfect seriousness, by an English visitor to my office one day. When I asked gently why he thought this feeling 'natural', he became rather annoyed. Not as annoyed as a businessmen's lunch meeting I once had to address, where one of the respected citizens present referred to the 'natural antipathy' that existed between different races. I asked him how, if there was such a natural antipathy, the millions of people of mixed descent in the British Commonwealth and the United States had come into being. People who describe themselves as being without prejudice rely upon having this kind of remark accepted without question. 'I'm not prejudiced, but –' is a popular opening for racist remarks, and it is characteristic of a particular kind of muddled thinking that might well be called Kindness to Inferiors.

Mr Temple, the visitor to the office, who would certainly have emerged from the survey as 'tolerant', was a classic example of the Kindness to Inferiors attitude. Politically, he was a middle-of-the-road progressive. He was very keen on social reform, decent housing and greater participation in government. He abhorred all snobbery and class hatreds, and worked hard for voluntary organizations concerned with good causes. He raised money for Oxfam. He thought the British Government should be giving much more aid to under-developed countries. His wife was a teacher, and his son the star of his school debating society, defending liberal causes. He was opposed to racial discrimination in jobs and housing, and thought everyone should have a fair deal, regardless of colour. For colour prejudice was, he knew, a bad and illiberal thing. He strongly disapproved of the South African government, though he was against digging up cricket pitches in protest against apartheid in sport, for that sort of activity, he thought, would only create a lot of antipathy among ordinary decent people towards the demonstrators. Yet he felt that, although it was quite wrong to treat coloured people unfairly, there was a difference between them and white people. You couldn't quite put your finger on what this difference was. But, like Everest, it was *there*. And if he was frank about it, he'd be very unhappy if his daughter married a black man. Not that he was prejudiced, he would tell you, of course he wasn't prejudiced. But –

There is a lot in common between Mr Temple's attitude to black people, and the attitude of liberal reformers in England, several generations ago, to the English working class. They should be treated fairly, paid a living wage, given opportunities to better themselves, such as scholarships if they were intelligent. But they were not the middle class. Their habits were crude, and they often smelt, though one would only mention this fact in a private whisper. Of course, poor souls, they couldn't help a lot of their faults, which were due to their having been badly treated in the past, and having never had the advantages of the middle class. One might say they knew no better. They should be treated politely, being greeted and not ignored if you met one of them in the street. This was the right thing: to behave humanely and decently to them, and see they were looked after in illness and unemployment. But it would not do for your daughter to want to marry one. If she did, you could only expect things to work out badly – as they do, for instance, in Somerset Maugham's short story, *The Postman*, where a nice, middle-class girl falls in love with a working-class boy, remains faithful to him even when he is sent to prison, and is rejected by him when he comes out.

Class is not caste, and just as many working-class children of the past have become cultivated, glossy-living, successful members of the middle class now, so it is perfectly possible, on Mr Temple's view of life, for some black individuals to become acceptable. They can be 'integrated'. He might shrink from touching a black person, and find it very natural for other people to shrink likewise, yet if he were asked to a reception at the House of Lords for political party faithfuls, and presented to the Prime Minister of a Caribbean state, he would be flattered to shake hands with him, and no doubt would feel a faint shock of surprise, making the handshake, to discover that there was no difference in the sensation between touching this big black man's hand and touching anyone else's. Mr Temple would not claim that some of his best friends were coloured people. The only reason he would not make the claim is because he is aware that the format of his remark is ridiculed by the progressive press. Yet, he might claim to know several coloured people and to get on well with them. And these friends, or, rather, acquaintances, of his are, he will tell you, the best kind of coloured person. They would be the first to agree what a pity it was that so many illiterate and insanitary villagers from rural Pakistan were flooding into our cities. They take a very balanced view of things. They are just like English people.

It is a shame, really, to ridicule Mr Temple, for he is quite a decent and conscientious man. And of course he can persuade most people that he is unprejudiced, when his remarks are compared with the remarks of the more open kind of racist, the sort of man who will tell you, 'I'm prejudiced, and I don't mind saying so. The whole bloody lot ought to be sent home.' Surely, good-hearted Mr Temple cannot be held accountable for much harm?

Unfortunately, he can. Mr Temple and his like may not be

feared by black people, as young fascist gangs with bicycle chains are feared, but they are as bitterly resented. You may not be wounded by cotton-wool condescension, but you can choke on it. The Kindness to Inferiors ideology is one which says, 'Just so far and no further. I will give you this. I will give you that. But you must not ask for more.' And the relationship is essentially a colonial one; the colonial power may perhaps be enlightened, willing to provide schools and incorruptible courts of justice, but it remains an imposed power which does not allow its own superiority and right of disposal to be questioned.

The Kindness to Inferiors attitude has been responsible for a number of errors, made in benevolence but without respect for black people.

One example is the proposal made within more than one local authority housing committee to deny Commonwealth immigrants mortgages from the local authority to buy houses in areas where there is already a substantial proportion of immigrant residents. The benevolent aim is to prevent the growth of 'ghettos'. Local councillors are aware that a ghetto is a Bad Thing, but their definition of ghetto is often a rather simple-minded one: a place where a lot of black people live. They are concerned to avoid concentration as such, if the concentration is of black people. They would not prevent Mayfair being occupied entirely by rich people, or a suburb being occupied almost entirely by highly-paid car factory workers, since a concentration of such groups does not 'cause a problem'. Concentration of black people somehow does. Very few local councillors would be prepared to admit that the problems of a ghetto are the problems of underprivilege forced upon a certain area when it is denied a fair share of the local community's resources, for this would hold local government, and not the residents, responsible for ghettos; for shortcomings in a district with understaffed schools, inadequate garbage-collection, poor street-lighting, a lack of open space and of nursery schools for young children, and inflated rents for damp and insanitary housing. No, a ghetto, in local authority language, means black people in large numbers, and must be avoided. So black people must be forcibly dispersed, by refusing them mortgages in the area where they want to live. If they are dispersed, there will be integration, which is a Good Thing, just as a ghetto is a Bad Thing. And to do them justice, they may be trying to avoid a concentration of black people in one area, not because they would wish to deprive that area of facilities, but because they fear another council, elected another year, might do so.

In practice, of course, such refusal of mortgages leads to ghetto conditions, in the sense of social deprivation, much more surely than would a concentration of black people in an area of reasonably decent housing. It is usual for large areas of suburban housing to be effectively closed to immigrant buyers. One reason for this is simply the price level; the best suburban housing will be beyond the resources of people whose savings for a deposit on a house have been acquired only after some years of manual work. (And only a very small proportion of immigrants are in non-manual work.) Within a medium price range, home-owners and estate agents between them are often able effectively to prevent an immigrant buying a house in an entirely white area. Immigrants will find houses to buy, and try to raise mortgages to do so, in areas that are being deserted by native English people for newer and smarter suburban property. A fifty-year-old brick semi-detached villa, still solid but in need of some repairs, is typical of the kind of house they might choose from the limited stock available to black people. And if denied this opportunity because some of their friends have managed over the last two or three years to buy villas in the same street already, the immigrant applicants will be thrown back on remaining in their present unsatisfactory furnished rooms. Refusal of a mortgage to someone both able and willing to be a house-buyer, on the ground that there are already too many people of the buyer's colour in one area, is straightforward racial discrimination. And no amount of benevolent intention on the part of the local councillors can alter that objective fact, nor can their desire 'to help the immigrants integrate' sound anything but infuriating hypocrisy to the black man who wants a house and is being told that he can't have it because there are already 'too many coloured people' living in the street where he has a chance to buy.

So what attitudes *are* all right? If the tolerant, well-meaning citizen can do as much harm, in certain circumstances, as the prejudiced one, what hope have we?

The 'tolerant' classification in the Abrams survey lumps together some people who are, on my definition, tinged with racism, and other people who are free of it: that small minority whom some Black Power leaders in England have referred to as 'the genuine white people'. The 'genuine', in my personal experience, are just as varied a collection as the more or less racist majority. I can think of one, a worker in a small factory, who might have stepped straight out of a wartime cartoon as an average Tommy: he first got to know 'coloured' people during the war, when instructed by an officer not to fraternize with the natives in India. Naturally, he will tell you, the first thing he and his mates did when told this was to go out and fraternize. He is now a minor union official in a small factory with a lot of West Indian employees, where he is not afraid to stand up for the rights of black union members. He once offered to help in a conciliation case between neighbours, suggesting a good clip round the ear as the best method with the Englishman who was persecuting his West Indian neighbour's family. I know two trade union officials, higher up in the hierarchy, who have put in a lot of time and trouble, often against opposition from some of their own members, to ensure equal opportunities for black people – just as I know another union official of the same rank who has systematically denied such opportunities in a straightforwardly racist way. Other 'genuine' people I can think of include several priests and teachers, though I regret to say that I also know strongly racist priests and teachers. In short, the 'genuine', or actively anti-racist people are scattered right across the rainbow of social difference; they may be old or young, male or female, well-educated or very little-educated, Christian or non-Christian, rich or poor. There is no section of English society that can be safely classified as either racist or non-racist; workers, students, police, housewives, professional men, all those classifications of humanity in which the communications industry deals will be found to contain a majority affected by racism to a greater or lesser degree in their individual attitudes, and a small minority free of it.

Individual attitudes, permeated by racial prejudice, have a great effect upon the quality of daily life and upon the possibility for social change. But individual attitudes are only one factor in determining whether or not we can talk of a whole society as a racist society. The other factor is the important effect of the policies of institutions, public and private. Ours is not a society of free individuals milling around able to control their own destinies. Whether you have a home or not, how it is built, where it is, how big it is, what sort of school you send your children to, what job you can aspire to, and many more fundamental questions – even whether you have the right to keep your own children with you or whether they are taken from you – are decided by organs of national and local government and by the controllers of public and private wealth. Having looked at the racism present in individual attitudes in England, we now need to look at our institutions, and ask whether or not they are racist institutions.

Part Two

To hinder another is not an act; it is the contrary; it is a restraint on action both in ourselves and in the person hinder'd; for he who hinders another omits his own duty at the same time.

– WILLIAM BLAKE

1. Emerson and Aurelia and Eveline

The office bell rang so softly that I was not sure if I had really heard it or not. When I went to open the front door, there were two people on the step outside, a man and a woman. The man was holding on to a piece of paper as though everything depended on it. They looked at me.

'Does Mistress Dummett work here, please?' he asked.

'I'm Mrs Dummett. Do come in.'

He handed me the paper carefully before crossing the threshold. It was a sheet torn from a memo pad, with my own name and the office address written on it. I brought the two of them into my office. They looked round the walls, where there were colour pictures from travel agencies of various Caribbean islands: moonlight boat rides, steel bands, big white hotels and blue sea, and dozens of laughing brown faces: an expense-account dream world.

'You been to Jamaica?'

'No,' I said, 'I wish I had.'

'It's a beautiful place,' he said, 'you'd like it there. Ought to go for a holiday some time.'

'I've got five children; I'd have to save a long time to get that far for a holiday.'

'Five children? You've worn well.'

There aren't many answers to that, so I asked if he had a family.

'We got three.'

'Boys or girls?' I asked the girl.

'We got a boy and a girl in Jamaica, and Wellesley – that's the baby – he's here.'

There was a pause. Neither of them had really smiled yet.

'I don't know if you can help us,' the man said.

'I'd like to if I can. What needs doing?'

'The lady at the Citizens' Advice Bureau told us to come and see you. We went to see her because the lady at the Housing Office tell us to see her. It's about our children. We been on the waiting list at the council for two years, and now they say we can have a house, only we told the council we got three children, but now we're worried because they say we can have the key at the end of this week, but the two older children are still in Jamaica. We been trying to get them here for one and a half years, maybe more. And maybe the council will think we're lying about our children, or don't want to bring them. Mistress Dummett, I paid the money for those children's fares eighteen months gone; the travel agency supposed to be helping, and I keep writing letters, but seems as though they're doing nothing over there.'

I said I thought I could help and asked for their names.

'Emerson Thoreau Weatherbourne.' He spelt it. And she told me hers: 'Aurelia Louise Weatherbourne.' I took their address, the names of the children, and their ages, Frederick, 11, and Rosanne, 9, and the address of the grandmother they were living with in Jamaica.

'Have they got passports and birth certificates?'

'That's just the trouble,' Aurelia Weatherbourne said, 'they got them all right, but the people at the High Commission there say Frederick can't really be our son because the names have got different.'

'You mean they aren't the same on the birth certificate and the passports?'

'It's like this. I had to send our marriage certificate when we wrote to say we wanted them to come here, and my birth certificate says – well, I'll have to go back to explain. You see I was born in the country, and the postmistress registered my birth, only she wrote down Amelia instead of Aurelia. She put

Amelia Brown, Brown being my mother's name. Only when I started going to school, my father didn't like me using my mother's surname, so I used my father's surname, and that was Morgan, so in school I was called Aurelia Morgan. And when I was married, it said Aurelia Morgan on the marriage certificate, only my birth certificate says Amelia Brown. I explained it all when I got my own passport and it was all right then. Only, you see, Frederick was born before we were married, and so he was registered as Frederick Brown –'

'Don't you mean Morgan?'

'No, because my mother see to it, and she used her name, that was my name too to begin with, Brown, you see. So the people at the High Commission say Frederick is my mother's son; they won't believe he's mine.'

She looked at me and I looked at her, and we both started laughing together. She was a good-looking girl in a vivid turquoise-blue dress, and her laughter was infectious.

'It's a mix-up,' she said.

'It certainly is. Well, what about the person who registered Frederick's birth? Couldn't they help get this straight?'

'That was the same postmistress that did my birth certificate too. She was an old lady, and she died.'

'Was he christened? Perhaps we could get help from the baptismal register?'

'Well, I don't know. Reverend Williams baptized him, and he went to New York when Frederick was still a baby.'

I wasn't going to suggest looking for a Reverend Williams in New York, ten years after he went there. It just didn't sound a very easy proposition. Still, someone must have replaced him. I put the kettle on for us all to have coffee, and Emerson Weatherbourne produced from his inside pocket a rubbed and frayed envelope stuffed with documents: certificates of birth and marriage, passports, letters, tax returns, duplicated postcards from the housing department, photographs of Frederick, Rosanne and Wellesley, and one of himself and Aurelia, younger and in very formal clothes, stiff and startled by the photographer's flashlight.

Once it was sorted out, there was plenty of information to prove that Frederick was the son of Emerson and Aurelia. But I had to pick out the kind of thing that would be acceptable to a British entry-certificate officer, and that meant relying on evidence from white people. It had, moreover, to be relevant to the demands of the Commonwealth Immigration Act 1962 and the White Paper of August 1965. We had only to prove that Aurelia was the boy's mother. Emerson was, in bureaucrats' language, a 'putative father' and had no rights of his own to have his son join him in England. It gave me an ugly feeling of connivance with the immigration regulations to have to argue in their own terms, but it was no earthly use doing anything else. I had tried too often appealing on compassionate grounds to have any belief in compassion left: this case was not so much a matter of compassion as of ordinary common sense, but I knew better than to look for much of that either. Emerson had consistently claimed Frederick and Rosanne on his income tax forms as his dependent children, also had evidence of money sent regularly to Aurelia's mother for their care, and by great and rare good luck there was a letter from an English teacher who had known the family. I assured them everything would be all right.

Some days later, Aurelia called at the office again. She had had a letter from the travel agency, demanding money. The fares paid in for Frederick and Rosanne would not be enough once Frederick had passed his twelfth birthday in a month's time; he would then be full fare.

'Can you get them to hurry up with the entry certificate, Mrs Dummett? I just don't know where to find the money quickly: I had to spend such a lot now we're getting a house, because we've only been in one furnished room. Also I sent my mother money to get the children new clothes to travel. If only they can get here before Frederick's birthday.'

I sent a telegram to Kingston, and followed it with a letter, asking that Aurelia's mother be sent an appointment at the High Commission in less than the normal six to eight weeks.

I didn't get a reply for several weeks, but before then Aurelia, full of smiles, brought the two children to see me.

'Thank you very much: I don't know what we'd have done. Shake hands, Frederick.'

The children looked worried and shy; they shook hands with me without speaking. I remembered an essay one of the West Indian girls at the College of Further Education had written: 'When I first come to England, I was very frightened. Everyone look very grave and all the buildings I could see were factories; everywhere had chimneys with smoke coming out, and I wondered where do the people live, because there isn't any houses, only factories.' I wondered how they would get on. A few weeks later, when I had to visit another family on the housing estate where the Weatherbournes had their new home, I stopped my car outside their new address. Six small English children, playing in the street, watched me as I went to the Weatherbournes' gate.

'Have you come to take the children away to a home?' asked one, who couldn't have been more than nine years old.

'No, of course not.'

'My mum says they ought to be put in a home. She says the Welfare's going to come. She rang up the Welfare, my mum did.'

I found Aurelia in tears. 'I wish we was back in the one room. They're horrible to me. The lady opposite rang the police and said she heard the children screaming, and it's all lies.'

She sat down on the sofa, one part of a brand-new three-piece suite in imitation mauve leather with upholstered cushions. The floor was covered in cheap, brightly coloured vinyl; one small woolly rug in the middle supported the room's claim to be carpeted. The only other furniture was an enormous radiogram. The children stood uncertainly, looking at her. Behind them, a big picture window, eye of a planner's dream, showed a panoramic view of grey sky, fences, and washing drooping from a clothes-line.

'We're the only coloured family in the street. We'd only been in a few days when the neighbour called in the police because he said our radiogram was too loud. That's not right, to call the police. They're all looking out of their windows and seeing the police come, and they think, "That's a coloured family the police is going to: what have they done?"'

I tried to comfort her, aware all the time of the two children listening to the sounds of their mother's distress, having it hammered home to them, within weeks of their arrival in England, that to be 'coloured', to be what they were, was to be unwelcome and on the defensive.

The front door bell rang, and I offered to go. Aurelia accepted, and went to the kitchen to dab cold water on her face. There was a woman I knew on the doorstep; though I didn't know her name, I had seen her frequently over the years in a greengrocer's shop where she worked, and we had often chatted to each other. She looked at me with some surprise; behind her, in the road, were two men and the van from a television rental company.

After we'd said hullo, and gone back and forth for a bit about how odd it was to meet just there, I found that she lived next door, but on the left of Aurelia, not on the right where the man who had complained to the police was, and that the television van had come to her door with a set that had been rented, but she thought they must have got the address wrong, and was it for this house?

I introduced her to Aurelia; she had indeed ordered the television set, and the woman from next door had no reason to stay. She paused, however, to look around.

'You'll soon get straightened out, dear,' she said, cheerfully but tactlessly, as she eyed the empty spaces in the tidy living-room. 'Where are you going to have the set? We have ours next to the window here. I expect your electric point is in the same place as ours, isn't it? Yes, here it is. You don't want too many trailing wires, do you?'

A singing kettle suddenly shrieked from the kitchen.

'I was going to make some coffee,' said Aurelia to me. She

turned hesitantly to her neighbour. 'Would you like a cup of coffee?'

'No, dear, that's ever so kind of you, but I oughtn't to stay here talking or I'll never get back.'

'Oh, have one with us,' I said, fearful that Aurelia might be hurt by her refusal, whatever had really motivated it.

'All right then, I will, but I mustn't be too long, or my husband will wonder what I've been doing all day when he comes home and finds no tea. Hullo,' she went on to Frederick and Rosanne, 'what are your names, then?'

The children, overcome with shyness, did not speak.

'Tell the lady your names,' said Aurelia sharply.

Very softly, they did.

'Rosanne, that's a pretty name. My grandmother was called Rosanna, a bit old-fashioned. You going to school, then?'

She talked on and on. She was full of goodwill, and the children, though obviously rather confused by her, began to look more at ease. She commended the teacups, which Aurelia brought in on an elegant tray, asked where they had been bought and for how much, and wanted to know how soon Aurelia would be getting curtains up.

'These are big windows to cover. It's nice to have a big window, but the council ought to think about what it costs to curtain them. You don't want everyone knowing your business, do you? Some of the people down this road spend half their time at the window, poking their noses into other people's business. I always say I've got better things to do. That old cat opposite, I heard her saying something to you the other day, but you don't want to take any notice of her.'

'She's been complaining of me,' said Aurelia, 'saying I don't treat the children right, and it's all lies.'

'Don't you worry about her; she's an old bitch. She still hasn't paid the Co-op for burying her old man, and that's three years ago now. Always making trouble, but I could tell you some things about *her*. Oh dear yes. The funny thing is, you know, she fosters coloured children sometimes. Hasn't got any now, but she had a little girl all winter, and two boys before that. So what call's she got to say she doesn't want her grandchildren playing with your kiddies here?'

Frederick and Rosanne were still listening. Learning about themselves.

The man who had installed the television set had left some time since. The kindly neighbour now suggested switching on for the children's programmes, and Aurelia obediently turned on the set. Grotesque flickers finally took shape as characters in a comedy sequence. An African king, feathered and painted, was making loud 'mmbaa' noises and pointing to a big cooking-pot, near which two white comedians sat, roped together, exchanging gags. Rapidly, the sequence faded, and a group began to sing one of the top twenty, while the camera raked an audience of cheering white children. Frederick and Rosanne sat solemnly watching, while their mother went on listening to the neighbour who eventually exclaimed that she must rush and get the tea laid or whatever would her husband say.

Dramatic chords heralded the news. One white face after another appeared: the newsreader, the Leader of the Opposition in a neat suit, an eye-witness of a big warehouse fire, and then a fuzzier shot, relaid by satellite from across the Atlantic, of uniformed policemen hitting out with truncheons, grabbing and dragging black people. 'Police were called in to deal with demonstrators at –'

I left Frederick and Rosanne still watching, and still learning about themselves.

Eveline Molton, whom I was to call on next, lived on the other side of the estate, and had been there already for two years. As she had five children, she worked her way quickly up the waiting list for houses. Her husband was on late work at the bakery, so I found her on her own with the children. She was a big strong woman in middle age, and was shouting instructions to three of the children while she cooked at the stove. There was a good smell of beef and onions.

'Take those things off the chair, Elizabeth, so Mrs Dummett

can sit down, and take Joseph upstairs this minute to wash his hands; you've been playing in that mud again Joseph; I've warned you once. Come in, I'm glad to see you: I hope you can help me. I want to go home.'

She turned down the heat under the saucepan, and came to sit with me.

'There's all this talk about sending us home; well, I want to go. Every winter my husband is ill, and the doctor says it's the climate, and he's not going to get better if we stay here. And he had to keep being off work for illness; I'm worried they won't keep him on. I try to get a job, but every time I go, it's the same thing: vacancy already filled. I did get a job washing up and kitchen work at the Pines Hotel, but the children's officer stopped that. And that's not right. I don't leave my children alone, and I wouldn't leave them with just anybody neither. My friend Betty had my children at her home, and she's got fireguards and everything, but the children's officer say Betty can't have them and I got to stop work, and she went to the hotel people so I can't go there no more.'

'Why wouldn't she let Betty have them?'

'She say some law, you can't look after more than two children or something like that. Betty has her own baby, and she look after one for someone else, and I got three too young for school.'

'That's right, there is a law about child-minding.'

'Well, what can I *do*? Seems so silly, I was so pleased to get that job, and Betty loves children, and my kids know her and they like going there.'

'If there was a nursery school, that might be the answer. But I know there aren't any nursery school places anywhere near here. What about the playgroup at the community centre? Could they go there?'

'I did go and ask the vicar. He very nice, he say the playgroup really full but they can make room for mine, only it's three and six a morning each child; that's two pounds ten a week for my three. Anyway the playgroup is half past nine to half past twelve, and I was working from seven-thirty for the breakfasts, so that's no good. I can't leave them on their own, that's two hours. Sometimes my husband's shift starts later, but not all the time, you see.'

I did see. Eveline was hemmed in by so many different difficulties there seemed no way out. Her difficulty in getting a job was no doubt partly because she could not go too far from home, and she had no skills except at needlework, though plenty of women got part-time work in shops and restaurants; the rest of her problem in getting a job was colour again. The Child-Minding Act, passed to prevent large numbers of small children being left for the day with minders who, it was held, fed and cared for them quite inadequately, was a blunt instrument that could equally well prevent adequate and reasonable arrangements for children; it dealt strictly in numbers. Would the Act have been invoked so readily with a white mother leaving her children while she went out to work? Perhaps yes, perhaps no. One would have to find out a lot about the local situation to be sure, not from the Children's Office but from local mothers themselves. It was nobody's fault that Eveline's hours of work, her husband's hours and the hours the playgroup was open just didn't fit. And the playgroup charged three and six a morning or it just would not keep open at all. It was subsidized by voluntary effort, but the law required a paid supervisor, premises of so many cubic feet, with so many lavatories and water-taps available; all this cost money. Perhaps the vicar would be prepared, on the quiet, to help out with the expenses for someone who had three children to be left there – but then there was the problem of hours again. It would not be easy to find a family willing to look after Eveline's family from seven in the morning till the time the playgroup opened, and then to take them to the playgroup. And even if one could, the Child-Minding Act would get in the way again. Many of Eveline's problems were shared by the white women on the estate, but in all their problems and insecurities they had at least some sense of solidarity with each other: they were not plagued all the time with the fear of rejection because of colour.

'I'm just fed up, and I want to go home. They don't want us here. My husband work hard, I work hard, but it's just miserable. Elizabeth's teacher, she say Elizabeth is a difficult child, always fighting. You know what happened? There's some of the other children always teasing Elizabeth, call her monkey from the jungle, say "Monkey, go home to the jungle", so Elizabeth hit them. I tell the teacher, and she say she sure it not true: there isn't any prejudice in her school. She say anyway Elizabeth shouldn't hit them. Elizabeth so miserable one day she just ran out of school and came home: I went to see the teacher, and do you know what she said? Elizabeth got behaviour difficulties, that's what she said, behaviour difficulties, and she thinks it's because I make Elizabeth look after the other ones at home, she too tired to enjoy school. I say Elizabeth not the one with behaviour difficulties; I know who got behaviour difficulties, it's those kids who can't be decent to others, always teasing. I see them after school, some of them, make a line with their bicycles across the path to stop Elizabeth and the other coloured children getting by, and call them names; they ran away when they see me coming that way from the shops, because I was real mad. One of the fathers came to see me, shouting at me on the doorstep here, and say I swore at his boy. I said you tell your son not to call my daughter coon and black bastard. He say the country's overrun with us and we ought to all get out and go where we belong. And I want to get out; I want to go home.'

It was one of those moments when I felt utter despair at my own helplessness. Not personal helplessness. I was able and willing to go and see the teacher; enlist the help of some decent local person on the estate, such as the vicar; help Eveline apply to the Jamaica High Commission to set into motion the slow, unsatisfactory process of obtaining aid with the fare home. But however busy I was, however many individuals I enlisted to use their voluntary good offices to help with the particular situation of Eveline and her job, Elizabeth and the school, none of these activities was going to solve the continuing problems of life for Eveline's family. As her husband was employed, there was no realistic hope of getting the fare paid by the Ministry of Social Security. For some time to come, if not for good, she was stuck with having to stay where she was. She would still be unable to have a job, Elizabeth would still be slowly destroyed by the heavy forces ranged against her – and so too would the other children later. What hope had Elizabeth of succeeding in school, of working well and winning praise? If she was lucky enough to avoid being sent to a 'special school' for her 'behaviour difficulties', if she stayed in the regular neighbourhood school, she would still be tormented by the other children; if she hit back at them, she would be called aggressive; if she defended herself by becoming withdrawn and apathetic, she would make no progress with school work. 'Elizabeth just doesn't listen, you know. Not a very high intelligence, I'm afraid. Of course, her background doesn't help. Poor little thing, she has to help at home, you know. All those children. I really think it would be kindest to *compel* birth control for these people –'

One small thing I could do. To be concerned with what was happening to Eveline, to be willing to try, was the only contribution I could be sure of making. And the first thing to respond to was what she most wanted herself, not what I might think best for her. She wanted to go home, and this opened a very doubtful prospect: would her husband easily find a job at home? would she? But it was what she wanted, and she had the right to decide.

'If you want to go home, I'll get forms for you and your husband to fill in from the Jamaica High Commission. Then they apply for you to get the fare from the Ministry of Social Security in London. It's easier that way than applying to the local office. But I'm afraid it may not be at all easy. Fare for you and your husband and all the children will come to – well, I'm not sure – over three hundred pounds, anyway. And the Ministry usually pays only if the State is having to pay the family's support. If your husband were out of work, and you were all on National Assistance, it would be fairly easy. Or if he were a permanent invalid. Or if the children had been taken into care, and the city was having to pay for their support in a children's home. But you aren't costing the government anything by being here, so they may not pay out the fare for you to go home.'

She was bewildered. 'What's all this talk, then, about sending us home? Can't we even go if we want to? If I could get a job, we could save the fare. But every penny my husband gets we have to spend to live.'

'Well, we can try. But I'll have to tell you now, it takes a long time. About six months.'

'I don't mind if it's six months, as long as I feel I'm getting away from here.'

'Well, perhaps in the meantime we could do something about a job. But that's difficult, because of the children. The only thing I can think of at the moment is some kind of needlework at home. I know there's a new shop making things for priests, a clerical outfitters; I believe I heard from someone the other day they wanted some of the fine work done by people at home.'

'You can tell them I do good sewing.'

But I was thinking, and perhaps she was too, that you had to do an awful lot of sewing to save the fare for seven people to Jamaica.

'If you do go home, will you be able to manage all right? Will it be easy for your husband to get a job?'

'I don't know. I think he can. And my mother got a little bit of land. It won't be easy. We got this house here, I know, but what good's a house when you're miserable in it? At least if I go home, I'll feel happier about the children. That's what hurts me. Somebody shout at me, I shout back, but I can't stop my children being hurt.'

When I left, the curtain at the window of the house opposite fell quickly back into place. The neighbours were keeping an eye on callers. The mood I was in, I could have thrown a brick at that window. Not that I knew anything about or against that neighbour in particular; I just felt helpless rage at the whole situation. Law-abiding habits are strong, and even if a brick had been lying about – which, on the Council's nice neat estate, it was not – I know I would never actually have thrown it. I was just frustrated by the knowledge of all the limitations on what could be done for Emerson and Aurelia's children, and Eveline's children. In some ways the children's parents knew much better than I could what difficulties they had to face. But there were other difficulties looming ahead which Emerson and Aurelia and Eveline did not yet even suspect, which I knew from familiarity with how English institutions worked.

These parents believed English education would open wide the door to opportunity. But the chances of the children getting to a grammar school, in the selective system still prevailing, were very low indeed. In all the city's grammar schools there were at that time not more than a dozen dark-faced children out of two thousand – half of one per cent. In the modern schools it would be a matter of luck which school they went to and what teachers they had, how well they could progress. Some teachers were wonderful, dedicated, hard-working, caring people. Others were convinced of the inferior capacities of the 'immigrant' children, and taught them accordingly. On emerging from school, they might, if lucky again, go on to further education. If given the aid of the Youth Employment Service, a lot depended on luck again. Some Youth Employment Officers tried hard to persuade employers to take 'coloured' young people. Others acquiesced in employers' prejudices, and simply did not mention to a dark-faced applicant the vacancies in firms where colour could be objected to. They might even anticipate or suppose colour prejudice on the part of an employer without first finding out, and play safe by not mentioning jobs where *they* felt it *unlikely* that a dark face would be acceptable. I remembered a phone call from a social worker in Buckinghamshire, very indignant because when he had telephoned a Y.E.O. about a boy wanting a job, he had been told of twelve possible vacancies suited to the boy's qualifications. The boy had gone to see the Y.E.O., and when his impeccably English name was discovered to be attached to a wholly African face, the number of vacancies possible mysteriously shrank to one. Even if Eveline's children emerged from school clutching pieces of paper that proved them in some way qualified, they were faced with the likelihood of discrimination. Without qualifications, they could hope for unskilled work, lifting boxes, trundling barrows – again it was a matter of luck how soon automation in the particular industry they entered would make them unwanted. The fact that a very few dark faces could be seen in positions of achievement was comforting to the English liberal heart. There was one dark clerk with the local authority; so you see, there's no discrimination. The police had one dark girl on the switchboard. A girls' grammar school had one West Indian pupil. Isolated instances like this did *not* mean equality of opportunity for Eveline's children. They served only to comfort white complacency. Such instances, it was thought, showed that a black person *could* succeed; if most of them didn't, it must be because of shortcomings of their own. 'We'd like to take coloured people here, but we don't get any applicants up to our standard'; this bland assurance by employers was enough to satisfy doubters. What exactly the 'standard' was, what prevented certain people from reaching it, these were questions seldom asked. An employer who had to admit turning down black candidates with adequate paper qualifications could always talk about 'character' instead. But where the schools had failed to develop, or had even largely destroyed, pupils' potential and pupils' self-confidence, an employer would hardly need excuses to turn applicants down.

But perhaps the most disturbing reflection was that Emerson and Aurelia and their children were *the lucky ones* compared with other families who shared their colour in England. They had a council house on a smart new estate. If fate had taken them to Birmingham, they would have had no hope of such a house, but would have been most likely in a damp single room, in a crumbling house due for demolition with roof-slates missing, faulty chimneys, doors swinging loose from hinges, no electric power wiring, combating chronic bronchitis with the help of oil-heaters, no other form of heating being available. They had all their children with them. Many West Indian and Asian families found themselves permanently separated, with one or more children abroad and the younger ones with them in England, because of the workings of the immigration regulations. Their children were attending neighbouring schools. They were not bussed miles away to schools of which the parents knew not even the name, as happened in Southall, or relegated to 'language centres' for immigrants only, away from normal school buildings, nor left at home not attending school *at all*, as had been the fate for months on end of many children for whom there was no room in the West Midlands, or whose passports showed them admitted for three months only (although in fact their settlement would have to be permanent) as happened to some children from East Africa with British passports. They had not been relegated to schools for the educationally sub-normal, like large numbers of West Indian children in London. The families had not, like some Pakistani families, had their windows broken so often that they had resorted to boarding up. These were the lucky ones.

But it was time for the children's party at the church hall. I drove back to the centre of the estate and joined the neatly dressed mothers, black, brown and white, leading their children by the hand into the rather discouraging premises next to St Peter's. Across the road was the glittering new community centre, its plate-glass doors already open for the youth club session. Expensive, bright-coloured curtains hung at the windows; outside, a keen youth worker in a track-suit and Woolworth plimsolls was uttering loud, hearty cries of encouragement to the straggling arrivals; girls giggling, boys playing and pushing each other off the pavement. They were too young for pubs, there was no cinema for three miles – and that served by a twenty-minute bus service – and no other local source of entertainment. The centre was used by some of the young people, and some of their parents, but many hankered sadly after the pubs, shabby and friendly, that they had left behind in the older parts of the town where they had been born. Their old houses had been bulldozed down, and some of the pubs too, and there were temporary car parks laid out across the sites of their old homes, soon to be replaced by new shops and offices, as smart as the new community centre, as neatly planned as the housing estate. The landmarks of their childhood had been razed to the ground; they had been uprooted from here and there and told to become a community. These were English people whose traditional life, with its good aspects and its bad, had been taken from them. The kind of social conformity most often driven home to them now was the conformity of the consumer, enjoined on them every quarter of an hour over the television, recalled by the advertisement hoardings and the shop displays. The estate was surfeited with smart cars, tinned biscuits, lemon squash, fitted carpets and washing machines; those who were too poor for all of these felt guilty and excluded.

But there were a few who came to the church, and it was some of these who now made up the party in St Peter's church hall. It had cream-painted walls, dusty bare boards on the floor, trestle tables and folding chairs, like hundreds of church halls all over the country. A gallant attempt at party decoration had been made with twists of coloured crêpe paper and a jug of chrysanthemums. Chipped cups had been neatly laid out ready for refreshments. This was to be the evening when the local children entertained each other and their parents, and after a good deal of whispering and fidgeting we had a few words of introduction from the vicar, and then the first turn of the evening, four English girls of about twelve years old singing the African 'Kum Bah Yah'. This was warmly applauded, and next, after a lot of nervous giggling, two children of West Indian parents sang the Welsh 'All through the Night'. More warm applause. Next was to have been a little girl of Indian descent, from East Africa, who was to dance, but she was overcome with shyness and hid her face in her mother's sari. She was pleaded with, but eventually three small English boys offered to sing, which they did with gusto, a song I'd never heard before, to the tune of 'Daisy, Daisy'.

> 'Daisy, Daisy, the coppers are after you,
> If they catch yer, they'll give yer a
> year or two;
> They'll tie you up with wire,
> Behind a Black Maria –'

The last two lines of this I unfortunately lost, because someone whispered to me how nice it was to see people of all races mixing like this, and it just showed that people *could* live together.

It was certainly a friendly and happy occasion. The little girl from East Africa was eventually persuaded to dance. There was more singing. The vicar concluded things by inviting everyone present to sing a hymn 'you all know', which unfortunately only a few people did, but those few managed manfully. There was a rush for the refreshments, with no distinctions of race: it was friendly, it was happy, and there was no doubt that everyone there had enjoyed the evening.

I had helped organize this event, though most of the work had been done by the vicar and his wife and a few of the parents. This was just the sort of thing my job was meant to be about. Promoting harmonious community relations. But could anyone seriously suppose, after leaving the thirty-five people in the hall and driving away past the hundreds and hundreds of houses, that this sort of thing was an adequate answer to any of the estate's problems?

2. People at a Conference: the Party

The lady magistrate was a little pink in the face after her second gin and tonic in the warm, crowded room. The edges of her make-up were showing. She had cornered a young, unhappy-looking Community Relations Officer and was telling him about his job. Her voice cut through the buzz of the party.

'I do so admire the work you're doing. I know it must often seem thankless and unrewarding, but steady, quiet effort, that's what's going to make these people accepted. If only the newspapers and television would stop harping on race, if they'd just *keep quiet*, it would all get better, wouldn't it? It only needs time. You can't expect people to get used to coloured people just overnight, can you? But British people are very fair: if the newspapers would only stop, we could get on quietly with living together. I always say, there are some bad coloured people – I see them on the Bench, of course, all the time – but a lot of them are very nice ordinary people; if only more people would just give a smile and extend the hand of friendship to them, we wouldn't have any trouble.'

To prove her point, she smiled broadly at a black man of about thirty who was trying to edge past.

'And where are you from?' she asked kindly.

'Brixton.'

'No, no, I mean where are you *really* from? Where's your home?'

'I'm an Ethiopian,' said the man, in a soft, unmistakable Jamaican accent.

'Oh, how fascinating. I love your King.'

The man succeeded in squeezing between the neighbouring couple and disappeared from sight.

'Isn't it interesting?' said the lady magistrate vaguely. 'I always say the best thing about these conferences is meeting people. Not the talks. Though we've had some very interesting talks today. It can only do good, can't it, for us all to learn more about each other? It's a pity that coloured man in the front kept interrupting; I thought he was really rude to the chairman when the chairman asked him to sit down. Someone ought to tell him that kind of behaviour will only get him resented: after all, we come to listen to the talks, don't we, not to see someone showing off, and put out just because *he* hasn't been asked to give a talk. I thought he was a little too big for his boots.'

She paused for another sip of gin and tonic, and the young officer took the opportunity to say, 'It *was* a pity he hadn't been asked to speak. The trouble with this conference has been that his point of view hasn't really been heard.'

'Well, you can't blame the organizers for not asking him. After all, you could see he wasn't going to keep any of the rules. He wanted to be the *only* person to talk. We should have been here all night. And I don't think that kind of person is at all typical. We had that very nice West Indian speaker, quite a different sort of man, very polite and reasonable, and really interesting. I shall find his talk most helpful in my work. I never knew before that the reason so many of these West Indian girls have illegitimate babies is because of – what did he call it? – different cultural patterns going back to slavery. You can't expect so much of them, can you, when they're not brought up to believe in marriage the same way we are.'

The young officer took a deep breath, but before he could get out any reply she went on, 'I have a lot to do with unmarried mothers. Do you?'

The officer was a phlegmatic young man. He did not scream, or throw his glass at the wall. He replied, 'No, I leave that to the sort of people who like to deal in the troubles of others.'

'The Moral Welfare people do wonderful work, don't they?' she said happily. Her world was full of people who did wonderful work.

'Excuse me a moment,' said the officer desperately, and ducked away towards the drinks.

A young member of Parliament, circulating rapidly round the party to talk to anyone who might prove useful, saw the lady magistrate on her own, and decided at a glance that she was not for him, and skilfully by-passed her, finding himself face to face with 'the coloured man' who had made so many interruptions. Here was someone to be talked to. He might well represent some interest group and be a useful contact for information, if for nothing else. And you never knew, you had to keep a weather eye open: some of these Black Power types were nobodies; others might really control some voting power.

'Hallo,' said the M.P. with practised warm cordiality. 'You're Mr Daventry. I was very interested in what you said this afternoon.'

Mr Daventry, not fooled for an instant, gave him a cold, expressionless eye. He was a thin, spare man with a strong brow, a jutting nose, and a short beard.

'Did I say something this afternoon?' he asked slowly. 'Seems to me I *didn't* say anything this afternoon. Seems to me that your fat friend in the chair didn't want me to say anything this afternoon.'

'Oh come now,' said the M.P., 'you must be fair to him. He had to let the Bishop speak, and we were running over time already.'

Mr Daventry's expression did not even ripple when he was told that he, a man with neither power nor money, had to be fair to the chairman, a well-known portly figure who sat on a dozen committees and received frequent passing mention in the press. He was too used to it. If the chairman told him to sit down and be quiet, he had to remember to be fair to the chairman.

'Well,' said Mr Daventry solemnly, 'I'm sure nobody would

have wanted to miss the Bishop talking about race relations. After all, he knows about it. I'm just a poor black man, what do I know about it?'

'Come now,' said the M.P. encouragingly, 'I'm sure you know a great deal about it at the local level, down at the grass roots. As a matter of fact, between ourselves, I had a word with the chairman afterwards and told him what a pity I thought it was he hadn't asked you, or somebody like you, to speak.'

'And what did he say?' asked Mr Daventry innocently.

The M.P., suddenly embarrassed at remembering what the chairman *had* said to the suggestion, improvised rapidly. 'Well, you know what it is with these conferences –'

'I do,' said Mr Daventry.

'The chairman himself wasn't really responsible for all the organizing. He was asked to take the chair after several of the speakers had already been invited. And one has to remember the public relations aspect. It makes a lot of difference to have someone like the Bishop here, as far as the general public is concerned.'

'That's right, everybody loves a Bishop,' said Mr Daventry. The M.P. instantly thought of the recent correspondence in *The Times*, where a bishop had come under attack from a number of enraged correspondents for a statement about South Africa; one correspondent had rather oddly written, 'Why does a Bishop have a special right to preach to the rest of us?' However, thought the M.P., this could hardly be in Mr Daventry's mind, since he wasn't very likely, a man like that, to read *The Times*.

'But it was a great mistake, I think, not to invite any representatives from immigrant organizations. Which group do *you* belong to?'

'Which group now? Which group?' answered Mr Daventry.

'I mean, are you in any West Indian organizations? You were saying a lot about young people this afternoon, I wondered if you ran a youth club or something of that sort.'

'Now where would I get the premises for a youth club?'

'Where do you live?' persisted the M.P., hoping still to get some useful information.

'I live in the Royal Borough of Kensington,' said Mr Daventry. 'I'm kind of a neighbour to the chairman here today. Only difference is, he lives in South Kensington and I live in North. We don't see a great deal of the residents from South Kensington in my road, except maybe round election times. Still, you know, we have a lot in common. Why, I believe that since the dustmen's strike, there are quite a lot of rats in South Kensington, just like we're used to having where I live. Only the residents in South Kensington seem kind of upset about the rats; they aren't used to them like we are. Why, we think of them just like pets.'

The M.P., after a second's uncertainty, decided this was a joke, and laughed heartily.

'Oh, what's the joke? Do tell!' exclaimed the M.P.'s wife, coming up at this moment, glass in hand. She was a lively brunette, in a clinging crêpe dress that had already earned a disapproving look from the lady magistrate near by. She was determined to be a wonderful wife to her husband and help him in his work: she knew, with greater certainty than anyone else knew it, that she was good-looking, amusing, intelligent, excitingly unconventional, and, behind the fashion-conscious façade, very serious-minded. Indeed, it seemed to her at times that she had almost an excess of the qualities an M.P.'s wife needed.

'Hallo, darling, this is Mr Daventry. My wife, Liz. Mr Daventry was just telling me about life in Kensington.'

'Oh, do you live in Kensington?' exclaimed Liz, still full of vivacious interest. 'How terribly smart. We live in Fulham.'

'I have a friend who lives in Fulham,' said Mr Daventry politely. 'Only trouble is, he's twice been stopped by the police when he's been going into his front door, because they thought it was too good a neighbourhood for a black man to be unless he was stealing something. He has this very high-class flat, you see. He's by way of being quite a successful musician. Funny thing, one time when the police stopped him, they asked him who he was, and he told them his name. And one of them belted him one and said, "And I'm the Emperor of China." Very witty, the police. My friend had a tooth knocked out.'

'Oh how absurd!' cried Liz. 'The police *can* be stupid, can't they? Something awfully embarrassing happened to a friend of mine once when she was climbing in at her own window, but it's a very long story and you really have to *know* the people, her and her husband, I mean, to find it funny. They'd just had a row, you see; they're always having rows –'

'Excuse me darling,' said the M.P. laying his hand on her arm, 'I must dash over and have a word with Wilcox; he looks as if he's about to go.' And he hurried away, now sure that there was nothing of use to be gained from Mr Daventry.

'Have you been speaking at this conference today?' Liz asked, when she had finished the involved story of her friend's encounter with the police.

'No.'

'Has it been good? It's such a shame I couldn't get to it myself, it's one of my days for good works, you know. An M.P.'s wife has to do a frightful lot, not just at election times, helping nurse the constituency. Hugh gets worked off his feet, poor darling, and of course he can't go round to all these little local dos the whole time. So I have to help out. Though I feel at times some of them would rather have someone more *respectable* than me, you know, someone wearing a hat and more *worthy*.' She looked thoughtfully down at her bosom, intending Mr Daventry to follow her glance and be reminded that she was terribly attractive as well as a hard-working wife. Mr Daventry however (oddly, she thought, for a black man, because everyone knew they were madly sexy) remained quite unmoved. Indeed, he did not seem to be paying any attention to her at all, but was staring over her shoulder. She half-turned, picking up a potato crisp by way of excuse, to see which woman he was looking at, but he was only looking at the blank wall.

Well, he couldn't even be bothered to listen, when after all she was talking to him just as if he were anyone else in the room wasn't she? She wasn't taking any notice of the fact he was black, was she? She'd talked to him the way she'd talk to any ordinary white person at a party. Who was he, anyway? Was he someone her husband needed to get on with? He didn't look very important, but you could never be sure. She held out the dish of potato crisps, and opened out another dazzling smile.

'Have a crisp,' she said.

Mr Daventry's eyes shifted back to meet hers, and for the first time since the conversation had begun, he smiled.

'You can't square me with a potato crisp,' he said. And, slowly and easily, he walked away from her, leaving her puzzled and angry with the dish in her hand.

The room was growing warmer all the time, the air louder, wreathed in cigarette smoke and heavy with the scent of gin. The crowd had thinned a little, though, and some of the conference visitors and speakers had begun to sit around the edges of the room, on the comfortable and expensive chairs with which the conference centre was lavishly furnished.

'Of course, the hardest thing,' said a social worker to her neighbour on the sofa, 'is going to be to get rid of the prejudices of the working class. They're so suspicious, aren't they, of anything new. And of course, one can understand. Personally, I find it very easy to get on with the West Indians, but I do have to admit I'm a little bit prejudiced against the Pakistanis. The trouble is with the ones who come from *villages*. So insanitary, very often, and utterly ignorant and illiterate. Some of my young mothers are quite sweet; not a word of English, but they smile and smile. But so *silly*. When I took along an interpreter the other day to explain about family planning, one of them just *laughed*. She couldn't seem to understand how important it was for her, with the new baby and two little toddlers with runny noses, and, you know, no trousers at all; of course the neighbours get upset. It isn't very nice. And the men, I feel, are a worse problem: they're so jealous of their wives. No, I do find it hard to like the Pakistanis. Though of course, I *never* show what I feel. They have no idea I see them differently from anyone else. Well, perhaps not anyone else; I find the Irish rather a problem too, to tell the truth. I mean, of course,' she added hastily, noticing too late that her neighbour's conference badge on his lapel was marked, 'Dr P. Kelly', 'I mean, of course, the *bog* Irish.'

Two of the conference organizers were agreeing with each other warmly on the success of the day. All the hard work of preparation had been worth it. Sixty people had come, which was remarkable for a conference on race; one of the pair had tried to organize a similar thing in the Midlands a few months before and had had to cancel it at the last minute because hardly anyone had wanted to come. Everyone had commented favourably on the lunch, though some had complained a bit at the price. Still, if a thing was worth doing it was worth doing well; it was always a great help to have a really comfortable hall, and all the arrangements for refreshments had gone extremely well.

'That chap – what's his name, Daventry – seems to turn up at all these things to interrupt.'

'Yes, you'd think he'd get tired of it. I thought the chairman handled him very well. The Bishop didn't have much to say, did he? To tell the truth, I couldn't help wondering if he'd got us mixed up with some other conference. I mean, overseas aid is very important but it wasn't quite the right note for today, I feel.'

'Well, it's the Bishop's thing really, overseas aid; he tends to see all problems related to it. It was a bit off the point, I agree. Still, it doesn't hurt to be reminded of the problems of the countries these people come from. Though, of course, then you get unfortunate remarks like that big red-faced man made: if their countries were so poor, why didn't they stay there instead of coming here to cause problems for us?'

'Was that the man who described himself as an average citizen of Wolverhampton?'

'Oh no, that was the questioner who said the trouble with immigrants was they didn't understand there were some streets where people like them shouldn't expect to be able to live; the

English working class knew there were some areas they couldn't reasonably expect to buy a house but these immigrants didn't. I believe he said he was an estate agent.'

'Ah yes. We had some very good questions, though. The session on immigrant children in schools was very good, I thought. Of course, having quite a few teachers here helped.'

'Pity there weren't more immigrant parents, you know; still, one can never get them to this sort of thing very easily. I did try to see if I could get one or two, but of course a day conference is difficult for a lot of people. Time off from work, and mothers with younger children and all that kind of thing. There was that one rather large lady in pink, West Indian, who got so emotional, I'm not sure who she was. You remember, who got so upset about the speaker saying West Indian children were from culturally deprived and inadequate backgrounds.'

'It's difficult, isn't it, to get across to someone like that the disadvantages her children *do* suffer from.'

The lady in pink, who was Mrs Daventry, was saying vehemently to a sympathetic listener, 'I wouldn't come to another of these things, not for a million pounds. Talk, talk, talk – what are they going to *do*? What about all the kids without jobs, hanging round and getting picked up by the police? What are they going to do about that?'

A young teacher, blonde and bright-faced, was exchanging accounts of classroom problems with a brown-haired girl in glasses.

'What do you think the headmaster said? He said rules were rules, and he wasn't going to have any pupils making the school look messy wearing unsuitable foreign clothes. He came into my class and told poor little Surinder to go home and change into something sensible. I was furious. I went to see him afterwards and tried to explain that her family would never allow her to come to school bare-legged, and if she wears a blazer on top she looks perfectly neat: I think shalwars are nice. I love my immigrants class; they're so polite and so keen to learn.'

'How many do you have?'

'Fourteen. It's too many, really, because they're all at different levels. Of course I meet some of the others, outside my English as a second language class. There's one dear little boy, Mohammed Asghar, a little half-pint, you'd never guess he was twelve. He wants to be a doctor. It's hard to know what to do, isn't it? I mean, he doesn't stand a chance of being a doctor. He *could*, of course, with a different background; he's terribly bright. He could hardly speak a word of English when he first came to me; he'd only been in England three months, and now he's really zoomed ahead. But I don't see how we can get him into the grammar school at thirteen plus; he just won't have done the work, you see, and although he's miles cleverer than a lot of the twelve-year-olds in the school, he's not been through primary school here and all his time with us has been in the English class, except for woodwork and P.E. and that kind of thing, so he's got a lot to catch up with. Maybe later on he could go to the technical college to do A-levels, but he'll need someone to see him through till then and make sure he gets the chance he deserves. I wish I could be there, but I'll be leaving in the summer to get married, and my fiancé is getting a job with an aviation firm near Bristol, so I'll have to leave this school and get another job down there. I'll feel so sorry to leave: you get attached to them, don't you?'

'I don't know about that,' said the brown-haired girl. 'I feel so worn out at the end of every day, I don't know how long I can stand the pace. Our school's in a real problem area. I must say, some of the immigrant children where I am seem a better class of child than the English ones. The whole area's gone down. A lot of local families have moved out to Woodlands and then of course the coloured families move in. I will say, they're nearly all very clean, and nicely kept. I wish all the English ones were the same. But I do find the coloured ones a problem. They just can't stand any criticism, you know. The West Indians are the worst. Very sullen, and won't talk to you.'

'Good gracious, I've never found that,' said the blonde girl, confused and put out by an attitude she had not been expecting. 'Not that we've got any West Indians, hardly; all mine are from India and Pakistan.' Then she thought to herself, 'But I shouldn't have said that; it sounds as though I'm allowing she could be right, talking that way about West Indians.'

'I think the Asians are a better type,' said the brown-haired girl. 'Their parents are keen on education, and they work hard. But the West Indians just seem to expect everything to fall into their laps. They talk big about being electrical engineers and that sort of thing, and if they find it difficult it never occurs to them it's because they just can't reach the standard. Oh no, they seem to think everyone around them's colour-prejudiced.'

'Perhaps they often are,' said the blonde girl pointedly.

'Well of course a lot of the neighbourhood is prejudiced,' said the brown-haired girl, missing the point, 'but that's only natural, with such a big coloured population there.'

'I don't see why,' said the blonde teacher. 'If you don't feel any prejudice against one brown neighbour, why should you feel it against ten brown neighbours?'

'It's the numbers,' replied the other simply, as though answering the question with a self-evident truth. 'It's all a matter of numbers, isn't it? I think they should be completely stopped from coming into the country until we've absorbed what we've got already.'

'Do you mean people shouldn't be allowed to bring their children here?'

'I don't think it's kindness to the children to bring them to an area like ours. They'd probably be much better off staying in their own countries; after all, someone must be looking after them there: grandmothers or aunts, or someone. Why can't they just stay there?'

The blonde teacher was at a loss for words, not because answers failed to come but because there were so many things wrong with what the brown-haired girl had said that she hardly knew where to start. If it wasn't already obvious to someone that it was natural for parents to want their own children to be with them, how did one begin explaining such a very simple human fact? And what did she mean by 'absorb'? Was it 'absorption' that was going on in the school referred to, with its despised class of white pupils, its 'better type' of Asians, its 'sullen' West Indians? What kind of beneficent social process was this? And how would it be improved by keeping some of the families permanently separated from their own children? And why were numbers so important, and how did you decide what number was good and what number was bad? 'Four legs good, two legs bad,' she murmured absent-mindedly, remembering what the sheep had been taught to bleat by the cunning pigs in *Animal Farm*.

'Sorry, what did you say?' asked the brown-haired teacher.

'Oh sorry, I just remembered something,' said the blonde vaguely, looking at the other and thinking to herself, 'A sheep, repeating things that are meaningless until they seem true. And she's *teaching*. My God, what will happen to the children she's teaching?'

'I hope you've enjoyed the conference,' said one of the organizers politely, stopping by their chairs. Most of the other delegates had left, and a white-jacketed waiter had begun to empty ashtrays and collect fistfuls of glasses from the tables round the room.

'Yes, thank you, it's been very interesting,' said the blonde teacher, with automatic politeness, and 'Yes, thank you very much,' said the brown-haired teacher.

The waiter, who was Spanish, went on clearing up as they left, and he hummed a tune as he worked, moving with the half-tones and subtle rhythms of a song that echoed North Africa and Southern Europe, a rich music of his own.

3. People at a Meeting: the Teach-In

It was a left-wing teach-in. Several of the faces were familiar from press photographs of the latest sit-in. Most of those present were young, many of them students, but there were also older faces to be seen here and there in the hall: veteran members of the Trades Council, middle-aged economists who still read the *New Statesman*; social administrators who took *New Society* instead; and liberal internationalists who had worked diligently over the years for peaceful causes. There were only a few dark faces in the audience, several of them local townspeople, and although the teach-in was on the subject of race, only a few dark faces were to be seen in the row of speakers.

The speeches were on different set subjects, but the approach of all the white speakers on the platform became steadily more repetitive as the long day wore on: racism was a tool of capitalism, used to divide the workers. In order to get rid of racism we must first get rid of the entire capitalist system. White workers, black workers and students must unite for the overthrow of the system. Students would activate white workers.

At last the repetition of this theme by a particularly young and dogmatic speaker so enraged a West Indian in the audience that he got up and interrupted with a shout: 'You don't know what you're talking about!' His next words were drowned by indignant yells in several parts of the hall. The West Indian tried to go on, but eventually sat down, muttering.

The speaker got a big round of applause and the chairman called for questions.

A white trade unionist then rose to ask his question.

'Mr Chairman, I happen to work in a factory.' (Ironic cheers from three students sitting on a radiator.) 'I've heard several of the speakers today say that students and workers are going to work together against racism. But quite honestly, in my factory, if there are two words that make all the men see red, those two words are "student" and "immigrant". And I'd like to hear something a bit more specific about how the white workers are to be persuaded to work against racism, or to see that it is being used by the employers to divide them. They think students are a lot of layabouts, and eighty per cent of the men are supporters of Enoch Powell on immigration.'

The speaker stood up again, without excitement; his weary expression said he had met this sort of ignorance before. But as he opened his mouth, the angry West Indian who had been shouted down, jumped up again.

'This brother's right,' he shouted, extending his arm towards the white trade unionist, 'this brother's right. The white workers of this country aren't against racism, because they've got rich by standing on our backs. The British worker's standard of living depends on exploiting the labour of black workers all over the world. When did the white British working man object to us being made slaves? Why is this country a rich country? why was it first with the Industrial Revolution? It was West Indian sugar that made you rich. The white working class in this country hates the black man. The white working man in this country would rather unite with the bosses than with the black man.' Furious shouts, but the West Indian raised his voice and went on. 'How many of you know about the Courtaulds strike at Preston? The black workers were told they'd got to work one and a half machines instead of one, and they were offered only ten shillings a week rise for doing fifty per cent more work. And when they came out on strike, who helped them? Their union didn't help them. The union fixed up with the management to bring in white workers to break the strike.' The shouts were getting too much for him and one of the students in the middle of the hall, who had not been doing much shouting, got up and called out loudly, 'I think we ought to listen to what this comrade says.' He pointed to the West Indian. 'After all, he ought to know what he's talking about.' 'I do know,' the West Indian shouted back, through cat-calls, 'but they don't want to hear. They don't want to listen to me because I'm a black man.' Cries of 'shame' from several parts of the hall. 'You're like the rest of them,' shouted the West Indian, glaring round at his interruptors, 'you don't really care a bugger about black people.' By now a lot of people had stood up, and the speaker had made several useless attempts to say something. The chairman began to bang the table and call for order. The noise gradually fell. As the speaker succeeded in beginning his reply, in the slightly facetious tone a man uses when he thinks he is dealing with rank stupidity, the West Indian got up and began to elbow his way out of the hall. Nobody followed him.

He was back again, three hours later, for the only speech to be given by anyone from the Caribbean throughout the day. This was a Black Power leader, wearing dark clothes and sunglasses. The West Indian in the audience began shouting encouragement to him after the first few minutes. 'You tell them, man.' The speaker was a skilful man. He stood, very relaxed, timing his words as only a veteran orator knows how, drawing laughs out of the audience at will. 'The only difference between Harold Wilson and Ian Smith is a difference – not of principle – but of tactics.' They listened closely to what he had to say about white power and imperialism. They liked the speaker's scorn for the hypocrisy that had cloaked itself as Western Christian ethics. The first jarring note was struck by the definition of the USSR as a white power country. Most of those present, either New Left or Maoist, applauded, but an elderly Trades Council man at the front got up and began to shout angrily. He was a man I didn't know personally, but he was a well-known local member of the Communist Party, a factory worker all his life, who had devoted great energy in former years to the Co-op education programme. He had the kind of dogged idealism that the Hitler–Stalin pact had not shaken, and the bad words in his vocabulary were words that went back to the thirties: Unemployment, Means Test, Mosley.

The student who had earlier called for a hearing for the West Indian began to speak urgently to the girl beside him. 'I wish they'd shut up. I want to hear what that man's saying.' The Chairman, heavy-handedly, tried to intervene, and eventually the Trades Council man was allowed his say. It was a rambling, but a moving, speech he made, much of it a personal history. He had dignity. When he had ended, the Black Power speaker addressed him gently, and then went on with his speech. It began to gather momentum. He attacked, scornfully, the idea of integration. Integration was a subterfuge for maintaining white supremacy. There could be no integration that meant anything at all until black people had true equality. Black Power was the slogan for a movement which was going to radicalize the black masses. It was no good having half-way reformists, black liberals, to lead black people; that sort of leader was a capitalist flunkey, acceptable to the establishment. Once the masses themselves were on the move, it would at last be possible to liquidate white power by violence. And that white power was not just the power of the capitalist. It was the power of the whole white racist society. White workers were white first, and workers afterwards. They would rather leave a black worker to starve than help him. The white worker was willing to join the white capitalists' armies, and go out with capitalists' guns and bayonets to kill his black brothers.

Almost the whole audience had turned against him now. One or two shouts challenged him. He shouted back at them,

'I'm telling you what's happening here and now. Those American soldiers killing the Vietnamese, most of them are workers, aren't they? Two out of three people in the world are threatened by starvation. And the two are black, and the one who isn't starving is white, whether he's a capitalist or a worker. There's a battle between the white capitalist and the white worker, yes, but they'll both stick together to fight against the black man wanting equal rights. There aren't even just communists any more, there are black communists and white communists. You don't understand, the world has changed: the struggle now is between black and white.'

Fury was gathering. One man, well-dressed and self-assured, rose and spoke for five minutes with a confident rapidity that prevented interruption. He gave a powerful account of how all the ills of racism went back to capitalism in the end, and how economic imperialism had grown while political imperialism had apparently waned, and of how the destruction of capitalism would ensure the destruction of imperialism and racism. Unwisely, he concluded, 'And we're willing to accept your help in overthrowing capitalism. Don't think we're not.'

The Black Power man leant easily against the table, and looked at him sardonically. 'So you're willing to accept me, are you? What do I say? Thank you very much? I don't want to be accepted by you, man. I know what that means. No, *we've* got to decide whether we accept you. I know your kind of drawing-room radical. All of you,' he went on, looking round the hall with intense scorn, 'you're the radicals of today. The Harold Wilsons of tomorrow.'

The West Indian in the audience laughed and cheered. So did a handful of others. But some of the audience were furious. No insult could have cut deeper. They were well-read; they all knew that the way they were talking was just the same way that the official leadership of the Labour Party had talked once, before it tasted power; some of them were already fixed up with good jobs that would lead to advancement, and the sting of truth was painful.

When I left the teach-in, the West Indian and I had a cup of coffee and a sandwich at the improvised buffet next to the hall. 'What can you do?' he said gloomily. 'Go in with these people or not?' 'They want us because they want to use us. I'm only going along with them just as far as I can use *them*. But that's not going to be very far. The trouble is, who else even wants to use us? We don't have so many allies we can pick and choose.

But those people' – he shook his head – 'they don't want to know *anything*. They want to *tell* us what we're supposed to do. And we've had enough of being told what other people want us to do. If those people in there *really* cared, they'd come to us and say, "You tell us what we can do." And we'd tell them. Remember that man who said he was a lawyer, this morning? Where's he going to have his practice? How many solicitors' offices do you see in the East End? No, he'll have his office in a white area, a rich area. Maybe he'll come and see us sometimes. Slumming. We see a lot of new faces around election times. They love to get our votes. They wouldn't ask one of us to stand, though. That might lose too many white votes for their party.'

Three students came out of the hall, and walked across to the buffet. One of them spoke shyly to the West Indian. He said he wished there hadn't been so much shouting, and he wished the West Indian had had a chance to make a speech of his own, because that was what they really needed to hear in there. The West Indian put his arm round the student's shoulder and offered him a drink, but the buffet had nothing but coffee and it was too late to go out to a pub. They began an animated conversation. More students, and two older men, came and joined in. It was a contrast to the meeting in the hall. All rather hesitantly, they made it clear they wanted to listen to the West Indian. He told them about the number of times he had been beaten up in London, about his friend, who had three times been charged and fined for offences under the Race Relations Act, Section I (prohibition of incitement) although white speakers could say what they liked and get away with it, about the West Indian children classified as educationally sub-normal according to tests that even English educational experts now admitted had been wrongly given. They listened. At last one of them said that he would be in London in the vacation, not far from where the West Indian lived, and asked what he could do for a few weeks that could help.

'You can come and help with our new playgroup.'

'*Playgroup?*' The student couldn't believe his ears. He

looked as though he had worked himself up to accepting a course in rifle practice, but not this.

'It's just at the stage where we need several people to help in getting it going. We've got a room for it now. It's taken a year to get that room. The local authority kept turning down the places we found; they didn't fit the health regulations. We've got someone to run it, and two sisters are visiting mothers now to fix up the times that are best and to find out which children will need volunteers to bring them along if their mother has to be at work. But we need to raise money and we need to get the room decorated, and some plumbing repairs done, and we need equipment. Now maybe you can help us with the equipment; you must know people who'd give something.'

The student was still bewildered.

'Well, if that's – I mean, I've not done anything quite like that before –'

'You'll learn,' said the West Indian, smiling, full of encouragement. 'Big toys, that's what we need. A slide. Some solid tricycles. Not broken-down stuff people think is good enough for black children. And wooden puzzles with pictures and letters that help the kids learn to read. And paints. And stories.'

'Well, if it's really what most needs doing –'

'Look, man,' said the West Indian, 'we're running this group ourselves. We're doing it because the whole future of our children and the sort of job they can get is decided by how they do in school. And how they do in school is decided by what stream they get put into. And what stream they get put into is decided by how they get on when they first start aged five. The teachers think they've got to be stupid because they're black. So they've got to be confident. They mustn't be frightened when they go along the first day to primary school. They've got to understand what's said to them, and answer back. And the best way I know to start them off like that is to have them in a playgroup first, so they learn how to answer back. So we're starting playgroups. You know what the Black Panthers do in America? You think they kill people, don't you? Well, they don't. They serve free breakfasts to school-kids, so the kids aren't hungry and falling asleep all through classes, so they can do their lessons. That's what we're trying to do: fill the practical need we can see in front of us. Now if you don't think that's the sort of excitement you were looking for –'

The student hastily said he'd be very glad to get toys and decorate the room for the playgroup. Actually, his father was in the furniture business, and maybe he could get some useful things cheaply. He still looked a bit dazed.

I saw him some months later. He had learnt more about the black community in the part of London where he had been painting walls than a whole sociology class who had been round the district the year before, interviewing people so as to make reports on the degree of integration locally, and the role of social services in encouraging such integration. He had learnt because, instead of setting out to study people, he had worked with them on their own terms, giving the help they wanted to get, and not offering the help he had thought most suitable to give. Without any self-consciousness he told me with real enthusiasm about the rocking-horse, originally a forty-five guinea toy from Harrods, that he had saved from being thrown out and had repainted and mended. Anger spilled out with his enthusiasm as he told me, 'But there's so *much* to do. And people don't know. I talked to boys of seventeen who had four jobs in a year, not because they couldn't work, but because they got made so wretched at every place with the way their workmates treated them, they couldn't stand it any more. Now they're called a problem. I used to wonder with those little kids at the playgroup – what's it going to be like for them? What's going to happen to them?'

I didn't know.

4. Institutional Racism

What is institutional racism? I remarked earlier that a racist society has institutions which effectively maintain inequality between members of different groups, in such a way that the open expression of racist doctrine is unnecessary or, where it occurs, superfluous. Racist institutions, even if operated partly by individuals who are not themselves racist in their beliefs, still have the effect of making and perpetuating inequalities.

What this means is that a racist institution has no need to put up a notice saying 'No blacks' if its normal methods of working exclude blacks from its operations or admit them only on unequal terms. In South Africa explicit printed notices appear, but these are, quite literally, adding insult to injury. The injury can be present without a printed notice. In England, as in the United States, it is perfectly possible for an institution to be racially exclusive in fact without a single written word, on a notice or an internal memo or a constitution, making this plain: it is, indeed, perfectly possible for it to be racist in spite of written statements and exhortations to the contrary. But we need to distinguish between the institution that is to some degree racist by general unspoken agreement and the 'institutional racism' that is the result of a system originally built without racial considerations being taken into account.

A business firm, with directors, managerial staff, accountants, salesmen, clerical staff, and manual workers may perhaps employ a number of Indians in unskilled jobs. None of them has ever risen, nor is likely to rise, to be a charge-hand or a foreman. There are certainly no instructions to this effect. Instructions are unnecessary. It is taken for granted that 'the men' will not accept anyone with a dark face in a supervisory position. Perhaps an Indian employee, with long service, good character and a high standard of work, may have the nerve to apply to be a charge-hand. If this involves authority over a group of Indians, it is likely he will be given the vacancy; if there is any question of authority over white workers, however, he will be turned down. There are always reasons to be found why it is only fair to give the job to someone else. There are no dark faces among the clerical staff or the accountants. Some West Indian girls who have applied to be clerk-typists have been turned down. It is always possible to say their spelling was not quite up to scratch, or their personal tidiness left something to be desired if (which is unlikely) anyone queries their refusal. The real reason is an embarrassed fear that the other girls on the staff might object, or that it wouldn't quite do. Again, the situation is *taken for granted*; there is no need to spell it out. There are no black salesmen; that dark faces would probably have an adverse effect on sales is a solid assumption. There are no black accountants partly because other local firms are also unwilling to have dark faces around, and it is difficult for someone doing accountancy training to get the practical experience that is a mandatory part of the qualifying course. There are no black managers or black directors. Nor, with the structure of the firm as it is, are there ever likely to be. For there is no opportunity to rise within it, if you are a dark person. And recruiting of young graduates from outside will draw very few black applicants, if any. For one thing, black candidates will take it for granted there is no point in applying for executive posts: they know in advance they will be refused. For another, there is a disproportionately small supply of young black graduates, and the reason for this lies not with the business firms at all but with the institutional racism of the educational system, which again is affected by the residential patterns of housing (since schools are mostly neighbourhood schools), while housing patterns are created partly by discrimination against black buyers and lessees and partly by the low incomes of many black applicants. And the low incomes are a result of low-grade employment. So there is a vicious circle. In this firm, racism operates by general unspoken agreement to debar black people from opportunities.

Such a firm is sure to claim to be non-discriminatory. After all, it employs Indians, so it can't have a colour bar, so it can't be discriminating. The term 'colour bar' has been responsible for a lot of harm in England just because it is generally used in this way. 'We have no colour bar' is taken as a statement of commitment to equal opportunity, but it does not mean that at all. In the case of such a firm, what it really means is, 'We have to employ Indians because we can't get English workers to do this particular hot and dirty job.' But the firm's policy as a whole is consciously to maintain a structure in which white people are always in control and always in the better jobs. This is assumed to be necessary, but not much thought is devoted to recognizing what the results will be. It is possible to maintain this situation yet to have some flexibility. If such a firm were to take on a single typist of Asian descent from Kenya, it could claim an integrated clerical staff, and give assurances that it had coloured workers at factory *and* at office level. This would not necessarily mean equal opportunity for all dark-faced applicants with all white-faced applicants for the jobs. It would not alter the structure itself, or the distribution of power within it, at all. One girl would have had the luck to get a job she wanted, and that is all. The next Asian applicant could be safely refused ('We've got one of them already, we don't want to turn into an all-coloured firm').

It is much easier for a firm like this to discriminate, as things are, than it would be if black people had equal opportunities in fields other than employment. If they had equal opportunity in housing and education there would be more applicants for high-grade jobs, and the firm would have to move in one of two directions: either towards becoming, somewhat unwillingly, an integrated firm with better – but perhaps still not equal – opportunities for black employees, or towards becoming an openly racist firm, forced into displaying quite obviously a policy of racial discrimination that up to now it has followed without anyone noticing particularly. (Anyone except, of course, the non-white would-be charge-hands, accountants, secretaries, salesmen and managers!)

But as things are the different effects of racism compound each other. Racism works by geometrical progression rather than arithmetical; the trouble is not just that you tramp round on the same day being turned down first for a home, then for a job, then for a place on a training course, but that each instance of discrimination against you increases the likelihood of discrimination working against you in some other instance. This applies to big things and small things. I remember a very well-dressed West Indian trying to pay by cheque in a branch of a high-quality men's clothing shop, and asking to do so in a very quiet and well-educated standard English accent; he was told he could not pay by cheque on a Saturday afternoon, and when I asked if I was also barred from paying by cheque there and then, there was some embarrassment and I was told it was all right because my bank was a local one. Subsequent inquiry revealed that the man's address was in Brixton, and the shop manager had felt this was not a very good class of address, and one could not be sure of a cheque from someone living there. Of course, one has to decide whether to take this doubt at its face value, but if one does it is clear that the racial discrimination which had kept this particular man living in Brixton when he would have preferred to live somewhere else had other effects on his life than actually fixing his place of residence. It had effects on his credit. Much more serious than this is the effect of a disdained living address on a black child who, after attending a school in a 'deprived' or 'twilight' area, writes off for a job to the firm I have described. The employer, recognizing the street address as in a disreputable part of town known for prostitutes, lodging-houses overcrowded with transient labourers, broken families and vandalism against property, turns down the job application out of hand, and picks an applicant from a nicer area. No question of racial prejudice on his part, he will say. He would not, as a matter of policy, take on a youngster from that particular bad area, whatever his colour. And the employer finds it no concern of his that the black youngster lives in such an area because local patterns of racial discrimination in housing exclude him from the more respectable parts of town.

It is at this point that we see institutional racism at work, the process that ensures racial inequality without wilful, conscious effort. To see it more clearly for what it is we need to imagine another employer of a slightly different kind. He employs a small office staff and has a workshop with a small number of skilled men; the cleaning is done part-time by an old-age pensioner and a man with a limp. The entire firm is white. The thought of black employees has never crossed the owner's mind. All the work is skilled, and the men belong to a trade union whose rules on apprenticeships prevent anyone becoming an apprentice after his seventeenth birthday. The boys who come as apprentices need a good standard of education: they have to be capable of precision work and know mathematics and physics, and some of them require technical drawing. The rule about age-limit on apprenticeships was devised long before there was any possibility of there being black teenagers around in the town. And of course the educational requirements are exacted by the nature of the work itself. The result is that boys can only enter work in this establishment if they have reached a certain standard of education, with written qualifications to prove it, well in advance of their seventeenth birthdays.

There is no policy of racial discrimination in this concern. Yet institutional racism is operative because under these conditions large numbers of black teenagers are unable to enter it. Some of them because they have been wrongly placed in ESN schools (of which more later); some because they have been in low streams of secondary modern schools and have never taken any CSE or O-level examinations, nor learnt anything like enough mathematics and physics to enable them to do so; some because they arrived in England to join immigrant parents when they were of school age, yet had their progress delayed by the complete change of environment so that they cannot reach the educational standard required until they are eighteen or nineteen years old; and some because they were delayed in school by difficulties with the English language, which kept them back in remedial or special language classes for a vital period of time and, again, delayed their hope of doing examinations until an age too late for an apprenticeship.

It is important to stress that all these experiences, causing either an inferior quality of education or a delay of two years or so in reaching the same standard of education as white contemporaries, are experiences that afflict young Asian and Caribbean boys and girls regardless of their quickness of mind, special talents and eagerness to learn. Some of those in ESN schools may be irredeemably slow-witted, but many more are intelligent children whose intelligence is unrecognized by the people giving them educational tests: because of language differences, because of cultural differences, or because of conscious or unconscious racist attitudes on the part of the testers.

Although conscious racist attitudes often are influential in determining where black children get placed in our school system, *they need not be present at all* when decisions are taken that are racially discriminatory *in effect*. I knew a boy from Trinidad who was set a test before entering a training course, and part of this test involved being able to recognize certain English wild birds. He did not know these birds, not from stupidity but because the years he had spent in England, on a housing estate in a city, and after the age at which small children even in urban environments here do nature study in school, had provided no occasion for knowing them. He failed the test. I do not suppose some cunning old racist sat down to devise tests that would exclude any applicants who had not spent their first ten years in England. The tests were set with quite different considerations in mind, but it turned out that in effect they worked against a candidate such as this boy from

Trinidad. Not, obviously, with just this one question: that merely provides one small instance of what the vague phrase 'cultural differences' can cover.

When we come to look at housing, a very straightforward example of institutional racism is provided by the rule in some places, giving priority to residents who have spent many years living in the borough, and demanding a qualifying period of residence from newcomers before their names can be formally placed on the waiting list and start working their way up in the queue for a council house. The idea behind this rule, demanding perhaps two years, perhaps five years of local residence before a family is eligible for the waiting list, is a readily understandable one that was devised without any racial considerations in mind. The idea was that people who had lived in a town all their lives, and perhaps had parents and grandparents living there before them, should come first in the queue for housing, before new arrivals from another town. And indeed the rule has worked in Birmingham, for example, equally to the disadvantage of people from Wolverhampton, the Highlands of Scotland, Jamaica, Spain and County Cork who have come to Birmingham to work. But obviously it works *consistently* against immigrants from overseas in whatever town they settle. The Englishman from another town may be able to exchange a council house in one town for another. While many English people are at a disadvantage under this system in getting a house, immigrants from overseas are *always* at a disadvantage.

In all the towns where jobs are plentiful in England there is an acute shortage of housing accommodation, usually at the price that the average wage-earner can afford, even more at the price that the lowest-paid can manage. It has ceased to be economically possible for private builders to build homes that can be rented by average and low earners; private builders can only make a profit if they build for people with considerably higher than average incomes. Even local authority building, which is subsidized, has to be let at rents, in places where land is expensive, that are impossibly high for many of the people for whom council housing is supposed to provide. Some council accommodation in the London Borough of Brent has been standing empty while local people are either homeless or living in appalling wretchedness because their council accommodation, even subsidized, has a rent of ten pounds a week. And in Birmingham elderly pensioners are shivering through the winter in their council flats because once they have paid the rent they cannot afford to switch on any heating. In this situation all the average and low earners suffer from the housing shortage. The vast majority of black people are in average and low-paid employment, and so here again, even before discrimination has been at work to keep them out of desirable residential areas, they are commonly at a disadvantage in housing. The housing shortage itself, of course, creates jealous competition and animosity between all those who suffer from it, and racial prejudice is frequently strengthened by this sort of conflict of interests. These are just a few of the factors referred to in the study of Sparkbrook, Birmingham, made by John Rex and Robert Moore in which they state,

> It is not our object to blame particular individuals for what has occurred. What we have tried to do with the aid of a form of sociological analysis is to show the way in which many of the reactions to the racial issue which we describe are to be expected in terms of the sociology of an industrial city . . . it may be that amongst the people of Birmingham whom we studied some discriminatory behaviour was due to innate and universal tendencies. And it may be that some of it was the product of personality disturbance. But it is also the case that a great deal of it was sufficiently explained once we knew something of Birmingham's social structure and conflicts, and the constellation of interests and rules which was built into Birmingham society.[1]

In other words, racist behaviour was produced by the working of social institutions that had grown up without race being an element in their design.

Such institutional racism is less easily recognizable for what it is in England than it is in the United States, because here it can be easily confused with the institutional inequalities of the peculiarly English class system. Indeed, some observers confuse racial inequalities with class inequalities and believe that the problem of getting rid of racism is exactly the same as the problem of getting rid of class prejudices and inequalities. If one works among the poorest people in a gloomy and decaying area of any of our big cities, this diagnosis is a tempting one. It can be made to fit the facts about the most glaring problems in such an area, but it does not explain anything like all the facts about our race situation in England. It does not explain white residents in a street banding together to keep out or persecute a black family moving in. It does not explain the refusal of a labouring job, quoted earlier from the P.E.P. report, to a black man when a white man, though emphatically not middle-class, was given the job. It does not explain the deep hostility to black people that is expressed in such remarks as these (by Mr John Sanders of the Birmingham Immigration Control Association):

> The Afro-Asians are feckless peoples with cultures different from our own. By our standards they are barbarous. No one really bothers about the Irish. They don't peddle dope, they don't kill chickens in the kitchen. This civilization of the North Sea and of Kipling's five nations is in danger of destruction through this flood coming in. It must be stopped.

It does not explain the legalized racism of our immigration laws. It does not explain why the selection committee for a parliamentary candidate would ignore the fact that a possible candidate was the child of a very poor family, but would give worried consideration to the fact that another possible candidate was black. Both possible candidates might have achieved middle-class status and be talented men; with the white one, his own attainments would be a commendation and his origins either ignored or played up for advantage in appealing to the electorate. It is unthinkable that a candidate's blackness would be played up for advantage by any of our political parties.

Of course black people and very poor white people do share

a number of wrongs. But the black people always suffer even more disadvantages than the white in any given situation and the white people have at least some hope of escape for their children if not for themselves; black people know that their children and grandchildren will still be black. The white poor may attain greater prosperity and security and higher status, but black people cannot become white. Their remedy cannot be complete if they make more money or gain a better education, because they still have to face dislike or contempt by reason of their unchangeable colour as long as there is racial prejudice.

What *is* true is that the institutionalized inequalities between classes have provided a ready framework for institutionalized racism, because institutions that work to the disadvantage of groups regarded as socially undesirable or unimportant obviously will work to the disadvantage of those who are thought racially unacceptable. The lowest class, so-called, of white people, a recognizable social group, will be lumped together with black people of many different social groups.

Some of the problems of racism in our society can perhaps be solved by a conscious effort to change attitudes through education. But institutional racism, which itself helps to create racially prejudiced attitudes, by keeping despised groups at the bottom of the heap, and then blaming them for not getting higher up, can only be affected by institutional change. Now if institutional racism is the product of institutions devised without racial considerations in mind, and having effects upon the population at large distinct from its effect on racial minorities, any change is going to affect the white population as well as the black. If, for example, the age-limit on apprenticeships were to be abolished, a number of white teenagers and adults would benefit from the abolition. If residence in a particular town for a defined period ceased to be a condition of getting straight on to a local authority housing list, white English people, forced by circumstance to move to a new place in order to find work, would gain by the change.

But changing social institutions is a very difficult matter: so many considerations come into play, so many interests have to be resolved. Tinkering about with an institution may make very little difference indeed: a meaningful alteration has to start from thinking out anew the whole purpose of the institution, and its whole complex of effects.

Tackling institutional racism cannot really be done except by institutional change. The same is true with other kinds of institutionalized inequality. If a public school decides to be very liberal and admit thirty working-class boys it is still a public school whose character depends on being an institution for the children of the rich people and run independently of the central and local government. It does not become an institution with equal opportunity for all would-be comers just by admitting a number – even a substantial number – of children whose social class and parents' income would normally make their presence in a public school unthinkable. The whole set-up of the place perpetuates itself: not just the requirement of large fees, but the curriculum, the private language, the accent, the choice of recreation, the manners, the assumptions about what kind of job and what kind of university the pupil will proceed to; all these factors ensure that the typical product of the school will become business-man, politician, lawyer, diplomat, higher civil servant, army officer, explorer, doctor or don, just as surely as the typical product of a secondary modern in a northern industrial town will be miner, factory worker, warehouseman, milkman, shop assistant and so on. A tiny minority, in each case, may cross the line but by and large these institutions have a strong formative effect regardless of the particular talents and inclinations of the pupils. Indeed their talents and their inclinations are shaped by the schools they are in. Public schools do not expect their pupils to want apprenticeships as plumbers, and secondary modern schools do not expect their pupils to want to write papers on Etruscan sculptures. The teaching is geared to what is expected of the pupil in later life. And what is expected is largely determined by the social class of the pupils' own parents, and partly determined by the social class to which the school wants its pupils to aspire. A grammar school, for example, may have a lot of pupils whose parents do manual jobs, but because it is a grammar school, heir to a middle-class tradition of education that in former days reflected the expectations of most of its pupils' parents, it expects its products to get non-manual jobs.

Our school institutions at present, with public, direct grant, grammar, technical grammar, modern and 'streamed' comprehensive schools, form a structure that upholds class differences and perpetuates them. There may be plenty of mobility between social classes, with people moving up and down between them, but the social classes themselves remain clearly distinct and identifiable.

A truly comprehensive educational system would be an institutional change threatening, if not to destroy, at least to change very considerably the English class system. That is why comprehensive education arouses such strong passions. Comprehensive education is basically about class, because the purpose of educational institutions is to prepare individuals for a place in existing adult society, not about intelligence testing. But the argument around it deals in all sorts of details, relevant and irrelevant, and often refers to education as if it were some known, solid commodity to be cut up and shared: the best pieces for the brightest children, say defenders of the status quo; fair shares for all, say the egalitarians. Yet education is not a quantifiable commodity at all, and whether children are bright or not is a judgement made on the basis of whether they have the qualities to succeed and gain entry to the higher social-class groups in the particular kind of society we have. Individual teachers who care about education as fulfilment of individual talents can do much for their own pupils, but cannot alter the entire system. In a society which valued poets and prophets instead of posts and profits many of our bright and successful people would be utter fools, and some of the inattentive, lazy dreamers at the back of modern school classes would come into their own.

Our present educational institutions are structured to the disadvantage of black children. Children with black faces *are not expected to do well* in our society. The highly prejudiced teacher will expect them to be failures because as black people they are sure to be stupid or lazy. The less prejudiced teacher, eager for the black pupils to do well, will still not *expect* them to become doctors, managers or fashionable portrait painters simply because in society as it is at present such an expectation seems hopelessly unrealistic, an idle dream. The teacher may wish such achievements possible, but will not seriously entertain hope of them. So he or she, while encouraging and helping the black child, may still steer the child towards hopes that are more realistic: 'Well dear, a lawyer, that's a very long and difficult training. What made you think of being a lawyer?' Only the teacher who combines a belief in the value of black children with the will and ability to help them over hurdles and do battle for them in gaining entry to higher education or worth-while jobs after they leave school, can do something to overcome – and this again, only in individual cases – the formidable difficulties in the black child's way. There are a few teachers who try to do this. But what are they up against?

'I was told by the Principal that I was going to help with remedial English for immigrant children ... I asked for guidance on what they had been doing. Nobody had a schedule or syllabus. Most people told me, "Oh, teach them anything."'

So begins an account by a West Indian teacher, Marina Maxwell, of her experiences in a north London school. (She left in 1968 to return to Jamaica.) She quotes remarks from other teachers on the staff, made in her hearing, such as this one about an older girl pupil (white) in the school: 'Oh, she's a tart. Really, imagine an English girl behaving like that – she has all sorts of boy friends – navvies, older men, even Negroes.' Another teacher referred collectively to the pupils as 'bleeding nuisances and black-faced buggers'.

'The school leavers' class,' writes Marina Maxwell, 'with whom I was working a Newsom programme of sorts, taught me what it is to be white and rejected. This is at the core of violence in schools: teachers, middle-class and climbing, care little for the "children of navvies", as one girl put it bitterly one day in a discussion. Every other day teachers asked me to sign this and sign that to recommend that "troublesome" children be sent to special schools, to backward classes, to be suspended or removed. I refused. No child should be judged against the background of the system existing . . . So often the noisy, unmanageable child proves, when given something to do and made to do it, the brightest and the most able. These children are being condemned to the lowest streams and the worst classes in schools.'[2]

An English-born student in social studies, Judy Bainbridge, has written an account of a primary school in a completely different area, Liverpool 8.[3] Liverpool is one of the cities that have a non-white population several generations old, living side by side with local white residents and with immigrants, recent arrivals of all nationalities. In such an area it is possible to see more clearly the effects of racial and colour attitudes quite independent of the factors that are associated with being a newcomer, language difficulties, 'cultural shock' and so on. A white resident explained to her, 'You see, we have no immigrants. Only coloured.' She observed that in Liverpool the immigrant, whether Jamaican or Nigerian or Indian, is seen as 'coloured' rather than as a member of a particular racial or national group. The 'half-caste' was regarded as being particularly unfortunate. A health visitor summed up this belief: 'The problems lie in the mixtures.'

Judy Bainbridge was, however, assured by a school nurse, 'Liverpool has no colour problem, but they all live in the poorer areas of course.' The receptionist at the Child Guidance Clinic could not tell which clients were West Indians: 'I don't know. They're just white or coloured.'

In the primary school she describes, this combination of ignorance with straightforward colour discrimination soon became evident in her attempts to find out something about individual 'coloured' children and their families:

> The teachers were perfectly willing to help, but, like the social workers, proved unbelievably ignorant about the people they worked with. The list of immigrant children kept in obedience to Ministry

regulations contained several inaccuracies. For example, two Guyanese children of mixed Negro and Chinese parentage were listed as Arabs. Some British-born children whose mother was English but whose father was Ghanaian were included, whereas some children born in Jamaica were excluded. Individual teachers displayed similar ignorance about children they had been teaching for a year. An African teacher, asked who were the West Indian children in his class, replied with some surprise, 'Well, all the coloureds.' Some of these 'coloureds' were of African descent, and most were Liverpool-born like their mothers before them. Another teacher told me how bright her West Indians were, and called Paul to come and read to me. Afterwards she told me that she had taught Paul's mother who had also been at the school, and who, I discovered later when I met her, had inherited her dark skin from a Ghanaian father. In this class, Philip was pointed out as 'the only West Indian who can't do anything at all'. Philip's father was from Sierra Leone, and his mother was of Sierra Leonean descent.

However, the teachers were not prevented from generalizing about West Indians by their inability to distinguish West Indians from others. 'Nine-year-old Carlton was described by his teacher as having "a typical West Indian streak of laziness".' The headmaster pointed out five-year-old Winston as a typically 'withdrawn' West Indian child: but Winston, Judy Bainbridge later found, lived with his deserted mother and three older children in one room and had no bedtime because, as his mother pointed out, there was nowhere for him to go to bed. It was not surprising if at school he was quiet and apathetic.

The school had a special language class for 'immigrant' children. (Placed there, presumably, on the same kind of inaccurate classification as produced the list of immigrant children under Ministry regulations!) The teacher of this class

was not qualified to teach English as a second language, and said she did not enjoy doing it, partly because it appeared she was aware of her own incompetence and partly because she disliked immigrants. Believing there were none outside the ports, she made it her responsibility to warn me of the dangers that awaited me in Liverpool 8. She said their houses were dirty, though she had never visited one. Also the men made unwelcome sexual advances, and she herself always wore flat-heeled shoes to school to facilitate her escape should she be accosted by one when she went to the shops in her lunch-hour. Neither of these allegations was convincingly confirmed in my experience.

When the teachers talked about individual children, the home was frequently characterised as a destructive influence. The Cs, for instance, had a 'very brutal' West African father and a 'loud-mouthed' Liverpool coloured mother. Nine-year-old Janet's teacher envisaged her growing up to be like her mother, while for Dennis, aged eleven, a criminal career was forecast. Neither child was expected ever to work for a living. All the Ts were said to grow up like their mother who was described as 'dirty', 'uncooperative' and 'hard'. Joseph D has been 'cleaner' since his father's death, which according to his teacher was 'to everyone's relief'. His brother Philip was described as a 'dead loss', except for 'sweeping up'. He was eager to learn, but 'had not a brain in his head'. His five-year-old sister was described as coming from a family who 'one after the other are ESN'. This opinion was not confirmed by the psychologist at the Child Guidance Clinic, where the D children were sent with dreadful regularity, although eventually one of the older boys was sent to a special school for boys of average intelligence who for some reason are retarded. The designation ESN seemed frequently to be used in an imprecise sense as a conveniently explanatory substitute for 'thick' or 'lazy' or other epithets much in vogue in the staff room. It is a convenient substitute because it places the child outside the teacher's area of concern: there are special schools for people like this. So at this school, Philip in one class, and Abdul and Alexandra in others, were assigned purely domestic roles while they awaited testing or re-testing for special schools.

These quotations do not really do justice to the wide scope, or to the full thesis, of Judy Bainbridge's study. But looked at as a description of what institutional racism can do, combined with racially prejudiced attitudes on the part of individuals inside an institution and operating it, these extracts give us a horrifying glimpse of what is happening in a place like Liverpool – where there is 'no problem'.

When a working party of the Liverpool Youth Organisations Committee produced a report on the situation entitled

Special but not Separate, which was a good deal milder in content than Judy Bainbridge's study, the local Education Committee decided to 'receive but not accept' the report on the grounds that, 'We have not got a colour problem in this city and anyone who wants to create one is wrong', and that the report was 'a contradictory, inflammatory and dangerous document' (report in the *Liverpool Daily Post*, 3 December 1968).

Oh, echoes of the old American South! (We've never had any trouble with our niggers till people started stirring them up.) One more quotation, this time from a Canadian teacher in South London, reinforces the impression of powerful pressures within the school forcing children, regardless of their real capacities, into the educationally sub-normal category. (I can, of course, be reasonably accused of giving only one side of the picture. There are other schools, some of them familiar to me, where it is possible for black children to be afforded some respect and real help. But the brighter side of the picture does not, by its presence, abolish the existence of the gloomy horrors overspreading a very considerable number of children in English cities whose fate is so far mostly ignored and entirely unremedied. And anyone who wants to consider the bright side only can obtain large amounts of information on it from official sources.)

The ILEA has announced in a confidential report that many immigrant children, particularly West Indian children, have been wrongly placed in ESN schools. The heads of the ESN schools thought that immigrants were four times more likely to be wrongly placed than other children. Statistics from the ILEA report as quoted in the *Times Educational Supplement* of 26 December 1969 by Michael Binyon indicate that the proportion of immigrant children in ESN schools has risen sharply in the last three years. As of September 1969 there were 36·9% immigrant children in ESN schools [again, far in excess of the proportion in the general population].

It doesn't take much imagination to explain how this happens. Most staff-room discussions, about West Indians in particular, centre around 'behaviour problems'. Often a child is recommended for ESN assessment on this basis alone. It is widely accepted by now that the IQ tests now in use are totally unsatisfactory. They have a distinct cultural, verbal, and middle-class bias.

De facto segregation is blatant in the comprehensive schools. It affects working-class children as well as immigrant children. I have heard educators use this fact as an excuse, but in the end it will not make the truth any less bitter.

This extract is from an article entitled 'U.S. Separatism in British Schools?' in *Race Today*, May 1970, by Carol Bergman, a Canadian then teaching in Battersea. In case anyone tries to take comfort in the fact that black children in London are at any rate no worse off than some white working-class children it is worth thinking over the implications of a situation where such an excuse is possible. It is a very frequent excuse, in more contexts than the educational one, but nobody seems to stop and think what it means. Maybe the black people are in bad housing, but so are some white people. Maybe this black man was refused a job, but they refuse Irishmen too. So everything is all right? There can't be racism at the bottom of it?

If we lived in a country where all were free and equal, with an equal chance before the law and an equal chance of decent livelihood and a reasonable place to live, with black people the only group to be excluded from Paradise, racism would be very easily visible. It would also be much easier to remedy and there would be a far, far better chance of public concern with the matter. But we do not. In spite of parliamentary democracy, free schools and the welfare state, we live in a society with great inequalities of wealth and of personal freedom. This is less obvious than it might be, partly because reverence for the *names* of our democratic institutions has clouded the *fact* that we are effectively ruled by a small group of politicians using Parliament as their rubber stamp, and a rather larger group of permanent officials belonging to the same oligarchy with powers usually unlimited by the courts. Our courts are run by middle- and upper-class people, subservient to the values and policies of the Government, and the police and the social workers apply different practices to the rich and the poor. What upper middle-class child, caught stealing from a shop, gets hauled before a juvenile court? And what poor child who is caught escapes this fate? How many social workers interrogate rich women about their sex-lives and the way they care for their children? How many poor women living in the worst housing escape such attentions, when living on welfare payments and without a husband? It is also less obvious than it might be because we have, instead of the 'two nations' Disraeli identified, a whole complex of nations within one. The fact that the class structure with all its snobberies and inequities is still with us, while mobility between classes has increased, has created new strains and stresses: between the working-class child who transfers to a middle-class job and his parents for whom he feels shame or embarrassment; between the middle-class parents whose children drop out of the system and the middle-class children who reject their parent's values; between the shabby genteel whose income has dropped far below his needs since inflation and the prosperous semi-skilled who can produce a roll of banknotes but be snubbed because of his accent. Resentments between different groups of society are strong and bitter; but the inequalities are not obvious to people who spend most of their time in a limited environment, meeting others of similar class and experience to their own. In a society organized as ours is, some are going to gain the great prize of worldly success, others are going to fall to the bottom and be destroyed; the majority, somewhere in between, are engaged in the struggle to stay as well off as they are, to get higher if they can but at any rate not get pushed further down. At the bottom of the heap are the 'deprived', the 'inadequate', the 'problem families', the 'delinquents', the 'alcoholics', the 'homeless', the 'handicapped': a mass of human beings pushed downwards by the pressures of social machinery and then neatly labelled as unwanted with one bureaucratic term or another. One of these labels now is 'immigrant' which means simply 'not white'.

In such a situation racism is, apart from its other important characteristics, one kind of injustice among many. It should be obvious that the existence of other injustices does not render racism non-existent. The very poor in England are insulted for their poverty, bullied by officials, exhaustively interrogated before they can get free school meals or a clothing allowance for their children, placed under intolerable strains and then told they are inadequate when the strains are too much for them. The black are persecuted for being black, and some of their experiences are the same as those suffered by the white poor: bad housing, official callousness, having their children labelled as culturally deprived, and so on. Other experiences are different. Racism has a number of special characteristics that differentiate it from other kinds of social injustice. The English poor are not told they can never belong and ought to leave the country. Nor do the English poor have to wear a badge everywhere they go, proclaiming 'I am one of a socially undesirable group.' The black person does, he cannot disguise his physical appearance; his colour is obvious when he gets on any bus, walks into any shop, talks to a white girl or drives past a traffic policeman. The English poor are wary of the police, and deeply afraid of 'trouble with the police' which would cut away the little security they retain, but the English poor are less likely to be in trouble with the police for the offence of standing in, and walking along, the street than black people in London. Many instances of police harassment of black people remain unknown to the public. Only some really spectacular error, as when an African diplomat in a white Mercedes Benz was accused of having a stolen car in Brixton in 1969, makes headlines. The police on that occasion took it for granted that no black man could have a Mercedes unless it was stolen. But they make similar assumptions all the time about black people, and not only about black people with low incomes.

There are large and important differences between the racial discrimination that black people suffer and the economic and social disadvantages that the very poor white English suffer, independent of the varieties of daily experience both groups may have. The point about racism, which cannot be too greatly stressed and which is very difficult for the white majority to understand, is that racism drastically alters personalities, the personalities *of both black and white*. Institutionalized racism warps and breaks the self-confidence, the sense of identity, the self-respect and independence of black people, while simultaneously distorting the nature of white people, stimulating their aggressions, feeding their resentments and fears, warping their judgement and encouraging them in self-deception. And these effects are compounded by the effects of racism in other countries and at other times. The black people in England now are the descendants of black ancestors who were colonized, and in some cases bought as slaves, by our white ancestors. Some of them are the cousins of black people in the United States who have been shot or imprisoned or sent to fight in Vietnam by a government including white cousins, many times removed, of ours. Only a handful of black people in England now are related by blood to Africans in Rhodesia and the Republic of South Africa, but all black people in England now feel some brotherhood with those Africans: because white people have identified them all, however varied, as black, they have now identified themselves all as black, and strong bonds exist between them though they have never met and know little about each other. And in this situation any act of cruelty by a white Rhodesian government against black African guerrillas, every beating by a white American policeman of a Black Panther, becomes symbolically an act by white British people against black British people. It need not have been so, had British governments in the 1960s had the sense and courage to stand out against racism in foreign policy and immigration laws and unite both black and white British citizens behind them. But now it has become so. It is as though both groups had been afloat on a raft which has broken in two; it seems impossible to get the raft joined together again, and worse, every movement of the tide pushes the two halves of it further and further apart. Black and white are now hardly within shouting distance of each other.

The fact that racism is now a major international issue, influencing all kinds of events and exchanges, is not the fault of England alone: far from it. The tragedy is that once England has become a recognizably racist country, which it now unhappily is, it has got to pay for the mistakes and cruelties of other people in other countries. Black people here have been told over and over again that they do not belong here, that it is important to keep more of them out of the country, that they should be 'repatriated', that, even if they stay, they stay on sufferance and will remain alien in our midst. Naturally, after all this, they cannot be expected to identify themselves with England in any way or consider themselves English. If they are to have any identity here they are forced into the position of choosing an identity as black people. The natural reaction to being told you are not wanted here is to reply, 'All right, I won't stay.' And some people are deciding for themselves to leave England. But others are unable to leave. Even if they had the fare home for their families they are faced with the alternatives of staying here with work, or returning to the country they left just because work was not available for them. Children who have grown up here have even less chance of leaving than their parents; they are told they do not belong here, yet where else do they belong? The predicament of East African Asian British citizens, living in limbo while shuttled between this country and Uganda or Kenya with no government willing to admit them, is not only an extreme of racist rejection at work; it illustrates the dilemma of all black people in England: there is nowhere to go. 'Foxes have holes, and the birds of the air have nests' – but what will happen to these sons of men?

Institutional racism works quietly: its effects may shout loud to black people but they are obscure whispers in the ear of the white population. However, there is one English institution which works continual, deafening propaganda against black people, and that is our immigration law. It is exceptional in that it is quite specifically and publicly racist, and backed by the full authority of governments. To understand what immigration laws have done to our internal racial situation is of the first importance. The magnitude of their effect will, I hope, become clear once we start looking at race, politics and the press.

Part Three

It is expedient

– CAIAPHAS

1. 'Immigration controls were working quite well, although they were far from perfect.'
2. For the Good of the People

1. 'Immigration controls were working quite well, although they were far from perfect'

It was not quite dawn. The edges of the sky were lightening to a pale translucent grey above the lines of houses, but the streets themselves were still obscure: long lines of terraced brick buildings, slate-roofed, fronting on to narrow pavements. There was not a tree or a blade of grass, and no birds to sing, so that the silence was complete, except outside number 37 Butchers Lane, where an old saloon car waited, its engine running, while the driver, a young Pakistani in a blue anorak, waited for his elder brother to come out of the house and get into the car.

A few upper windows were lit already, for the postman at number 30 had to leave early for work, and the lorry-driver opposite had a long run to do. But Mr Khan and Mr Malik were the first to move, with a long drive ahead of them to London airport, where Mr Khan's twelve-year-old son Ajaib was due to arrive on the flight from Karachi. Mr Malik switched on the headlights as he pulled out from the kerb and the illumination moved ahead, showing first the lines of doors and darkened front-room windows, then the little general shop on the corner, its dark blue blinds pulled down, its exterior vivid with painted signs advertising shoe polish and dividend tea and Aspro, then the intersection of more streets, all exactly the same. In five minutes they had reached a main road with larger, bay-windowed houses interspersed with shops, brand-new petrol stations and one or two seedy cafes, all lit a ghastly blue by overhead street-lamps. Five minutes more and they were on the concrete ribbon of the London road, lit now by bright orange above, hemmed in on either side by desirable cream-coloured semi-detached homes, mile upon mile of them.

It did not look very like a promised land. How was Ajaib imagining it all as he sat, at the same moment his relatives were on their way to meet him, in the PIA plane coming in over the coast of England? As a matter of fact Ajaib was thinking about the new calf at home. He felt sick and nervous, and listless with sleep. Never in his life before had he travelled on an aeroplane. The excitement when he left had been enormous; the whole family there to see him off, his mother and two aunts crying, a muddle of shouted last-minute instructions and endearments and messages for England, the important feeling of his smart new clothes bought for the journey. Although he had already travelled two hundred miles from his own village to reach the airport at Karachi, he had not been tired but full of energy and excitement as he took his seat inside the plane – so comfortable, so grand, so unlike anything he had ever experienced before. The stewardess, beautiful in her Punjabi-style airline uniform, had smiled at him and spoken to him. He was overwhelmed with it all.

He was on his way to England. Several people from the village had been away there for several years, and they earned enormous sums of money – 250 rupees a week. They sent money home; they had houses and radios and cars. Ajaib's mind was a confusion of images: great pink and white palaces, shining cars, cities with gleaming pavements.

The plane flew through darkness, and as hour succeeded hour and his stomach, unused to travel, felt queasy, his excitement slowly ebbed. The plane, so strange and fascinating at first, began to look like an enclosed confine in which he had passed years of his life. The incessant roaring of the engines made him somnolent, yet he could not sleep. His limbs were heavy; he longed to get up and walk about, to get out of the plane, but he could not. All the others on the plane were strangers to him, and he, whose life had been spent every day since birth in a small village community, was discovering the loneliness of urban civilization. His thoughts seemed to be moving slowly, around and around on the same theme, as though they were heavy with the same heaviness that was in his limbs. At last he was sick into a paper bag and then, although his head still ached, he felt a little better.

Mr Khan and Mr Malik were now driving along in full daylight on the motorway, in the thick of the morning traffic. They had plenty of time to spare. Their car, and Ajaib's plane, were gradually converging upon Heathrow Airport, a great sprawling network of runways and roads, signs and lights, scattered buildings, depots, oil tankers, garages, coaches, taxis, cars and thousands of people moving hither and thither in a complex pattern of purposes, representing a total daily expenditure of unthinkable hundreds of thousands of pounds. Ajaib's ticket, his new clothes, and other incidental expenses, had cost a very modest fraction of this, about £180, saved by Mr Khan out of his earnings as a bus conductor. Even sharing his living expenses and the mortgage payments with other members of the family, it had taken a long and steady effort for Mr Khan to save the money he needed. He had, before saving, to send home something regularly for his wife, for Ajaib, for his elderly father and for his younger son Abdul. Ajaib was to come to England first, because it was not possible to save enough for all the family to come at once. The immigration rules would not allow Ajaib to come in after he was sixteen and in practice it became very difficult once he was much over twelve; Mr Khan had a friend whose fifteen-year-old boy had been refused admission because the immigration officer suspected he was older than his passport said, and brushed aside as meaningless the evidence of the birth certificate issued in Pakistan. So the prudent thing was to bring Ajaib first; Mr Khan's wife was eligible to come any time to join him, and the younger boy had some years in hand before reaching the age where he risked refusal. With Ajaib arrived, another year of saving might, with care, allow him to send for his wife and Abdul together; then they could all be reunited at the house in Butchers Lane; Mr Malik was saving to move to another house. It all took a lot of planning and a lot of work. Luckily he could do quite well with overtime as a conductor, and he was used to living economically. Ajaib would have to go to school, and then perhaps he could go on to further education; in England he could learn well and have a better chance in life than his father had had. Just a few more years of effort; then Ajaib would be earning and helping to support the rest of the family.

The car dipped into a short tunnel, and emerged into a network of converging roads. Mr Malik, who was young and self-confident, a thoroughly urbanized character after a few years in England, steered it expertly along the lane that led to the multi-storey garage for the overseas building. Ajaib's plane was less than fifty miles off.

Inside Number Three Building cleaners were at work, mopping the smooth floor, washing down the plate-glass walls with rubber wipers; two Pakistanis in white cotton jackets moved never-endingly round the café section clearing dirty cups and plates and collecting the crumpled sticky papers that had wrapped high-priced mass-produced pastries. Mr Khan and Mr Malik sat for ten minutes over a cup of coffee and then went down to stand at the exit from the customs hall through which newly arrived passengers filed, day and night, in unending procession. About a hundred others were waiting, many of them also from Pakistan or from India; a few Australians, a German business-man, English families, a mother trying to keep track of two impatient small children who kept running in different directions. Through the plate-glass it was possible to see the upper part of a great staircase from which the newly arrived left immigration officials behind them and proceeded down to the customs hall.

Australians were coming through now, porters wheeling their baggage ahead of them on metal trolleys. There were loud greetings and hugs and embraces. Some English, some Americans, a group of Japanese wearing labels on their jackets, a business-man with a sleek portmanteau who shook hands with the waiting German before they walked off together. And then a pause, while the waiting group strained their necks to look for arrivals from the PIA plane, which had landed half an hour before, within five minutes of the plane from Sydney.

Now they began slowly to come through. Three women in vividly coloured tunics and shalwars, one with a thick white shawl; several of the waiting Pakistanis hurried forward to greet them. A prosperous looking Pakistani man of middle age in a dark blue suit and sun-glasses. Then three younger men, leaner, less affluent-looking, returning perhaps from a visit home; they too had friends to meet them. One by one the PIA passengers gradually came through; Mr Khan started forward at sight of a boy, but paused; it was not Ajaib. At last there seemed to be no more to come and Mr Khan's son had still not appeared. Anxiously, he tried to enter the customs hall to ask someone if he could make inquiries, but a customs officer curtly barred his way, and told him he was not allowed in.

Mr Malik went to the PIA desk to find out if Ajaib's name was on the passenger list; it was some minutes before he could get attention, and when he did he was told by a business-like but indifferent man at the counter that Ajaib's name was indeed on the list, so he must have arrived. Mr Malik, by now very worried at what might have happened, returned to his elder brother outside the customs hall, and found him talking to an Englishman. 'He is here: come with me,' said Mr Khan and with no further information he followed the Englishman. Mr Malik, puzzled, followed in his turn into the customs hall, across it and up the enormous staircase at the far side, to a balcony divided off from the great arrival hall beyond. Through a gap in the partition, where immigration officers stood, Mr Khan could see his son sitting dejected, with his bundles at his feet, on a massive couch. Mr Khan started forward but again his way was barred. He was about thirty feet from Ajaib, and called his name; the boy looked up slowly, bewildered, and saw his father being held back as he tried to come towards him.

Worried, confused and fearful, Mr Khan had difficulty in taking in the fact that someone was addressing questions to him. He heard a voice, but the words had no meaning. He was jolted into consciousness when the voice, raised louder, uttered slowly and deliberately.

'Come along now, do – you – speak – English?'

'Of course he speaks English,' said Mr Malik indignantly, 'he is here five, six years.'

'Then he can talk for himself, can't he?' said the immigration officer. 'Now then, if you can speak English, you can give me your full name, can't you? And your address.'

'Bashir Ahmed Khan, 37 Butchers Lane', and he gave the town's name.

'Is it your own house?'

'My brother and I, we share it.'

'You share it, do you? Who's the legal owner?'

'We have joint mortgage.'

'And your brother's name?'

Mr Malik tried to interrupt with his own name, but the immigration officer impatiently silenced him.

'I'm asking Mr Khan the questions. I don't want any answers from anyone else. Now, then, is this an all-male household? Lots of lodgers?'

'No lodgers,' said Mr Khan.

'So there's just the two of you living there, is that right? How many rooms do you have?'

As Mr Khan reflected, Mr Malik eagerly put in 'six', just before Mr Khan said 'four'.

'*Will* you be quiet?' said the immigration offcer to Mr Malik. 'Now, you don't seem to know how many rooms there are in this house you live in. How many? I want *you* to answer,' he said to Mr Khan.

'Please, may I see my son? He is here waiting, I have not seen him for five years.'

'All in good time. Now, your brother's name here is Abdul Malik, you are joint owners of 37 Butchers Lane, and the two of you live there in four rooms, or six, is it?'

Mr Khan could not keep his mind on the questions. 'Four, five, six, what does it matter?'

'We'll get through this a lot quicker if you can just try to give a straight answer to a straight question. I have to satisfy myself of certain facts before your claim that this boy is your son can be established. He tells a very confused story, and perhaps you can help to clear it up. Now, how many people did you say live at this house?'

'Four people.'

'You just said you didn't have any lodgers.'

'I never say – I mean –' Mr Khan was confused. He and his brother Malik, his nephew and his cousin lived in the house. There were no lodgers, only members of the family. He tried to explain, but his English became less clear as he tried: he was anxious about Ajaib, sitting alone and despondent, and he stuttered, forgot the right word for 'cousin' and referred to his father's brother's son; the immigration officer did not seem to be following him at all.

'Wait a moment,' said the immigration officer, and left to make a telephone call. Mr Khan and Mr Malik waited, smiling, waving and trying to make signs of encouragement to Ajaib across the floor that separated them, until another immigration officer brusquely told them to stop making signals, and moved them across to a seat at the side of the balcony out of sight of the boy.

New people from another flight began to come through the barrier; they were kept less than a minute at a time as their passports were scrutinized, and they moved on chattering loudly, laughing, down the stairs to the customs hall. Long minutes went by until the first immigration officer returned.

'I've just been on to the police near your home,' he said. 'I'm told 37 Butchers Lane is a terraced dwelling with two ground-floor rooms and two upstairs. So it's a four-roomed house.'

'There is a kitchen,' said Mr Malik, 'and we have added bathroom with improvement grant where the coal-bunker used to stand.'

'Well, that's still four rooms,' said the immigration officer impatiently, 'never mind about the kitchen and bathroom. I'm also told there are seven people living there.'

Mr Malik and Mr Khan indignantly began to deny this together. 'You can ask who you like – I will telephone my solicitor, he will tell you there are only four persons –'

'Then why do the police say there are seven people?'

'How do I know why the police say this? It is not true: they are lying,' said Mr Khan.

It is a serious tactical error to tell any official that the police are lying; from that moment on, Mr Khan's chances plummeted. But his indignation was justified. There were only four people in the house, that house which Mr Malik had truthfully according to his own lights said to have six rooms, and which Mr Khan, using the same method as the immigration officer of not counting the kitchen and bathroom as rooms, had described as having four. The phone call to the police had gone to a desk sergeant who remembered calling at 37 Butchers Lane when a chimney had caught fire two months before, when three of Mr Khan's friends had been staying the night because they had come from Glasgow for a wedding. The police sergeant had simply assumed that all these Pakistanis, who looked pretty much alike to him, lived at the house. But Mr Khan and Mr Malik were not told the date from which the police information derived; they did not connect the statement that seven people lived at their home with a transient visit that had taken place two months before. As far as they were concerned the police were giving a false story, and this was somehow connected with the fact that they were not allowed to speak to Ajaib, and with the fact that they were being cross-questioned as if they were criminals. Mr Khan was allowed to telephone his solicitor, who promised to telephone the immigration officer back immediately and vouch for his character. The solicitor did so, but when questioned over the phone by the immigration officer about the number of persons living in the house, had to admit that he had never personally visited 37 Butchers Lane since Mr Khan had lived there.

Next, the immigration officer questioned Mr Khan about Ajaib.

'When was he born?'

'1954.'

'Yes, I want the exact date of birth, not just the year.'

'It was in summer.'

'What was the exact date?'

'It will say in his passport.'

The immigration officer was impatient and suspicious. 'Surely you know the date your son was born?'

How could Mr Khan explain? Birthdays are not celebrated in Pakistan; birth certificates were not normally issued – certainly not in rural areas in the 1950s. There was no need to know the exact day of anyone's birth; it was as if an English person were asked in what phase of the moon he had been born. But Mr Khan did not know how to explain this, for to him it seemed so natural that an exact birthday was a matter of no consequence, he was unable to imagine himself into the state of mind of the immigration officer, who seemed to attach so much importance to it. Ajaib was obviously under sixteen; what was the fuss?

'When was he born?' the officer repeated.

'1964.'

'Oh, so your son's only two years old, is he?'

Mr Khan was unaware of having made a mistake in the number. He was angry. 'What do you mean? My son is twelve years old! Only a fool would think he is two years old. What are you trying to say?'

The interrogation dragged on. Mr Khan was asked the name of his wife, his wife's sisters, his wife's mother, and the date of his wife's birthday. The last question again he could not answer. He was told to wait again. The time dragged on. The immigration officer was questioning Ajaib, with the help of a tall, burly interpreter, who was in fact a retired English business-man who had been twenty years in the Indian sub-continent.

This was the third time Ajaib had been questioned, asked

over and over again for the name of his mother, his aunts, his mother's birthday, how many years he had been in school, how many cattle the family owned, how many brothers and sisters he had. Some of the questions he found hard to follow; the English interpreter spoke Urdu with a marked accent, and Ajaib had spoken his local dialect of Punjabi all his life and found many words hard to comprehend. Moreover, he was tired out and feeling rather dizzy. His sickness had almost entirely worn off but he had not been given anything to eat since arriving – nearly three hours ago now. The journey had exhausted and disoriented him. He was only twelve and he came from a small village; here he was in a nightmare world of glass and leather and plastic, being questioned over and over again by strangers who could not speak clearly enough for him to follow, and whose tone of voice was hectoring and hostile. It was extraordinary that he could manage to reply at all. But he was aware, obscurely, that it was very important for him to try hard for something must be seriously wrong; his father was being kept away from him, but if only he could answer the questions these men kept asking, giving the answers they wanted, he would get the chance to speak to his father. So he tried. But even more than his father, he became confused. The men repeated the same questions over and over; he tried to answer right, but he could not always guess what they were trying to find out. Asked his younger brother's name, he gave the pet family nickname that all the family used at home; how was he to know that when Mr Khan was asked the same question he would reply with Abdul's official name? Asked about the number of cattle, he was not sure whether to include the new calf or not; one time he included it, one time not, so that his answers seemed contradictory.

After five hours, Mr Khan was told that the immigration officer would refuse Ajaib admission. 'We don't think he's really your son. His answers and yours to simple questions about the family are seriously conflicting. Also, we are not satisfied with the accommodation you have, which is already overcrowded.'

At this point, at last, Mr Khan was allowed to cross the floor and embrace his son. They both wept. Mr Khan did not know how to explain to Ajaib what was happening; he could scarcely comprehend it himself. He was allowed to give the boy some food. They had an hour together. Then Ajaib was led out to the PIA plane to be sent back to Karachi.

It was all routine to PIA. This happened every day at Heathrow Airport. Ajaib was the third child that day to be refused. The airline had to bear the expense of carrying passengers who were refused entry, but there were generally places enough in the planes.

This was 1966, when the immigration laws were a great deal more liberal than they have since become, if it makes sense at all to say 'liberal' of rules that could produce events like these over and over and over again. These were the Immigration Act 1962, and the White Paper on Commonwealth Immigration of August 1965, which were designed to cut down the numbers of Commonwealth immigrants arriving, and simultaneously to improve harmonious community relations in Britain. 'We must be fair to those already here' had been the agreed formula. Mr Khan was already here. It was fortunate, perhaps, that nobody came to tell him kindly that night that the immigration regulations were intended to make things better for him in England. And it might well have puzzled other residents in Butchers Lane to work out how their community relationships would be improved by the fact that Mr Khan, grieved, angry and bitter, was not to be allowed to have his son join him, and had lost at a stroke a hundred and eighty pounds of savings for fares and expenses that nobody was responsible for returning to him. Mr Khan had watched white people walk through immigration without difficulty while the passengers from Pakistan had long delays, and he and his son had been forced to endure an ordeal and an unjust decision that would affect the rest of their lives.

In the same week, Eveline's sister in Birmingham had a similar experience. Her youngest brother, Harry, who was only nineteen, was due to come on a visit. Different members of the family had been pooling funds from their savings to pay the fare. Harry was a favourite of the older sisters; lively, talented, full of jokes, and making a great success of his education. He had no wish to come to England to settle; he had prospects in Jamaica, but the holiday visit had been being planned for over two years with money gradually paid in to the travel agency in Kingston. Harry came over by boat and arrived at Southampton. Eveline's sister had travelled down from Birmingham to meet him. Harry was held back, interrogated, and told he was suspected of trying to enter for permanent settlement, as he had relatives already in the country. He explained over and over again that he had come on a visit. It was no good. The word of a black person counted for nothing. The decision was entirely up to the immigration officer, and if the immigration officer chose to believe Harry was coming for permanent settlement, no evidence was of any use, and no appeal possible – except to higher up in the Home Office, but Harry did not know this, nor did Eveline's sister. Harry was returned to Jamaica; the money spent on *his* fare, and the preparations made for his stay were again completely lost.

And in the same week there were bewildered old men come to join their working sons who were interrogated, told they were not really the age they said they were, and returned to India. And there was a boy from India who was made to undergo medical tests, having his teeth examined and his wrists X-rayed, to determine whether he was over sixteen or not, and who was then told he was over sixteen (which he was not) and returned to India. The X-rays were to determine whether fusion of the epiphysis had taken place or not; such tests determine physiological age, but as for deciding a person's exact age by the calendar, they are subject to at least an eighteen-month margin of error either way – so I was assured by a leading expert on child growth to whom I wrote on the matter. They could, then, easily be interpreted so as to allow a boy whose calendar age was seventeen to enter the country, even though under the regulations he was not entitled to, or to exclude a boy of fourteen or fifteen who was in fact eligible.

And in the same week the police called on a girl from St Kitts who had come over to join the man who wanted to marry her only to find that the man in question had decided to marry someone else in the meantime. The police told her she could not stay in England, as the regulations demanded she should get married within three months of arrival if her status, on admission, was that of a fiancée. She cried, but it was no use. It would be an offence against the law for her to take employment, or to remain in the country. She had to go. She didn't have the fare. The police told her to make arrangements about the fare.

And in the same week, a young Australian girl working as a library assistant in London was chatting to a friend on the telephone about whether to move around the country taking temporary jobs or whether to stay on at the library and save up for a few weeks free of work; whether to go back to Australia in three months' time or six months'. She was hardly aware of being subject to the Commonwealth Immigration Act and the White Paper regulations. Indeed, in practice, she was not. She had entered the country without difficulty, taken a job without question, and assumed as a matter of course that she could stay or go when she pleased. But then she was white. She did not have to worry. But the Jamaican woman who cleaned the library, whose brother not understanding the situation had asked for her help after he had been refused a work voucher, knew how easy it was for the Australian girl, and knew why. She overheard the telephone conversation as she worked, and silently drew her own bitter conclusions.

It was one week like other weeks. And while some white English people were complaining that coloured immigrants were flooding the country, the non-whites like Mr Malik and Mr Khan and their nephew and their cousin, and Eveline's sister, and Eveline and her husband, and their other sister and *her* husband, and their friends, and the Indian families whose elderly parents and sons had been refused, and the friends of the girl from St Kitts, and many more, all knew that *they* were suffering the consequences of these laws called immigration regulations because of their colour, because it was a colour unwanted and despised. This was the situation that the Government, and officials, and many well-meaning voluntary workers, described as fostering the growth of harmonious community relations. It could hardly in fact have been a more explosive mixture.

In the same week, Mr Menotti, an Italian with a small tailoring business, who had entered England some years before on a work voucher as a hotel waiter, had saved, had readily obtained permission to stay on after a couple of years, and had acquired the flat above his business premises, went to the airport to meet his wife, his son of seventeen, his younger daughter of sixteen and his son of twelve. There were delighted emotional greetings; they travelled back to the flat and ate an enormous meal together. They were aliens, and not Commonwealth citizens. An alien could bring his dependents in up to the age of twenty-one. None of Mr Menotti's children, nor his wife, spoke a word of English, yet oddly enough nobody in the House of Commons nor in the press was to be heard protesting about the difficulties being caused by Italians flooding the schools and causing difficulties to staff and other pupils, or about their occupying jobs despite language difficulties with orders and works notices. Because so many of the staff were Spanish, a certain mental hospital about this time put up painted notices in its buildings and grounds, in two languages, English and Spanish, but no one commented locally: no special committees were formed to applaud the idea of doing so as a constructive step in Anglo-Spanish community relations, and nobody on the other hand complained of a waste of paint and time. Nobody was demanding a stop to 'alien' immigration, though far more work vouchers were being issued to the Menottis of this world than to the Khans. And yet – and yet – the notion that the Commonwealth immigration laws had nothing to do with racism or colour prejudice, the belief that the problems in community relations were happily solved by arranging language classes and interpreting services and social get-togethers for certain 'new arrivals' (some of them present in England for half their lifetime already) who just happened not to be white, these ludicrously false and silly notions were solemnly accepted by all but a handful of the liberal-minded. (The illiberal, of course, saw more clearly that racism and colour prejudice *were* involved and were content that this should be so, though they would have found widely varying verbal means of expression to justify the conviction that black people were undesirable and had got to be kept out or, if here, made uncomfortable.)

But since 1966, when events of the kind that I have described were occurring not just in one awful week, but every week, the situation has continued to change. It changes, indeed, so greatly and so frequently that there can be no hope of writing about it and being up to date with a description for longer than a few months at best. The practical application of the written regulations varies in ways which only a person doing casework all the time in immigration law can understand or appreciate. So that even though the written rules may remain the same for a year or two years at a time, what actually happens to people trying to migrate or to bring their own wives and children or other relatives to join them is a matter of uncertainty. This is partly because so much of the law is in fact left to the discretion of an individual immigration officer or entry certificate officer. It is partly because the rules are so complex and subject to change that it can easily happen that officials responsible for administering them actually get them wrong. And it is partly because many parts of the law are so badly drafted in relation to actual circumstances that there is no reasonable way of applying them: for example, the use of the exact birthday as a dividing line between persons eligible and ineligible to migrate is a completely unworkable system when applied to a country in which exact birthdays are unrecorded for a large proportion of the population, and simply have to be guessed. However cruel or however kind the immigration officer may be, given such a rule to use he is certainly going to decide wrongly on both sides of the line a good many times in the terms of the law itself.

There has, then, been a steady development of the situation for the worse; first because the laws themselves have been changed to become more and more restrictive, second because the discretion to be used in the application of the laws, fairly flexible just after the 1962 Act, has become more and more a weapon for exclusion, third because even the restrictive rules themselves are sometimes bent by officials in ways which keep people out rather than let them in, and fourth because the laws and their regulations can be such that the people to whom they are supposed to apply are quite unable, through no fault of their own, to comply convincingly with the conditions laid down.

Day after day in the late 1960s, distraught families at Heathrow were being approached by touts with offers to help them get the detained relatives they had come to meet admitted: their services would cost fifty pounds down, and another fifty pounds if the relative was in fact admitted. The efforts of such paid advocates was sometimes an obstruction if the family asked also for the help of one of the organizations not demanding money, the National Council for Civil Liberties, a local Community Relations Committee or a voluntary organization, for the Home Office would find itself approached by different people on behalf of the same immigrant. While representations were being made to the Home Office, the would-be immigrant would be detained in the police cells at Heathrow; after five days, he or she would be moved into a prison if adult, a remand home if a child. The point of this procedure was that such a person was not technically inside Britain at all, having failed so far to satisfy the immigration authorities of his or her right to enter. Although anyone accused of a crime can apply for bail and if granted it can remain at liberty, these would-be immigrants were given *no* chance to remain at liberty or go to their families while their cases were under consideration; the Home Office suspected them one and all of being likely to vanish. These were people who had attempted to enter the country in a normal and legal manner and had committed no crime against this country's laws, yet who were kept locked up in penal institutions, sometimes unable to communicate in any language with warders or fellow-prisoners, sometimes unable to eat the unfamiliar food, sometimes fearful that the food contained ingredients forbidden to them by their religion. One Indian woman spent three weeks in Holloway prison, with her two children who had accompanied her each in a separate remand home, none of them able to see each other. Oh yes, the immigration laws were very important for improving community relations; only a few fanatics or extreme leftists could object to them. (Actually, most of the white people I knew at this period who were concerned about the horrible things that were happening were almost comically moderate, middle-of-the-road, solid English people whose basic sense of fairness and decency was outraged by the treatment of intending immigrants and their families, but who tried in vain to rouse public attention and action.)

Strong protests to the Government, however, about the immigration restrictions in the 1965 White Paper had been made from within the Labour Party by some constituency parties and backbench M.P.s; too late to prevent the White Paper provisions from being carried out, but resulting, at the very end of 1965, in a Government decision to set up a committee of inquiry into immigration procedures. The committee, under the chairmanship of Sir Roy Wilson, took evidence and reported in the summer of 1967 that an appeals procedure should be introduced, and that the Government should give financial assistance to a voluntary body representing immigrants themselves so that it could assist those threatened with refusal to prepare their appeals before an independent tribunal. Although an organization exactly fulfilling the recommendations of the Wilson Committee had just been formed under the name of the Joint Council for the Welfare of Immigrants, representing over 150 immigrant organizations as well as multiracial groups, churches and the National Council for Civil Liberties, the Government did not take the opportunity to give the financial help its own committee of inquiry had recommended, nor immediately to introduce legislation on appeals.

Long delays, further discussions, further investigations, were eventually followed by the Immigration Appeals Act 1969 which set up an appeals machinery of some complexity and also, on an amendment, made it compulsory for intending immigrants from colonies and independent Commonwealth countries to obtain entry certificates to Britain before leaving their own countries. An advisory service was set up with government money to assist those refused to prepare their appeals. But the appeals were to be heard in Britain, while the refused person was still in the country of origin. The harrowing scenes at Heathrow and other ports of entry were virtually brought to an end; refusals became remote, and being out of sight could comfortably remain out of mind even more easily than before.

Meanwhile, the restrictions themselves had increased. By 1968 intending immigrants were all subject to health checks, unless they were dependent relatives or returning residents, and refusals on grounds of ill-health were being made. The number of work vouchers available each year, theoretically 8,500, was in fact steadily reduced to half this number. Employers who were themselves immigrants were systematically refused work vouchers for halal butchers and cooks for Indian restaurants and by 1968 again the Ministry of Labour was refusing to issue work vouchers except for work of social or national importance, a restriction that was never legislated upon and which effectively reduced the numbers even more. And in March 1968 a new, full-blown Act of Parliament was passed, the Immigration Act, which denied the right of residence in Britain to British passport-holders without parents or grandparents born in Britain, and so effectively excluded thousands of citizens in East Africa not merely from their right to live in Britain, but, in a grim and real sense for many of them, their right to live at all.

The Joint Council for the Welfare of Immigrants, despite its lack of money from any official source, has kept going since its foundation in 1967 on voluntary contributions, some help from charities, and the work of its two full-time employees backed by volunteers. From one small, inadequately furnished office it has kept up a spate of activity that unceasingly helps individuals in distress, lobbies for amendment to the immigration laws, seeks legal redress from, for instance, the European Court for the victims of discrimination, and battles for publicity for the plight of the excluded and the harassed. Its reports on East Africa deserve to be read in full, but these extracts give some idea of the suffering directly created by our immigration laws:

> We are eighteen Asians of British nationality who tried to enter Britain legally but after waiting for more than 18 months without any proper reply from British High Commission in Kampala, Uganda, we had no other choice but to push our way into England, so we left for U.K. On our journey while passing through Austria we were asked and pulled out of the train at the border town Jesinica and were asked to consult the British High Commission. So we reached Belgrade and saw the deputy Commissioner and he said that he couldn't do anything as the higher authority in U.K. has refused them to issue any vouchers. We are on the road since last fifteen days and now we are penniless and the stage has come that last 3 days we have taken a loaf of bread and water and we are sleeping on the pavement of theatres and sometimes on benches in the garden. The strength of the people are getting weaker and one of us is so sick we had to admit him in hospital and the doctor has said he is so sick that he will have to stay for 21 days in hospital. We don't know what will happen to him.

And the situation continues to get worse. Of the general election period in the middle of 1970, the report says:

> The behaviour of the British Government during the month immediately preceding the General Election on June 18th showed a sharp deterioration when it came to their treatment of British citizens from East Africa. Up to that time, deportations had been carried out like clockwork, but it had been possible in some cases of extreme hardship – such as a woman with a baby – to obtain special consideration. From mid-May to June 18th, however, deportations went ahead at all costs and nothing could be done to stop them. One journalist even remarked that deportations were so commonplace that they were just a bore.

It is not possible to go into details about what happened to the 200-odd people who were caught up at the ports during the Government's election fever. JCWI has a record of these and in only two cases – one of a middle-aged man with diabetes and heart trouble and the other of an elderly man and his teenage daughter whose case had been taken up in April by Lord Brockway – did deportation fail to take place. In the first case, Lord Brockway himself had to intervene and the person concerned, although he was not deported, spent a month in prison where he lost a stone in weight.

There are, however, a few typical cases which are quoted below.

A girl called A.P. She left Uganda on 23rd May. She arrived at Dover and was subsequently put into Holloway Prison. Later she was taken to Heathrow pending deportation to Uganda. She was kept there several days because it was not possible to arrange her passage back immediately. When seen by JCWI's representative at the airport she was in a state of chronic anxiety. She was eventually deported to Entebbe and returned to Heathrow by the Ugandan authorities. She was then returned to Holloway Prison where she spent several weeks.

A.M.P. (aged 21) left Entebbe on 23rd May. He travelled to Dover via Athens and Frankfurt. He spent a week in Canterbury Prison with nine others and was then taken to Pentonville. Later the whole party was deported via Frankfurt, Cairo, Entebbe, Nairobi, Dar es Salaam and Port Louis. They were returned to Heathrow by the same route and put back in Pentonville Prison on 15th June.

R.V.K. came to Britain via Holland. From Harwich he was sent back to the Hook where he was kept in detention for several days. He was then deported back to Britain. From Harwich he was taken to Heathrow and deported to Entebbe where he was refused admission. He was taken on to Nairobi and then deported back to Heathrow via Entebbe. From Heathrow he was returned to Pentonville Prison.

As for Kenya, JCWI reported in 1971:

Today there are hundreds of families living in one room, with all their remaining belongings stacked pathetically around. Everything saleable was sold long ago to buy food. All that is left are a few mattresses perhaps, clothes, murti (religious statues) and the family photographs.

This report makes clear that such families are living at subsistence level, unable to buy milk, meat or even fresh fruit and vegetables. 'The children are under-nourished and show signs of extreme withdrawal and lassitude. Their parents, who go without themselves in order to provide for them, eat even less.' Families like these have in many cases well-educated, trained commercial or professional workers as their heads: they have been reduced from a hard-working, middle-class and apparently secure way of life to a state as demoralizing and mentally unbearable as it is physically deprived.

With immigration laws like these, spokesmen for 'extreme' views on immigration control, like Mr Sandys, Mr Powell, Mr Ronald Bell and so on, are merely putting the icing on the cake with references to how 'the breeding of millions of half-caste children will merely produce a generation of misfits and increase social tension', (Mr Duncan Sandys 1967) or to 'a nation busily engaged in heaping its own funeral pyre' (Mr Enoch Powell 1968 on allowing in excessive numbers of immigrants).

But 1968 was only another stage in a process which shows no sign of ending, the process of blocking the entry of black people, at whatever human cost, and making life miserable or insecure for those already here. In January 1969 Labour's Home Secretary, Mr Callaghan, announced that in future the Commonwealth citizen who married a British wife, or any wife with a right to reside in Britain, would not thereby become eligible to reside in Britain himself. Although a woman could still become legally resident in Britain by marrying a male resident here, a man could not acquire any right of residence by marriage. Women who married Commonwealth husbands then had the choice of leaving Britain or of living permanently apart from their husbands. And 1971 produced another full-scale Immigration Bill ostensibly to place alien and Commonwealth immigration on the same footing, but in fact to preserve the worst features of existing legislation for both aliens and Commonwealth citizens, to create new divisions and incredibly complex new kinds of status in which there will be not two but many classes of citizen before the law, and to remove some of the protection provided by the Immigration Appeals Act. At the time of writing the 1971 Bill is not yet law and may still be amended. But if it is passed in substantially its proposed form, it will create fear, insecurity and unhappiness far beyond even what our existing immigration laws have succeeded in achieving. Nor can it be reasonably expected that the process will end here; there is no logical or likely end to the demands of the anti-immigration interest until there are no black residents left in the length or breadth of the country. Any situation short of that one will still provide fuel for the burning message, 'Keep Britain White'. The fact that our whiteness may be our winding-sheet if we continue policies so sure to lead to hatred, bitterness and retaliation does not seem to bother anyone. Even someone dead to all sense of decency might see reason to alter our present immigration laws because they are so plain stupid from the point of view of our own self-interest. However, wisdom seems in as short supply as honour.

Postscript: a news item in *The Times* of 30 October 1970. It was not important enough for editorial comment:

Indians Barred

The wealthy Indian parents of an engineer in Britain have been refused permission to attend their son's wedding because it is feared that they may try to stay, an M.P. said yesterday. Mr and Mrs R. Desai, who live in Tanzania, were refused entry permits to see their son, Mr Pinakin Desai, of Grosvenor Road, Rugby, marry in Norwood, London, tomorrow.

Mr William Price, Labour M.P. for Rugby, has appealed to the Home Secretary for an explanation.

'Mr and Mrs Desai bought return tickets and signed all the necessary papers but at the last moment the permits were cancelled by the High Commission in Dar es Salaam', Mr Price said.

Mr Desai said: 'It is unbelievable the authorities should think my parents will try to live in this country. My father is an accountant and a family man. He has a large house and offices in Dar es Salaam.'

Mr Price said: 'This is one of the meanest decisions taken by any government in recent years.'

The decision has to be revoked today or Mr and Mrs Desai will not catch an aircraft to Britain in time for the wedding.

Our Nairobi Correspondent writes

Six British Asians from Uganda, including two children said to be in need of medical attention, were being flown to London late last night after a week of being shuttled between Kampala and Nairobi. None has an entry voucher for Britain although all wish to enter the country.

The six left Kampala by road for Kenya on October 22, and were returned on an aircraft. But their permit to enter Uganda was withdrawn and when they were returned to Kenya their visitors' passes were revoked.

The party included three men who seek work in England and Mrs S. Patel and her two children aged 18 months and four years, who hope to join their father, who works in a Wembley factory.

Visitors Genuine:

The great majority of Commonwealth visitors and students arriving in Britain are genuine, says a study published yesterday that summarizes and analyses the evidence amassed by the Select committee on Race Relations and Immigration during an inquiry, cut short by the general election, into control of Commonwealth immigration in the last Parliament.

The authors, Mr Arthur Bottomley, Labour M.P. for Middlesbrough East, and Sir George Sinclair, Conservative M.P. for Dorking, say that in 1969 there were some 1,400 refusals of admission to people seeking admission as visitors and students, as against 370,000 admitted.

Mr Bottomley said yesterday that immigration controls were working quite well, although they were far from perfect. 'Limitations must be applied across the board and be fair to all Commonwealth countries,' he said.

2. For the Good of the People

In October 1967 a report was published at the request of the Race Relations Board and the National Committee for Commonwealth Immigrants, and at the expense of Marks & Spencer Ltd, by three distinguished lawyers: Professor Harry Street, Geoffrey Howe, Q.C., and Geoffrey Bindman. The purpose of the Street Report was to examine legislation against discrimination in other countries, and to make recommendations to Parliament on the most suitable types of such legislation to be introduced here. The authors made the point, which was to be frequently emphasized by the proposers of anti-discrimination legislation for this country, that the importance of such a law lay not only in its implementation, but in the educative effect it would have upon public opinion: the weight and authority of Parliament would have declared against racial discrimination.

> Legislation of the kind that we have proposed is intended, far more than other laws, to have a positively favourable influence upon the entire range of public attitudes towards discrimination. For this reason it is more than usually important that the law as a whole should be widely accepted, and as little misunderstood as possible.[1]

Earlier in 1967, an American civil rights lawyer, Joseph L. Rauh, had developed the same point at a conference in London on racial equality in employment (again organized by the NCCI and the RRB):

> No facts play a more important part in the creation of opinion than the laws themselves. The mere declaration of policy influences

most people. Second, law is perhaps the greatest educational course in the democratic society. We learnt this the hard way because, as I told you earlier, our law – our law of slavery, our law of segregation – taught inequality for hundreds of years, and only another law can offset the ugly teaching of the earlier law. Third, government teaches best by example. When a Government as an employer hires Negroes, it teaches. And when a Government passes a law on racial equality, it teaches ... I not only believe that law can affect discrimination, I deeply believe that law can affect prejudice.

Now, several years later, these remarks make melancholy reading. It is true that the Street Report and the Employment conference were riding on a wave of success towards the passing of a wide-ranging anti-discrimination law, the 1968 Race Relations Act for which the NCCI, the Race Relations Board, the Society of Labour Lawyers, CARD and other lobbies had been pressing. The powerful sponsorship of Roy Jenkins, then Home Secretary, was to bring the Bill before Parliament very shortly after their demands had gained wide publicity. But whatever effect the implementation of the law's provisions was to have, its educative effect on public opinion was doomed to failure. Although the Bill was passed, it was the philosophy of its opponents which captured public attention and there has been ever since a widespread popular white belief that the Race Relations Act of 1968 created a specially privileged class of black people who, reasonably or unreasonably, could not be refused anything.

Why did this happen? Was Joseph L. Rauh quite wrong in stating that public opinion followed the law? Was the truth rather that law limped after public opinion?

The interplay of law and public consent poses a difficult question. But in this particular case, it is quite clear from the history of the 1960s that the failure of the Race Relations Act to educate the public in favour of racial equality was due, not to the fact that governments play no part in educating public opinion, but to the fact that governments had succeeded all too well in educating public opinion *in favour* of racial discrimination for a full seven years before the Race Relations Act of

1968. The passage of the Act contradicted the whole trend of official policy towards black people on the part of both Conservative and Labour Governments during the decade. The legislation that *had* succeeded in educating public opinion in the wrong direction was the legislation which wrote racial discrimination into our immigration laws.

For a full understanding of British immigration laws we have to look back at the first measure ever introduced, in 1905, whose intent was to stop Jews coming into the country. The Aliens Act of 1905 was later followed by Aliens Orders, made at times of emergency under threat of war, whose intent was to keep Germans out of the country. Finally from 1962 onwards there has been a body of law built up, partly by legislation, partly by the 1965 White Paper, most of which was put into effect under powers conferred by the 1962 Act, and partly by executive orders, whose intent has been to keep black people out of the country.

It is worth stressing intent, because in no case has the wording of the law been so ungentlemanly as to specify that certain races or nationalities should be excluded as such. Elaborate prevarication has established laws which operate clumsily, and more or less effectively; the fact that they do not achieve a hundred per cent exclusion of the unwanted group can be produced indignantly as proof that they are not really discriminatory to answer any liberal questioner, while the fact that they effectively keep out all but a few of the unwanted can be used to answer critics from the other side who want a hundred per cent exclusion.

Before 1905 movement in and out of the country was free from control by statute. The statutes introduced at intervals since then have had the effect of restricting movement to such an extent that it is now possible to find a couple of hundred immigration officers working through a twenty-four hour period at London Airport alone, and thousands of police man-hours a year are devoted to checking on the movements, accommodation and employment status of migrants, students and visitors. The elaborate machinery and daily work required to implement the immigration laws, keeping a sizeable staff of Civil Servants permanently busy as well, is all devoted to one end: keeping out, or getting rid of, unwanted *categories* of human beings. The work, whose cost to the nation must be financially extremely high, is not devoted to the furtherance of any policy other than exclusion. This country, since freedom of movement was abolished, has never had an immigration *policy*, in the sense of a plan for controlling population movement in the interest of the nation's economy, its foreign policy or its social needs. All such considerations have been subordinate to the interest of exclusion for exclusion's sake.

Lobbying about most laws is concerned with the wrongness of, say, charging exorbitant rents or the rightness of building more schools, and individuals affected by such laws are not in any way singled out for blame or praise for what kind of people they are; the actions they have chosen to make are specified as desirable or undesirable from the point of view of public policy. Our immigration laws are concerned with classifying individuals for what they are and *for what they have no choice but to be*; born with a particular skin pigment, born in a particular country or within a particular community, and with declaring such characteristics to be so undesirable in the eyes of the law that the mere physical presence of anyone exhibiting them, regardless of his behaviour, may be declared unlawful.

An immigration law which was framed on any basis other than racism would not necessarily have such characteristics. If, for example, a British government decided to close the borders to all but people with certain skills in short supply, such as doctors, dentists, plasterers, carpenters and physicists, and then admitted new residents – together, of course, with their dependent families – strictly on the basis of professional skill in these jobs, the law could be considered as a good or bad one from the economic point of view but it would not be a law of a racist or nationalist nature. It might not be a good law to have but it would be very different from what we have got – a situation in which any pretence that immigration control is to control crude numbers coming in, or is concerned with allowing only skilled people in, is invalidated by the plain fact that Irish immigration, consisting largely of people without skills, has always been completely unrestricted and has produced the largest single immigrant group of all. (I hope it will be evident from the rest of my argument that I am certainly not in favour of banning the Irish – that would just be another manifestation of racism: the reason for emphasizing their freedom of movement is simply that their status makes nonsense of every argument, except the specific racist appeal to keep coloured people out, which has ever been advanced in favour of controlling immigration.)

The kind of lobbying that is directed against people for what they are goes on to identify problems within the country as being created by the physical presence of certain people rather than by the commission or omission of any acts of policy. The *Daily Telegraph*'s heading for a letter from Sir Cyril Osborne on 11 October 1961 (a letter of which 5,000 copies were specially printed and handed out by Sir Cyril and others to delegates as they arrived for the Conservative Party conference in Brighton) was:

IMMIGRATION LUNACY – Even nearer an Afro-Asian Britain

And Sir Cyril's attitude was expressed plainly earlier than this when the *Daily Mail* printed his remark, 'This is a white man's country and I want it to remain so', in February of the same year. Also later, in December, in the *Spectator*: 'Those who so vehemently denounce the slogan "Keep Britain White" should answer the question, "do they want to turn it black?" If unlimited immigration were allowed, we should ultimately become a chocolate-coloured, Afro-Asian mixed society. That I do not want.'

The fact that Sir Cyril has denied having any colour prejudice will surely blind very few people to the nakedly racist character of these remarks. But when the *Streatham News* reported Mr Christopher Chataway, M.P. for North Lewisham, on 27 October 1961, as demanding some limitation on immigration with the words, 'We do want this to be one country', the manner of expression is very different and yet the kind of law being asked for and the motivation for it were clearly concerned with exactly the same measures as Sir Cyril's cruder propaganda: 'coloured' immigrants must be kept out of the country somehow; they did not really belong to it.

On 6 October the *Daily Telegraph* reported that Mr Norman Pannell, M.P. for Kirkdale, prophesied 120,000 coloured immigrants coming into the country that year. The *Telegraph* stated:

> There are 40 resolutions on immigrants on the agenda to the Conservative conference. The one chosen for debate expresses concern at 'the very serious problems being created by the uncontrolled number of immigrants flowing into the United Kingdom' and asks the Government to take action. Only one resolution supports the policy of free entry from the Commonwealth.

This brief extract from the *Telegraph* is characteristic of a great deal that has been published in the last fifteen years, in that it refers in one place to 'immigration', which might mean the total immigration of all nationalities and colours, and in the next passage to 'entry from the Commonwealth', but clearly referring to the same issue both times. Immigration has become a term which is most frequently used to mean not immigration proper, but immigration of dark-coloured people; but by using 'immigration' and 'Commonwealth immigration' sometimes as meaning different things and sometimes as meaning the same thing, English politicians, press and public have developed a very satisfactory manner of disguising their own racism from themselves. At all times the propaganda in favour of 'controlling immigration' has been understood on every side to mean 'cutting down on coloured immigration', yet as with the wording of the law itself the defender of control can exclaim indignantly that he never mentioned colour but only the number of people coming into the country; while if he is attacked from the right, he can point out that everyone understood his remarks to refer to coloured immigration. This usage has served to confuse many English people, who began with some latent colour prejudice but who could without difficulty have adapted to living happily in an equal multi-racial society. They have been warned constantly by politicians that this is an over-crowded little island, and that people coming into it cause problems, and they have come to identify the people who cause problems by arriving here with people of dark colour. People like this start from quite a different position from the one held by Sir Cyril Osborne: he is in favour of a white man's country, and therefore denounces coloured immigration and justifies his attacks by talking about coloured immigrants as bringers of vice, disease and housing shortage. But some of his audience, starting from the position that they have 'nothing against coloured people', are aware of problems in society such as a housing shortage, are readily persuaded of the simple (though false) argument that more people entering the country must mean fewer houses for English people to live in, and then being persuaded (again falsely) that 'immigration' and 'coloured immigration' mean the same thing, come to the conclusion that it is necessary for the well-being of the country that coloured immigrants be prevented from coming in. Starting from a non-racist position, they are brought to arrive at a racist position, not just because a few wild extremists on the Right advocate it but because over and over again they have seen British governments, both Conservative and Labour, with all their authority endorse by the legislation they have passed the validity of the arguments that the extremists have produced and are thus fully convinced of the necessity for exclusion.

What, in the whole debate on non-white immigration, has been regarded as openly fascist one year, has become a few years later a respectable and moderate opinion – not because it is in itself moderate but because the whole of public opinion has shifted further and further towards acceptance of racist positions, to a point where anyone making practical demands for racial equality, in terms that would have seemed mildly liberal in the 1950s, is liable to be called an extreme leftist, or a hysterical champion of coloured immigrants against the interests of the native English. Furthermore, what was the opinion of a few individuals, expressing hostility in terms of colour, at one time made hardly any impression on public opinion, but became much more effective as a form of public education in racism *after* immigration control had begun. In 1958 Lord Salisbury claimed to be speaking for the common man in opposing the uncontrolled immigration of 'men and women of African race', but very few common men were in fact supporting him – at any rate outside Birmingham and the West Midlands, and even there the activities of such people as the Birmingham Immigration Control Association represented a minority view. At the time of the Notting Hill disturbances public opinion acquiesced in condemning the white youths convicted of assault there. Had the British government chosen that moment to introduce a Race Relations Act, the effect on public opinion would surely have been to strengthen and extend the belief that racial discrimination was unjust and undesirable. And with such an Act on the Statute Book, the chance of openly discriminatory immigration laws being passed later on would have been greatly reduced. But the opportunity was missed. Advocates of anti-discrimination legislation were begging for it before the hour was too late, in the mid-sixties, but the hour by then was already too late for anti-immigration propaganda had succeeded in pushing the government to make Britain's first race law a racially discriminatory measure: the Commonwealth Immigration Act of 1962.

The rapidity with which extreme views were accepted by large numbers of respectable and responsible people as moderate and acceptable ones is demonstrated by the fact that Sir Oswald Mosley's election programme in 1959 had become official Conservative Party policy by 1969, and was only one step beyond Labour Party policy of 1965. The Labour Party had, of course, strenuously opposed the 1962 Immigration Act but only three years later and now in power, they were introducing far more severe restrictions than 1962 had ever envisaged. The Rose Report, *Colour and Citizenship*, says of Mosley:

His Union Movement had been as surprised as anyone by what

had occurred in Notting Hill, but they were brisk enough in their efforts to exploit the situation. Early in 1959, Mosley announced his intention to contest the North Kensington seat at the forthcoming General Election, his platform epitomized in the statement, 'we are going to treat these people fairly but we are going to send them home'.

Mosley polled less than 3,000 votes, and lost his deposit for the first time in his career. Perhaps his mistake was to advocate repatriation too soon. Sending people 'home' was indeed the only possible logical consequence of finding the physical presence of dark-skinned citizens undesirable. Limiting immigration was perhaps going to reduce the numbers of new arrivals; it could never succeed in removing the dark-skinned people already here. But if advocates of controlling immigration began from the premise that the presence of dark-skinned people in this country was a bad thing, it was clear that sooner or later they would have to find some more effective means of getting rid of them than just stopping their friends from joining them. But the argument for repatriation has to be a blatantly racist one: it cannot proceed from any assumption except the undesirability of black people's presence as such. It can only be used once the majority is prepared to endorse, or at least stand passively by and tolerate, plainly racist policies. The argument for controlling black immigration, on the other hand, can be used very effectively to please those who are racist and to deceive everyone else. The argument 'we are going to treat these people fairly but we are going to stop them coming into the country' was explicit Labour Government policy from 1965 to 1970, and its premise, 'the Government believes the presence of coloured people constitutes a problem but it wants the country at large to behave as though it did not constitute a problem', was the basis upon which an official policy of integrating the immigrants was built. Its central contradiction made the work of trying to achieve racial equality in England absolutely impossible. It also left the Government wide open to attack when it introduced its Race Relations Bills (1965 and 1968). I remember an employer at a conference asking the very pertinent question, 'Why is it wrong for me to refuse to have any of these people in my firm when the Government is refusing to have them come into the country? If the Government doesn't want them, why should I want them?' When Birmingham City Council passed a motion in the summer of 1968 declaring that it did not want any more immigrants allowed into Birmingham, there were Government spokesmen who expressed their distaste, but they were in no position to condemn Birmingham: the local government there was only demanding for its own area the same policy as the national Government had proclaimed best for the nation.

Once the Labour Party and the Conservative Party had begun to compete with each other to see who could be toughest on immigration, it was inevitable that the area of dispute would move deeper and deeper into racist territory. Each new measure limiting immigration comes as a foretaste of the next, more restrictive one, and it becomes very unpleasant indeed to speculate what measures for getting rid of the physical presence of non-white people will be advocated once their immigration has been completely halted, and once a repatriation programme has got under way – as will surely happen. Racism is a violent and dangerous animal; once let loose, it is impossible to control, and those who hope to pacify it, or to use it for their own purposes and then tie it up again when not wanted, are making an appalling mistake.

What Mosley proclaimed as National Front policy in 1959 has become by 1971 a policy that many people who think of themselves as moderate, unprejudiced and honourable would uphold with equanimity: 'We must treat these people fairly, but we must send them home.' The National Front has, indeed, been left far behind in racist demands by a number of people who use different party labels for an ideology just as loathsome. It is not only the tone but the content that makes interesting comparison in the following two quotations from well-known twentieth-century political thinkers:

All the symptoms of decline which manifested themselves already in pre-war times can be traced back to the racial problem. Whether one is dealing with general law, or monstrous excrescences of economic life, of phenomena which point to a cultural decline or political degeneration, whether it be a question of defects in the school-system or of the evil influence which the press exerts over the adult population – always and everywhere these phenomena are at bottom caused by a lack of consideration for the interests of the race to which one's own nation belongs, or by the failure to recognize the danger that comes from allowing a foreign race to exist within the national body ... All the great civilizations of the past became decadent because the originally creative race died out, as a result of contamination of the blood.

And second, as reported in *The Times*:

He said that the British public and government had been consistently misled over the size of the coloured population ... In all its history, our nation has never known greater danger ... No government has the right to alter, or permit to be altered, the character and identity of a nation without that nation's knowledge and without that nation's will. It is a moral issue and it is a supreme issue. It dwarfed every other political subject.

The first quotation is from Adolf Hitler's *Mein Kampf*, and refers to the Jews. The second is from Enoch Powell's speech in Carshalton, Surrey, of 16 February 1971, and refers to Britain's coloured population. Both authors identify racial impurity as the most important of all political issues: the first puts down every political evil 'always and everywhere' to lack of consideration for the interests of the race to which one's own nation belongs or to '*the danger that comes from allowing a foreign race to exist within the national body*'. The second refers to the size of the coloured population as *the greatest danger this country has ever known.* Strong words indeed! A greater danger than the threat of defeat by Nazi Germany in 1940, and all that would have entailed for this country? We must suppose so; the words will bear no other meaning. Yet to some, patriotism that would regard the threat of rule over England by the Nazis as less of a danger than the presence, living and working peaceably within this country, of a number of dark-skinned people from various countries (whether they be one million or four million) must seem a very odd kind of patriotism indeed.

Yet words such as these are not regarded by most people with alarm. Their precise manner of expression may be deplored, but there are plenty of respectable people of all kinds ready to express views that look towards exactly the same direction. *The Times*'s leader of the same day condemned Mr Powell's words strongly, and yet in terms that treated his speech as 'once again trying to rush the Conservative Party further than it now wants to go'. *The Times* objected, quite rightly, that a repatriation programme as demanded in the speech would be

> a bullies' charter. Every unscrupulous landlord who might think that his property values would rise if his coloured tenants left, every group of thugs who would like to drive coloured people out of Britain, would feel that if life here could be made sufficiently wretched for their victims then these unfortunates would simply take their payment from the state, and go. Too much of this sort of thing goes on already to risk encouraging more.

True enough. The leader then added, perhaps for fear that this consideration would not weigh very heavily with all its readers, that a repatriation programme would be very expensive for the taxpayer (newspapers frequently seem absolutely unaware that coloured as well as white people pay taxes) and might 'prove a means of paying the fares of immigrants going home on holiday'.* As a critique of a speech that clearly identifies racial purity as the first priority of our national life this leading article, no doubt intended and widely received as a powerful condemnation, appears to me, I must admit, an utterly inadequate response.

That has been the trouble all along; the response to racist demands in a prolonged public debate, ostensibly concerned

* A remark that betrays complete ignorance of the way the procedures work: it has long been the practice when deporting or repatriating people that their passports are withheld by the British authorities before they travel, and are confiscated by the home Government, or in some cases by the carrying company, afterwards.

with immigration rather than with race, has *always* been inadequate. The first notorious Powell speech of April 1968 was answered by James Callaghan, Labour Home Secretary, with an annoyed defence that the Labour Party had been very successful in cutting down the numbers of Commonwealth immigrants coming in, and by Mr Heath, leader of the Opposition, with a speech deploring the manner of expression Mr Powell had used, but not condemning outright his policies – which were, indeed, only a little different from official Conservative policy on immigration at the time. The Labour Government had just passed – or rather rushed, in a six-day travesty of the Parliamentary process – the 1968 Immigration Act which denied entry to Britain of British citizens from East Africa, unless their parents or grandparents had been born in Britain (a neat way of dividing brown from white). Mr Callaghan had said of that Act that it was in breach of obligations solemnly undertaken – yet he clearly thought the exclusion of Asian-descended immigrants of such great importance that solemn undertakings were well worth breaking. Newspapers that had judiciously asserted the right of Britain to control immigration in the interests of better integration had little ground to stand on if they wanted to attack demands for repatriation, or to attack claims about a high coloured birth-rate. They themselves had acquiesced in treating 'numbers' as an important issue where coloured immigrants were concerned; they were not in a position to say convincingly, all of a sudden, that numbers were irrelevant. They could only say the numbers alleged by Mr Powell for the future were probably wrong, and get bogged down in a meaningless debate about how many babies people were likely to have – as if a reduction in the birth-rate of babies who were not white would magically improve 'race relations'.

Powell is only one voice among many. Writing a few days after the quoted speech Nigel Lawson, in the *Sunday Times*, thought that repatriation grants for coloured immigrants would not be a practicable policy, but suggested instead 'repatriation' grants for white people living in coloured areas so that they could move to white quarters. White hostility existed, so it had to be accepted and 'appeased' by measures such as this; other ideas would be to allow new immigrants into the country as temporary workers only, to 'remove that archetypal focus of white resentment, the West Indian layabout living off the Welfare State', and to abolish all the efforts of paid workers in race relations who actually make things worse by persuading 'affected whites' (that is, white people hostile to coloured immigrants) that 'the whole establishment is against them'. Mr Lawson made several gross mis-statements of fact in this article, of a kind all too familiar in this type of propaganda; he complained that Commonwealth immigrants enjoyed a favoured status; he accused the 'race relations industry' of dismissing hostility against coloured immigrants as 'a first-generation problem', when for years people in the so-called industry have been saying exactly the opposite, and he implied that the ruling establishment was sympathetic to coloured people and hostile to the white majority. The main point of interest about his article was, however, that in dissociating himself from Mr Powell he produced an analysis and suggested solutions that would seem startlingly outspoken, say, from Governor Wallace of Alabama, and all under the by-line of a Member of Parliament and former editor of that once moderate journal, the *Spectator*. No more convincing and melancholy example could be found of how far over to the Right leading opinion has moved in a decade than that an article of such extraordinary untruthfulness and silliness should appear in a leading newspaper generally associated with realistic reporting on race issues, with a plea for *laissez-faire* gone mad – white hostility exists so it must be appeased. (Heroin addiction exists so we must help people buy and sell heroin? Robbery with violence exists so we must appease robbers by making it easier for them to rob? Where does this sort of argument go? If such comparisons are thought absurd, that can only be because white hostility to coloured people is accepted as a morally blameless position, without its own serious practical consequences in misery, injustice and violence.)

Powell supporters frequently blame the press for pandering

to the prejudices of the left-wing intelligentsia (a term of opprobrium used for all who do not support Powell). Yet in fact the press has played a considerable part in the movement of opinion towards racism. In part, it may have done so by following opinion rather than leading it; if the press reports what politicians are saying, and prints letters from readers with a variety of views, it inevitably follows certain trends and then gives them impetus by the very fact of reporting them. However, the press bears a heavy responsibility for failing in the first duty of a free press over the whole decade of the 1960s; for it has failed to identify as a matter of public interest the problems already existing, and the likelihood of far worse problems in the future existing, of injustice, hostility and persecution resulting from racial propaganda and racist immigration policies. It has accepted the basic premise of Sir Cyril Osborne and his like that the public interest of this country is the interest of a White Britain, and in doing so has betrayed the interests of both black and white. It has played up 'race angles' in stories in such a way as to encourage dissensions and fears, while ignoring race stories that demonstrated with equal possibilities of sensational treatment, and hard news value, the harm being done by racism, especially in the application of immigration regulations. Throughout the sixties, papers were simply uninterested in stories of children being forcibly parted from their parents, bullying by immigration officials, (unless these affected European au pair girls with influential English friends) the medically unsound 'age' tests used to determine whether children trying to come here had passed their sixteenth birthdays or not, the placing of children in remand homes and adults in Holloway or Brixton prisons while their cases were under consideration by the Home Office, sometimes for weeks on end, and when no crime save attempting to enter the country to join relatives had been committed. A very occasional small paragraph could be found in some papers; the *Guardian*, eventually, began reporting such cases more prominently, but the featuring of such news was generally so intermittent and unsupported by comment that the general public remained completely unaware of what was happening. Meanwhile stories of illegal immigrants, boatloads of Pakistanis who had been conned into paying out their life savings for a passage to England, have been constantly in the big headlines on the front pages, reiterated week in, week out. Such stories, which have increased as the figures for 'legal' immigration have decreased, have played a large part in persuading the general public that a flood of dark and dangerous newcomers is constantly arriving to threaten the well-being of the country. Meanwhile the plight of the East African British passport-holders since March 1968, referred to in occasional feature articles, has never been a major issue on which a newspaper chose to crusade, and the effects in human misery and openly racist national attitude which the 1968 Act has had, both upon the people affected, living in desperation and poverty, and upon opinion outside this country towards us as a nation, have remained virtually unknown.

Some newspapers, some of the time, have been honourable exceptions. Whereas Midlands newspapers in Birmingham and Wolverhampton have reflected, where they have not encouraged, widespread racial hostility among white people, provincial newspapers in other areas have sometimes championed the cause of equality. A remarkable leading article in the *Oldham Evening Chronicle* on 12 October 1961 referred to the debate then in the forefront of publicity, on controlling Commonwealth immigration for the first time, and discussed the issue with what later proved to be an accurate prophetic insight:

It is usually denied that control of immigration is a reflection of racial prejudice. Those who call for control insist that they do so for economic reasons. These are generally taken to mean fears of unemployment and of immigrant workers taking the bread out of English workers' mouths. This is an understandable fear, but it is based on very dubious grounds. The demand for labour in this country is greater than ever before, and there is every reason to believe that it will increase year by year. It should also be remembered that the immigrants of this country – who still number less than one per cent of our total population – are usually doing the dirty or ill-paid jobs that Englishmen do not want any more. Those who are not in this category are mainly the doctors and nurses from the Commonwealth who are helping combat the grave shortage of medical staff in our hospitals.

Health checks and a bar on those with criminal records are sensible measures with which no one can quarrel. But the most important weapon the Government seems likely to adopt is a system whereby would-be immigrants will have to satisfy the Ministry of Labour that they have a job to come to.

This too can be a reasonable and sensible measure if it is interpreted liberally when put into practice. It will certainly enable the Government to take effective action if there ever comes a time when unemployment threatens. But it is equally obvious that in practice the system may well enable white immigrants to get in easily enough, while coloured would-be immigrants will have a hard time of it.

Perhaps this is what people want. But if so let us not pretend that there is no prejudice behind the move. Men of liberal views will be disposed to regret the motives that underlie this movement towards restriction.

The *Oldham Evening Chronicle* was quite right. After the passage of the first restrictive law, it *did* become easy in practice for white immigrants to enter the country while coloured would-be immigrants had a hard time of it. The need for labour did not decrease. Firms that had been recruiting systematically from the Caribbean began to advertise in the Irish press instead for workers, or to apply for Europeans: in 1967 48,000 work vouchers were issued for white European workers to come here, and less than 5,000 work vouchers for the entire Commonwealth, though Australians and New Zealanders were waved rapidly through immigration without being asked for vouchers and without any questioning about their length of stay or intention to take work. When late in the sixties there was some attempt to tighten up on Australian immigration by the Home Office, immediate loud and indignant protests were heard from quarters that had never opposed the need for 'keeping the numbers down'. George Brown's National Plan in the mid-sixties forecast the urgent need for 200,000 more skilled workers if the economy were to improve. (We are still bedevilled by a lack of skilled workers in the right places, and with under-use of a willing work-force whose desire for re-training has not been met – some white, some black.) Moreover, the economic regulator that made migration in the fifties responsive to the job situation in Britain – immigration figures fell sharply in the Selwyn Lloyd 'little depression' of 1957 when unemployment rose temporarily – was distorted by the use of restrictive laws. In late 1961 and early 1962 Commonwealth immigration tripled as a result of publicity in other Commonwealth countries about the impending legislation, and many tried to come simply in order to beat the Act. After its passage considerable numbers of Asian immigrants began to send for their families to join them, in the belief that it was best to settle permanently in this country rather than to risk returning home to an uncertain economic future when re-entry would be rendered impossible if at any time they wanted a few years' work in Britain again. The net effect of the 1962 Act was a crude numerical increase in Commonwealth immigration. The much more stringent controls in the 1965 White Paper succeeded in keeping many families permanently divided, and causing hardship and suffering not only to people overseas who wished to migrate but to families already here who found themselves unable to bring their own children to join them, or who found that younger brothers wanting to come as students were turned down because of a suspicion that they might stay beyond the period of their course of study and commit the crime of working in this country.

The regulations themselves have all along been an inadequate guide to what actually happens; many people who have a right under the immigration restrictions to come have been turned back from ports of entry or, more recently, denied entry certificates in their own countries. Immigration officers have been given the unpleasant task of implementing a policy that insists on racial discrimination as a criterion. My own experience suggests that while some have found this a distasteful job and have been ready to yield to representations on behalf of individuals when possible, many others have developed a zeal for keeping non-whites out at any cost that ensures the refusal of entry to many who are legally entitled to enter as visitors, students or relatives. When Powell made his April 1968 'Tiber foaming with blood' speech, thirty-nine immigration officers at London Airport issued a public statement of support for him – an extraordinary event, considering the rule that civil servants may take no part in politics, and more extraordinary still when the Home Office reaction was to transfer (not sack) the leader of the group to another port, and to leave the other thirty-eight where they were, daily dealing with would-be immigrants.

Politicians and newspapers together have continued since 1965 to propagate the theory, now widely believed, that immigration and community relations (a euphemistic phrase for the relationships of black and white within this country) are two separate issues. The fact is that the propaganda in favour of restricting coloured immigration together with the practical effects of the working of the law have combined to embitter and alienate black and brown people in Britain, and to reinforce or to create racially prejudiced attitudes towards black and brown residents already here on the part of the white public.

Part Four

Reading maketh a full man

– FRANCIS BACON

1. Comics

'Africanization has even reached children's comics in Zambia,' stated *The Times* 'Diary' for 2 March 1971. Well, what will they think of next! Imagine, comics about African children for African children. And with African heroes. I am not sure what the 'even reached' means. I suppose most people's idea is that since Africans started being prime ministers and civil servants, just like Europeans, they have systematically been copy-catting in every department of life until they finally thought of putting themselves into comics too. The news item continues,

> A monthly educational comic for schoolchildren, called *ORBIT*, has recently been launched in Zambia and includes a comic strip showing Zambians in outer space and another entitled 'Mike Chanda, Charter Pilot'. Another regular feature is an 'Alphabet of African Freedom Fighters', which, in remarkably sober language, tells the story of men like Chief Awolowo, Ben Bella and – next month – President Kaunda.

I like that bit about 'remarkably sober language'. What would have been expected? Hysterical black man's language? Or perhaps the crudely chauvinistic stuff that we are used to in some English comics about our own heroes? But I fear that, in whatever sense this news item was meant, many readers will have taken it as a report of something surprising, silly and bizarre: a publication intended for Africans, and intended to introduce children to scientific and technical aspirations, that is not in European terms. No doubt many English people would laugh heartily at the notion of a comic describing Africans in outer space. Ridiculous! Everyone knows it is white man's technology and know-how that has taken man into space and that black people are not capable of that sort of thing – though they might eventually be helped by, and copy, the white man sufficiently to achieve a fairly small ramshackle rocket, or to provide one token crew-member in an enterprise from a white, or possibly Chinese, base. Well of course they wouldn't have the money to do more. And wouldn't it be rather risky to use them? Or to let them try?

It may be difficult for English people to remember that English comics have featured English space-pilots since long before men of any nation got beyond the stratosphere and that, as a matter of fact, England does not have an astronaut programme, or the money to launch one either.

I guess that an 'Alphabet of Freedom Fighters' will strike most people here as a very political kind of item for a children's comic, reminiscent of propaganda in Communist countries. We don't have any political content in our own children's comics.

Or do we? A fair equivalent in this country for an older schoolchildren's comic is *Look and Learn*. In the first issue of 1971 there is an account of the assassination of Admiral Darlan in a series on great men who have met a violent end: 'The Victor at Waterloo', a sketch of the Duke of Wellington; and 'The Devil's Wind', an account of the Indian Mutiny, in which we read of Bahadur Shah, 'a decrepit, opium-sodden old man of 82, who lived on a pension supplied by the East India Company', and of mutineers 'raging through the streets like a great tide, eagerly hunting to death every man, woman and child of European parentage, or of the Christian faith. While the city was being destroyed by them, blood was also being shed by the native troops whose task it had been to defend it.' Fifty European prisoners in Delhi, 'were finally led out into a courtyard where a throng of exultant natives immediately cut them down, one by one, with their swords. Only one woman and her three children escaped by calling themselves Mohammedans.

The bodies of the rest were carted off and thrown like rubbish into the river.' The account ends by remarking that the mutiny 'might never have happened if the British had not insisted that their sepoys should use a bullet considered unclean by all Mohammedans'. And the article is part of a series called 'Twilight of an Empire', a series on 'the tumultuous story of British India and how the British themselves helped to bring about its end'. Whatever one may think of the content and presentation (is this, perhaps, 'remarkably sober language'?) it can hardly be called politically neutral. Was the violence in 1857 a furious outbreak against greased bullets, and against nothing more? A later article in the same series gives a glimpse of British atrocities: 'the British soldiers went on an orgy of looting and murder. Defenceless civilians who had not even taken part in the mutiny were shot down or hanged, or else were robbed of everything they possessed in the way of portable valuables.' But this sentence, coming as it does in a feature headed 'The treachery of Nana Sahib', who is described as 'a man with a pathological hatred of the British race', is hardly enough to turn the whole series into an objective or accurate account of the events of 1857. And why, oh why, is Indian history always in terms of the British Empire? And of 1857, at that? Varied from time to time with Clive, the Black Hole of Calcutta, and thuggee and suttee? Would an English comic describe Hereward the Wake as 'a man with a pathological hatred of the Norman race'? I rather think not.

Look and Learn is a highbrow comic, as comics go, and caters to a minority taste. The more popular comics, written for entertainment pure and simple, are usually more anarchic: they do not revere authoritarian British figures (like General Sir Hugh Wheeler, in the above *Look and Learn* episode), but frequently send up teachers and policemen and also the rich, personified in such characters as Ivor Lott and Lord Snooty. The heroic figures are often sportsmen, especially footballers. The observations in Orwell's classic article on 'Boys' Weeklies' still hold remarkably true: in more than thirty years since he wrote, the popular culture of the word of comics has hardly changed at all, and some of the same characters still appear week by week. 'Probably the content of these shops [small newsagents in poor quarters] is the best available indication of what the mass of the English people really feels and thinks', Orwell wrote of the 'twopenny weekly', including not only comics but the whole range of publications with a special appeal, sporting papers, women's story papers and so on. In spite of the enormous and obvious impact of television over the past twenty years, it remains a striking fact that the weekly papers of this kind still sell, and still adhere to conventions that change much more slowly than the pace of cultural change in general would lead us to expect. It is still possible to find in children's comics schoolmaster figures with gowns and mortar-boards who must have been as unreal in daily experience to elementary school pupils in 1939 as they are to secondary modern pupils now. There has crept in another conventional teacher-figure, a sour-faced woman in glasses, and sometimes also a man without a gown but with the exhausted look that real teachers sometimes develop. Whatever the conventional appearance and dress, the function in the folk-story of the teacher has remained unchanged over a very long period: a pompous ass, an unfair tyrant, a ruler who has some favourites and some scapegoats in the class, a comic figure, an authority to be outwitted and bamboozled – but always a representative of the ruling order in life, whom one is naturally against. In one comic I found a villainous figure described as 'the truant-catcher', who lurked around in wait for children avoiding school; this is a rare example of a local-government social-worker type, and again the presentation is of an enemy to be avoided. Policemen in the frankly comic stories are part of the Dogberry tradition: pompous asses again, usually rather tubby, and very different from those public guardians in the television police programmes, 'Z Cars' and 'Softly, Softly'. In fact, 'L Cars', in *Sparky*, features two of the most ludicrous and incompetent cops, Frederic and Cedric, one could conceivably devise. The police officers in charge of them are sergeant-major figures, perhaps a shade more competent but just as absurd. The thrilling stories, in which the drawing aims to be naturalistic, more often present policemen as heroes and they are made to look quite slim and sometimes handsome. But these belong to a separate category. The purely comic series in comic papers is peopled by figures as conventional as the characters of the Commedia dell'Arte: Ivor Lott has a top hat and an Eton jacket and comes to school in a big car, rather implausibly accompanied by a butler in a striped waistcoat; and this is all part of a firmly drawn literary convention, which readers perfectly well understand.

In all this there can be found no open political propaganda, though there are political assumptions of a very important kind; the people in power are always out to get you, and you have to try to get the better of them, though you will often fail. If you can fool them, even without much material benefit to yourself, this counts as an important moral victory. This view of life represents a genuine popular culture, esteeming independence and bloody-mindedness, which I personally find one of the few hopeful features of our political scene. It is based on two simple principles. It is very important to be fair and loyal to your friends, but you can bend the rules a bit in dealing with people in authority. And secondly, people who think themselves important are in fact ridiculous.

But the popular weeklies contain story material, meant to be exciting rather than funny, which rests on different assumptions; the line Orwell drew between one set of weeklies and another still exists and is sometimes seen to divide items within the same paper. Orwell complained of a lack of working-class heroes; of the cult of the bully-boy, the powerful, the superman character, and of stories about adventures in far-distant and utterly unreal venues – the Wild West, the Africa of the Foreign Legion, and not far-off places as they really existed in the modern world, nor contemporary Europe.

Some changes *have* occurred in thirty years, but considering how enormous the political and social change of that period has been the similarities are quite remarkable. Working-class heroes can be found, but certainly not in the sense that Orwell was looking for, of people who were heroes in terms of realistic contemporary social life. The working-class heroes are footballers, like Val Hudson in 'Forward from the Back Streets', featured in *TV21 and Joe 90*.

Football stories apart, the adventure tales in comics still fit Orwell's general catalogue. We still have Tarzan, science fiction, the Wild West, boy adventurers in distant, primitive parts of the world, Cavaliers and Roundheads, and, instead of the Great War stories Orwell mentioned, we have moved forward to Second World War stories – still, of course, with German villains.

The important thing to observe is that the material most widely read in England *now*, and at the most formative period of life, is very much the same stuff as it has been *for more than fifty years*. It has become more violent since the days of *Chums* and the *Boy's Own Paper*, but for the most part has not become one whit less nationalistic and xenophobic. The conventions about social class, about Great Britain's supremacy, and about foreigners, have remained constant in spirit and even, very often, in specific presentation. Billy Bunter, the Fat Owl of the Remove, lives on in strip cartoon instead of prose, in *Valiant*.

And hard though it is to believe one's eyes in reading it, the *Beano* in 1970 was publishing an episode in 'Billy the Cat' which reads like a Frank Richards story through a distorting mirror; at Burnham Academy, a boys' boarding school, there is a 'foreign prince' named Prince Ali and wearing an uncertain form of Indian dress with a turban, for all the world like our old friend Inky, the Indian boy Rajah, more formally known as Hurree Jamset Ram Singh in the Greyfriars stories. The story is a very, very pale imitation of the Greyfriars tradition; it borrows some of the trappings, but it is a tired confection. The boys in it are not strongly characterized, even in simple terms, and the hero is a curious fantasy figure: William Grange, a schoolboy who, by night, puts on a black leather suit and becomes an acrobatic crime fighter with the ability to fly through the air: he is called Billy the Cat.

Orwell commented that Greyfriars was nothing like a real public school; Burnham Academy is several more stages removed from reality, only sketchily recognizable as a school at all, and the mixing-up of this kind of school narrative with an element of completely different style, the fantastic, magically-powered, helmeted and leather-clad supernatural hero, produces something so odd that the presence of anachronistic Prince Ali scarcely seems surprising. You could throw in the Texas Rangers and the Queen of the Fairies without upsetting the balance of the story much. None the less, Prince Ali's presence is interesting. He does not talk in the high-flown parody of Bengali diction that Inky used, long ago; the joke about supposed Bengali pretentiousness is really a dead joke now and Ali talks colloquial standard English; he is neither sinister nor stupid and has, in so far as the story allows for this at all, a recognizable character as a boy rather than as an Indian. I think there is some significance in this. *Beano* is one of the comics that represents what I have called genuine popular culture, anti-authoritarianism, and the desire to make fools of the powerful. There is no glorification of bullies in *Beano* and its like: bullies, sneaks and teacher's pets are all despised figures though, realistically, they are not always worsted in the weekly stories about them. Prince Ali may be a prince somewhere out there in India, but here he is a boy at the mercy of crooked kidnappers and guarded by a bumbling detective; it is up to schoolboy Billy to help him. *Beano* type comics find foreigners funny, but they do not represent them as utterly brutal. This is a marked contrast to what we might call the *imposed* popular culture of comics like the 1970 *Victor*, with their heroic soldiers and policemen, Germans and Italians who deserve to be blown to bits, and sinister Orientals or bloodthirsty redskins. What more unlike a bloodthirsty redskin could there be than *Beano*'s Little Plum, who, year in, year out, wrings more laughs than one could believe possible from the simple device of adding 'um' to every phrase, as all comic redskins must?

('What um goal-keeper!') And what more unlike a heroic soldier than *Dandy*'s Corporal Clott? Or Barney's Barmy Army in *Beezer*?

But this distinction between two kinds of culture in comic weeklies, one anti-authoritarian and guffawing, the other rough, tough and admiring the strong, is a distinction useful only up to a point. The two different styles sometimes overlap. The clichés and conventions of the former do not change at all: even though pantomimes and seaside postcards have undergone some modernization, these comics still keep to rules they have observed for decades. However, the clichés and conventions of adventure fiction are showing signs of change. One reason for this may be that the conventions have become so tired that they have less and less chance of creating excitement in the reader; authors are mixing together different elements from a variety of known conventions in an effort to create something new, but the results get odder and odder. 'Billy the Cat' is one example of this mixing of conventions: the Batman hero and the Greyfriars hero are rolled into one. But other examples abound. 'The Wild Wonders', in *Valiant*, has two boy heroes, Rick and Charlie, who, together with their guardian Mike Flynn, have travelled to Tregovia in order to help Sid, a British secret agent, rescue scientist Dr Julian Jolliffe who is held prisoner there. So far so good. A recognizable type of adventure in every detail. Because of the arduous life they have been living the boys have developed into super athletes. Just as well, because the Tregovian agents chasing them through the countryside are wearing *motorized boots*. An odd touch, which seems rather incongruous with the old-world foreign villain style of talking these agents use: 'All right, accursed children, ve know you vos in there.' Fleeing into the undergrowth, the boys are scared by two owls, but are then reassured when one bird remarks: 'All this crashing and banging. Pah! What's the world coming to? A chap can't get a decent day's sleep any more!' and the female owl replies, 'We'll just have to move to a quieter tree, dear.' How do the boys understand the cross-talk of these owls? 'Thanks to their amazing ability to communicate with birds and animals, the wild boys could understand what the owls were saying', the narrative explains. The boys describe their difficulties, and the owls promise to help them against the spies, one of whom by now has got quite near and is muttering to his colleague, 'Popov, get ready. I zink I can hear zem coming out.' The owls succeed in stealing the transmitters that control their motorized boots, and the spies are rendered helpless. Mike Flynn and Sid arrive on a motor bike; an aeroplane overhead which is looking for all our heroes fails to spot them and flies away again, and not far away an army vehicle is drawing near, stuffed with Tregovian soldiers (looking remarkably like Russian generals, every one) saying, 'There has been no word from Nitski and Popov for over an hour, so zey must be in trouble. Full speed to Groznik Heath! We will trap those accursed Englanders even yet.'

Are the fugitives doomed to capture? Be sure to read the next thrilling instalment! So *Valiant* exhorts the reader. But how many thrilling instalments can you get out of a mixture like this without them becoming incomprehensibly complicated or obscure? The motorized boots have come out of some mixed traditions of science-fiction apparatus and seven-league boots; the talking owls are pure Disney; the spies have Russian names and their soldier rescuers talk the stage Russian of the Edwardian era, peppered with the word 'Englander' which was a standard World War One period way of indicating that *German* soldiers were talking. Mike Flynn looks more like a boxer or footballer than an adventure story guardian figure; he is young and beefy and seems to have strayed out of quite a different kind of story about how the team won the Cup. Comic weeklies now are full of this kind of garbled tale, and some of them have begun to use a few up-to-date concepts mixed with the old and tried formulas. Splash Gorton, the beatnik swimmer, is an outstanding example. Splash Gorton's name looks back to Flash Gordon; but his appearance, with long, wavy hair, moustache and frilled shirt, is something new. Real beatniks never wore frilled shirts, but Splash is an amalgam of characteristics that might vaguely be thought modern, while as a sportsman he is rooted in a tradition of athletic heroes.

Whether this search for novelty is the reason, or whether there is now in progress a deliberate move away from racially contemptible non-white stereotypes in comic weekly adventure stories, the fact is that the treatment of non-European people in these stories is undergoing a change.

The indications are as yet only slight and they are not very consistent, and yet a change is undoubtedly under way. Over and over again, reading through whole issues of comics, one is amazed to find how true Orwell's analysis still holds. Yet his national and racial classifications of sterotypes in the *Gem* and *Magnet*, inspected again with reference to contemporary comic weeklies, are less applicable. The excitable, bearded Frenchman has vanished; not that the French are portrayed more realistically, but that they scarcely appear at all. Nor have I discovered any treacherous Spaniards, pigtailed Chinese (except in the purely comic cartoons), stiletto-carrying Italians or stupid Danes. Nasty Germans are quite plentiful, either as bull-necked Teutons or as corruptly elegant and monocled Gestapo chiefs. And there is a new class of foreigner, not readily identifiable as belonging to any particular nation, and who indeed may belong to a fictitious one. The comic black man has continued to appear for a long time in the comic cartoons, generally in some form of the cannibal and cooking-pot joke, where white men in sun helmets are placed fully clothed in boiling water and funny witch-doctors are foiled by tin-tacks sprinkled in their path. But the faithful Negro in prose narrative seems to have gone, and even the cartoon cannibals are less frequent.

Hostile African natives remain in some adventure stories. *Whizzer and Chips* had a serial called 'Wonder Car' in 1970 in which the three child-heroes, Colin, Porky and Patti were in Africa. The children rescue 'some men on a raft who were being attacked by natives, only to discover the men were escaped convicts'. The 'warlike natives' are drawn for us:

dressed in leopard-skins or loincloths, with long shields, spears, bangles, necklaces and head-dresses, they are straight out of an old production of *King Solomon's Mines*. The children easily scare them off by starting up the engine and the horn of Wonder-Car. Episodes of this kind follow a long-established pattern.

But there are signs that comic papers are somehow losing their nerve about this traditional presentation of warlike, primitive savages. Is there an uneasy feeling abroad that it is not quite the thing to show black people in this light? What can explain an extraordinary story in *Smash* called 'The Fighting Three' in March 1971? It is stated quite definitely at the beginning of the story that it takes place in 'darkest Africa'. Yet the inhabitants of the lost city of Akitula, where Hambone and Weasel are taken after being captured by sinister masked figures, are drawn uncoloured, with slightly Mongoloid features and long white beards. The nearest physical type to which the drawings approximate would be the hairy Ainu. Certainly they look nothing like any kind of known inhabitants, greatly varied though these are, of the African continent. The white heroes' friend, McGinty, is tied to a sacrificial slab; when he frees himself and tears the mask from one of the sinister figures, this turns out to be a white rival, Jed Brady. The local priests are not too sinister; they talk correct English, though they are not very sophisticated since they believe that a hoard of old spoons, beads and mirrors found under the sacrificial slab is a great treasure; it was brought many years previously to the temple to be traded for gold. So here we have the old cliché about the foolish natives being given worthless Birmingham bric-à-brac in exchange for precious metals or jewels – yet the local characters, who should, to fit this convention, have been black-skinned and dressed in feathers or leopard-fur, are instead rather dignified, long-robed, non-black, racially ambiguous people.

In contrast, the *Victor*, in March 1971, brings Alf Tupper, champion runner, to Africa in a completely different way. To begin with, Alf is in Tanzania, a named, identifiable country and not a vaguely generalized dark continent. Secondly, Alf is working as an engineer to the Kilimanjaro Mountain Railway, and has come to the area in search of a witch-doctor named Meru, who he hopes can cure his injured leg. The witch-doctor is not a villain or a complete figure of fun, but someone who really might have some acknowledged medical powers. Meru has set Alf the task of collecting ingredients for 'a healing brew', and these tasks make the framework for episodes in the story. But more surprising yet is the character of Gari Omolu, who is not only one of Tanzania's greatest runners but also a research scientist. We know at once he must be a decent character if he is a great runner; he is not going to be one of those sinister or crazy scientists. And sure enough, Gari Omolu appears with a normal friendly countenance, wearing a bush shirt just like Alf's – and greets him as an equal: 'Hello, Alf!' He continues, talking in standard English, 'Now that you've repaired the rocket, we've having a hyena hunt. Care to come along?' When powerful Alf kills a hyena with a spanner just as it is about to spring on Gari Omolu, the Tanzanian remarks, 'The beaters will go back to New Moshi and tell the tale of how Alf killed the hyena with one blow. Soon they'll forget about the spanner, and they'll tell of the white man who clubbed a hyena with his fist!' The beaters are an undifferentiated lot, and they speak rather inadequate English: 'Alf could shoot Klip, take all hair' and 'Alf only kills with fists. He will punch the Klip.' But remarkably, the concept exists that African characters are varied kinds of people: the beaters are uneducated but unobjectionable, Gari is a sophisticated and decent fellow, and the witch-doctor, though joked about a good deal by Alf ('You'd make a super demon king at a panto in London next Christmas') is not without some individuality and authority. The whole story is, of course, as ludicrous as any other comic story, and it would seem absurd to an African reader in the same ways that it seems absurd to an English one – but it does *not* portray Africans as uniformly dim-witted or hostile, and succeeds in making one of them a sympathetic and straight-forward character, to at least the same extent as the English hero, Alf. Alf, of course, has superior physical strength, but Gari is intellectually superior to him, without being boastful or devious about it. An extraordinary reversal of the kind of story where a white man's cunning outwits the primitive brute strength of the black man.

The same issue of *Victor* includes 'The Eye of Kubla Khan', in which Ralph Monckton and his older friend Wat Tyler are travelling with the Polos to China. No sinister orientals here. The travellers are amazed at the size and beauty of Peking, and are kindly welcomed by the Khan – who again speaks good English, of a formal kind befitting a ruler – and he gives the boys permission to scout ahead of his army, in search of Ralph's father who is held by rebels in the Shensi Mountains. There is a quite different kind of story, too, later on, about fourth division team Scundale United and how it is helped to win the vital match against first division Sunderville by a scheme that two friends, Simon Jones and Ram Singh, hatch together. This is the usual kind of football story; the striking thing about it is that Ram Singh plays in it the part of an ordinary boy, not of an Indian stereotype. His appearance comes in useful when, in furtherance of their money-making scheme, he and Simon dress up as a Maharajah and a Field Marshal respectively, but this is a natural part of the story, and there are no undertones of racial feeling whatever. Ironically, the same *Victor* has no less than three war stories about the English fighting the Germans (who are made to look quite reasonable people, but who keep saying 'Himmel'). Anyone who knew nothing about England asked to look at this comic and define our attitude to foreigners, would conclude that we seemed to have little colour prejudice but had an entrenched military hostility towards Germans.

Perhaps as a result of the American film industry's changing treatment of American Indians over the last twenty years, a heroic Indian, Johnny Cougar the wrestler, appears in *Tiger*. Hero though he may be, he talks in a babylike third person and says things like 'Now must think heap fast.' He has as much life and reality as a cigar-store Indian, and is worth mentioning not because he gives the impression that American Indians are rational and varied human beings, for he does not, but because it is worth noting at least that an American Indian can be resourceful and reliable in a technologically complicated society. He is at any rate one step away from the scalping, tracking, wig-wam-dwelling stereotype.

In some ways the conservatism and powerful conventions of the word of children's comics have been a safeguard against deteriorating racial attitudes. If comics were sensitive to political and social change and quick to record it, we could have expected to see over the last fifteen years a sharp increase in racist presentation of fictional characters. But this has not happened. The serious educational prose of the *Look and Learn* series on British India, presumably well-intentioned, seems to me much more likely to do harm to the reader's racial attitudes than the adventure strips current in the really low-brow comics. I guess that *Look and Learn* is trying to give a serious, liberal and balanced picture of the world; its informative snippets on 'What happened this Week' bring in a wide variety of characters: Stalin, Castro, John Foster Dulles, great British inventors and so on. But it too is following its own conventions, less obvious than those of the low-brow comics but just as important: this is Britain, the land of wild flowers, brave sailors, social reformers, sportsmen, inventors, and St George. It is really rather stuffy. 'The Sound of Things to Come', an article on music for young people, described in terms of a line from Holst through Benjamin Britten to Stockhausen and completely ignoring the music most young people care about, remarks, 'Jazz musicians improvise their music around a theme. This form of composition is being used more and more by the serious musicians of today.' Serious music, the worth-while kind of music, is plainly Western classical music. The drawing of a jazz group accompanying this feature shows all but one as white musicians, and nobody would ever guess from *Look and Learn* that black Americans were the creators of the twentieth century's most fertile and lively musical tradition. The world has not really changed, except in superficial ways; there are still bad Red Indians (in great quantity and detail), and if English hero Rob Riley, in a strip adventure, has a black friend, this friend is given the implausible name of Ham! (Evocative of hewers of wood and drawers of water, and not the name of any black person I have ever met or heard of.) And Ham hovers in the background as a black-faced stooge while Rob gets all the action. The rest of the world may exist, but it does so as a mine for pebbles of information, useful in general knowledge quizzes; there is an illusion of reality more dangerous to the thoughtful formation of attitudes than the utterly fantastic world of the out-and-out popular comic. Many middle-class people comfortably assume that they are liberal and the working class is prejudiced where race and colour are concerned. The difference between this middle-class style of weekly children's paper and the popular papers illustrates how this illusion arises: the middle class thinks it knows the facts and has superior knowledge, when often all it has is a knowledge of the left-overs of dead propaganda, masquerading as factual information and presented with respectable dullness instead of vulgarity.

Comics are cut off from reality and probably no child would want to read them otherwise, but although millions of people may have had their attitudes to foreigners partly formed by stereotypes in the comics they read as children, and may therefore be handicapped by a hopelessly false picture of what the rest of the world is like, it is not unreasonable to hope that children growing up now will be in this respect a little – just a little – better off.

2. Fiction: Words and Pictures

It is obviously going to be impossible, in one brief chapter, to give either a systematic or a reliable account of the effect upon racial attitudes of the kind of fiction we look to for recreation. To begin with, such fiction is to be found in so many different places: films at cinemas, old films and new programmes on television; paperback books, magazines, books from libraries; fictionalized strips and brief films from advertisers; cartoons and, for a minority, stage plays. It would require long and detailed research to produce an analysis of all this, and such an analysis would have to take into account the very difficult matter of finding out exactly who reads and watches what, including both old and new material, and the even more difficult matter of assessing how influential upon viewers and readers these various kinds of material are. Some research along these lines has already been undertaken; more is under way, at, for example, the Centre for Mass Communication Research at the University of Leicester.

But I think it is worth attempting some comment on this very large and complicated issue, if only to point out some of the difficulties in generalizing about it. To begin with, I find it rather worrying that some of those who talk about the effects of the 'mass media' assume that there is an élite and educated group reasonably free from these effects, and therefore pure and free from outside influence in the formation of their own views. My personal experience suggests that, however bad the effects may sometimes be of 'mass media' material about race and colour, these effects are certainly no worse than the effects of supposedly literate, liberal, and sophisticated material influential upon the highly educated minority. And such a minority, believing itself better educated than the rest, develops a self-assurance of its own liberalism and tolerance that is a worse obstacle in the way of genuine understanding than is the scorned 'masses' viewpoint which can discern no difference between an Indian, a Pakistani and a man from Trinidad. A measured and judicious discussion, supposedly, of the rights and wrongs of an Immigration Bill in *The Times*, that assumes the terms of discussion must be on the detail of how least illiberally to get people out of the country, instead of talking in terms of its being a racist notion to want to get rid of black people at all, does as much harm as an outright demand for repatriation on the grounds that this is a white man's country. Too much ground has been yielded before the argument begins. Similarly, fiction (in the widest sense) that is produced by someone believing himself to be very liberal and free from prejudice, when in fact he has got no further than thinking blackness is a quality people must learn to tolerate, can do as much harm as an old-fashioned piece with a Wog villain and a Haitian master-mind using Voodoo to further an international conspiracy and Dr Fu Manchu and witch-doctors and so on. That popular television series, *Till Death us do Part*, indignantly defended by the BBC as a programme to work against prejudice, is a perfect case in point. The idea was supposed to be that viewers would ridicule Alf Garnett and identify with the young couple, his modern daughter and son-in-law. But instead, Alf Garnett became a folk-hero. The programme had exceedingly bad effects; words like 'coon' freely used by Alf, were repeated by white men to black work-mates, the racist clichés that sprinkled his conversation passed into the vocabulary not only of adults but of child viewers, and thousands of black people were angered and distressed by this popularization and repetition of the crudest kind of race jokes. However, the BBC seemed to think that critics were being very naïve and unsophisticated in not understanding that the programme was meant to be making fun of racism and seemed quite uninterested in the evidence of those who should, after all, know best what effect it was having – the people at the receiving end of the racist jeering and hostility.

Another instance was the programme, presumably meant for a fairly sophisticated taste, that went out first on the BBC2 'Beachcomber' series, in which three men from 'Filthistan', dressed in the stage Eastern style that Wilson, Keppel and Betty used to have for their soft-shoe dancing, went through a tedious series of episodes in which living on National Assistance, immigrating illegally, being stupid, and talking in a funny accent, were the somewhat unsophisticated stock jokes that clearly referred to Pakistanis. Had the National Front wanted a spot of its own on television, it could hardly have done more effectively, since it would have had exactly the same points to make about what Pakistanis were like, but would probably not have thought of using such an effective music-hall style format to put the notions across, and would instead have adopted a hectoring and solemn style that would have put viewers off. Had the same programme included a similar caricature of gibbering Jewish moneylenders battening on the Gentile country that had foolishly allowed them in, there might have been some uncomfortable awareness of something wrong. But again the assumption was that you had to be pretty illiberal and humourless not to take it in good part that jokes based on the most damaging of racist lies were going out as entertainment, while any other sort of material about people from Pakistan – in particular, the employment on television of people from Pakistan taking a normal part in plays, features, news reporting etc. – was absent.

A number of ham-handed pieces of fiction with a serious dramatic, rather than a comic, intention have also been in evidence. *Softly, Softly* had a 'liberal' feature about skinheads and Pakistanis; the programme was clearly directed against skinheads, but the Pakistanis in it were involved in trafficking illegal immigrants – really, by now, the British public must believe that every Pakistani to be seen is either an illegal immigrant or an entrepreneur for bringing people across the Channel. Another *Softly, Softly* episode had a Black Power agitator, talking in a form of dialogue that was completely unlike anything I have ever heard any black person use, and being listened to patiently by the Superintendent; anything less like reality I have seldom seen in a semi-documentary piece of fiction; if a Black Power leader gets taken to a police station, the last thing that is likely to happen to him is that he should be listened to, and indeed few white people on being taken down to the station after a 'disturbance' get the chance to expound their philosophy of life to a Superintendent. I felt sorry for the black actor playing the part in this episode, but on the other hand a black actor who wants work at all has to face the fact, I suppose, that he is constantly going to be cast in features about the 'race question'; nobody is likely to ask him to play anything else, even Othello. The part of Othello goes to a white actor like Sir Laurence Olivier, who first blacks up for the part and then plays it in an eye-rolling, hand-jerking caricature of a black rapist straight out of *Birth of a Nation*. (A number of white critics were impressed by how 'Negro' he made the role.)

In short, it is a dangerous fallacy to believe that the 'quality' press and the less lowbrow programmes are going to be free of racial prejudice, while the stuff churned out for the 'masses' must be closely scrutinized for its harmful effects. The more education that people over thirty have had, the more they have been exposed to racist ideas implicit in fiction, and the more they have absorbed an account of English history which takes for granted the superiority of the English and the low achievements of non-Europeans.

Much, of course, gets absorbed indirectly and unconsciously so that the first sources of particular notions are quite forgotten. How many readers of *Robinson Crusoe*, an enormously popular best-seller for many decades but now, since popular periodicals and television, probably a minority taste, even remember what Crusoe was doing before his shipwreck? He had landed in West Africa, where he was received in a friendly manner by the black people living there, and given food and water. Leaving these 'friendly Negroes' he was then taken on board a Portuguese ship and travelled to Brazil, where he discovered 'how well the planters lived, and how they grew rich suddenly'. A few years later he decided to go back to Africa, appointed by a group of other planters whose prosperous ranks he had joined, to buy some Negroes on commission, 'They offered me that I should have my equal share of the Negroes, without providing any part of the stock.' The difficulty was a purely financial one; Crusoe's plantation was doing so well that it was already worth three or four thousand pounds sterling, and this being so, 'for me to think of such a voyage was the most preposterous thing that ever man in such circumstances could be guilty of'. However, he agreed to go provided the other planters entered into a contract to care for his plantation, and off he went. 'We had on board no large cargo of goods, except of such toys as were fit for our trade with the Negroes – such as beads, bits of glass, shells and odd trifles, especially little looking-glasses, knives, scissors, hatchets and the like.'

Nothing could be more matter-of-fact, and if the reader accepts the same premises as the fictitious author, he will agree that there is nothing odd about buying people as slaves for monetary gain, nothing bad about so treating people of whom your only experience of them has been that a group of them befriended and fed you when you were hungry, and nothing contrary to good, sound commercial practice in offering cheap hardware in return for other people's life and liberty. But the slaving trip never came off, for Crusoe was shipwrecked in the Caribbean. Here, like a good European, he proceeded by meticulous hard work and thought towards the conquering of his material environment with very cleverly adapted technology. And so passed many years until the sight of a naked footprint in the sand frightened him with the thought of another human presence. He does not appear to have had a moment's pleasure or hope in the presence of another human being. His fear was of savages, and later he indeed witnessed the wretched creatures dancing round a fire and preparing to kill and eat human victims. Observing the chance to rescue one who fled, and who swam faster than his two escaping companions, Crusoe remarked, 'It came now very warmly upon my thoughts, and indeed irresistibly, that now was my time *to get me a servant*, [my italics] and perhaps a companion or assistant; and that I was called plainly by Providence to save this poor creature's life.' After succeeding in doing so, 'I began to speak to him, and teach him to speak to me. And first, I made him know his name should be Friday, which was the day I saved his life. I likewise taught him to say Master, and then let him know that was to be my name.' Extraordinary! It evidently never occurred to Crusoe for a moment to ask the other man what his name was. No, Crusoe would give him a name, a name that glorified Crusoe's deed and identified the other in those terms, and Crusoe's own name was to be not Crusoe but the title of a ruling relationship, Master! Friday became a willing servant: 'his very affections were tied to me like those of a child to a father, and I daresay he would have sacrificed his life for the saving mine upon any occasion whatsoever'. Crusoe taught Friday English, which he learnt to speak 'broken'; again, it never seems to have occurred to Crusoe to learn Friday's language, or to have any curiosity about it, nor about the knowledge which a Carib Indian (if that is what Friday was) might reasonably be expected to have of fishing skill, medicinal use of local plants, and other knowledge natural to a native of the locality. Instead, Friday was taught how to work the plantation and to wear clothes. Later, in a battle with the cannibals, Crusoe saved a Spaniard and Friday's father, and 'My island was now peopled, and I thought myself very rich in subjects. And it was a merry reflection which I frequently made, how like a king I looked. First of all the whole country was my own mere property; so that I had an undoubted right of dominion. Secondly, my people were perfectly subjected; I was absolute Lord and law-giver; they all owed their lives to me and were ready to lay down their lives, if there had been occasion for it, for me.'

Lo the poor Indian! Crusoe, although revolted by the unnatural cannibalism of these savages, had doubts about his right to kill them, and decided not to set a gunpowder booby trap, partly because he was short of powder, but partly because he was not certain whether he had the right to judge them for what seemed to him unnatural practices; perhaps their nature dictated cannibalism, and they were free of guilt. Friday's loving nature and noble, handsome appearance remind us of an American observer's comment on American Indians; 'Two contrasting images of the Indian – as Noble Red Man and as Blood Thirsty Savage – have prevailed in the minds of whites in the past five hundred years.'

Crusoe's remarks about his right to rule, and his conviction that those over whom he was absolute lord and lawgiver were utterly devoted to him as to a father, provide a text-book exposition of our old friends, 'Western values'. I am not going to attempt to go through all such instances in widely read fiction, but any reader who begins to be on the look-out for implicit or explicit attitudes towards race and colour in English fiction will be struck by how much unnoticed or forgotten material there is in familiar stories. The opening of Thackeray's *Vanity Fair* sets the scene with a bandy-legged black servant: his name is Sambo, and he grins. But he is not the only non-European character to appear; Miss Pinkerton's Academy includes among its pupils a Miss Swartz, 'the rich, woolly-haired mulatto from St Kitts'. She is a pathetic character, good-natured, stupid, and fantastically rich: she cannot spell, can sing only three songs, and overdresses in ridiculous gaudy finery, but many are eager for her acquaintance, and old Mr Osborne is eager to marry his son George to her, in spite of her colour and her stupidity, because of the vast fortune from the West Indies that she has at her command. But George Osborne, loyal to his beloved Amelia, refuses: 'Marry that mulatto woman? I don't like the colour, sir. Ask the black that sweeps opposite Fleet Market, Sir. I am not going to marry a Hottentot Venus.' Despite this scorn, and the unkindness visited on Miss Swartz by girls who are jealous of her money, she is not an unsympathetic character; her role is to show up the greed and the hypocrisy of the satirized English characters in the book. Yet one cannot escape the impression that, to Thackeray, it was ludicrous that a 'mulatto woman' should have pretensions to elegance and ladylike accomplishments, and that nothing except greed for riches could have made any Englishman conceivably want to marry her. She is pathetic because she is pretending to be white, but cannot manage it.

Vanity Fair has, incidentally, some interesting sidelights on the importance of both India and the Caribbean to the social history of the time. Captain Dobbin has returned from the West Indies after yellow fever; Joseph Sedley, an incompetent ass if ever there was one, has made money as a collector for the East India Company and brought home with him a taste for curry; and there are other references, besides those to Miss Swartz, which emphasize the flow of wealth into England of enormous fortunes, acquired without difficulty or the need for merit, in possessions or trading posts overseas. 'The black that sweeps opposite Fleet Market' reminds us that multi-racial Britain is not a new phenomenon. Such references can easily pass unnoticed in the general interest of the story, as can a hundred other casual remarks in English fiction. Jane Austen mentions the West Indies only once – and this is the furthest point from England she ever names – in *Mansfield Park*. Kind, honourable Sir Thomas Bertram maintains the wealth of his estate, the likeable but almost incredible sloth of his handsome wife, the upkeep of Mrs Norris, his two spoiled daughters and his free-spending son, and the modest support of the heroine, Fanny, from a plantation in the West Indies to which he has to go when trouble arises on the estates. What the nature of this trouble was, we never learn, but the existence of a plantation, worked by slave labour on behalf of an absent owner, is accepted without question as part of the natural order of things by an author whose intelligence, sensitivity and strong moral principle are evident on every page. These *assumptions* in fiction have their effect: the importance of the West Indies in the early nineteenth century was to provide England with wealth; and to ask what life there was like, for anyone except the planters, need not even cross the mind of the thoughtful civilized person.

Brown and black people were far too remote and strange to be understood as human beings – witness the terror in *Cranford* at the appearance of an Indian servant in a secluded English village.

But the remoteness and strangeness of other peoples was to be used as a device to thrill in stories of adventure and mystery: their presence could provide exotic excitements, as it did in *The Moonstone* in which the Indian guardians of the diamond, with their mysterious powers of seeing things in a pool of ink, are presented so vividly. These Indians may be exotic, and we learn very little about them, but they are not racially stereotyped, and not sinister by reason of their nationality: it is clearly understood that the theft of the Moonstone was a desecration by a wicked adventurer of another religion which ought to have been respected. The same attitude is not always true of the hundreds of stories which have followed the eye-of-the-god theme.

Rider Haggard's *King Solomon's Mines*, first published in 1885, also fathered a long series of imitations, this time about adventure in Africa. The traditional adventure story about Englishmen in Africa has something in common with the American myth of the West: the brave, hardy and resourceful pioneer, using another people's country as a background for his exploits, threatened by spears and magic, winning because of guns and superior mental powers combined with great courage and adaptability. There are good and bad Africans; some noble, some savage, as with the American Indians. But the attitude even to the noble is that they must be kept at a distance. Captain Good falls in love with the lovely black girl, Foulata:

'Good never was quite the same after Foulata's death, which seemed to move him very greatly. I am bound to say,' narrates Allan Quatermain,

that, looking at the thing from the point of view of an oldish man of the world, I consider her removal was a fortunate occurrence, since, otherwise, complications would have been sure to ensue. The poor creature was no ordinary native girl, but a person of great, I had almost said, stately beauty, and of considerable refinement of mind. But no amount of beauty or refinement could have made an entanglement between Good and herself a desirable occurrence: for, as she herself put it, 'Can the sun mate with the darkness, or the white with the black?'

They can, of course, as the large population of mixed descent in South Africa bears undeniable witness, but they shouldn't, as the present South African Immorality Law, forbidding marriage between different 'races', declares. So, Foulata, it was lucky that you died. Would it have been equally lucky in the story, if Captain Good had died? I think not: as a white man, he was less expendable than a black girl. 'Her removal was a fortunate occurrence.' No flowers for Foulata.

In twentieth-century English fiction, black people are still found in thrillers and tales of adventure as exciting and exotic elements, and are also still evident in satire: in Evelyn Waugh's novels there are symbolic and stereotyped black people, whose part is to show up with particular vividness the nastiness and folly of the white characters: part of Margot Metroland's corruption is that she has a Negro chauffeur as a lover, and the crowning horror of the cannibalism in *Black Mischief* is, of course, in an African setting. At a later date, after the independence of a number of African countries from British rule had been established, some novels dealt with Africans, no longer as savages or as symbols, but as politicians – often inept and corrupt, and with a strong underlying flavour in the story still of barbarism just under the surface: jungle man in a European suit. Whereas most fiction might be said to affect attitudes not so much by its express opinions as by the assumptions underlying its narration, this passage from best-selling Nicholas Monsarrat's work bludgeons home a point of view:

Without Britain, Pharamaul would have been nothing: now at last it was something. It was on the map as a separate country, where before it had been two half-starved warring tribes, eternally at each other's throats, fighting murderously for goats and sand.

The process had taken a long time, and lost the lives of many good men: generations of the younger sons of England, pitchforked into this barren waste and told to get on with it ... Britain, having come to pacify and discipline, had remained to educate and develop.

Pharamaul is a fictitious, plainly African state, featured in *The Tribe that Lost its Head* and the sequel, from which the above quotation comes, *Richer than all his Tribe*. A good deal of sadistic excitement is provided in these books, notably in horrid mutilations practised by the natives, and there is plenty of more straightforward sexual titillation too. Black may not be beautiful but it is certainly naughty and stimulating to the white people in the story.

If it is possible to generalize at all, we might conclude that the presence of black people in much English fiction has been of a symbolic kind. They are present, not as recognizable human individuals in the same sense that white characters are, but as elements in the story which make a point about particular qualities associated with blackness – whether savagery or nobility, stupidity or cunning.

A complete contrast to Monsarrat, except that the kind of white people portrayed must in fact be based on very similar original models, is to be found in John Masters's popular series of novels about India, from *Nightrunners of Bengal* to *Bhowani Junction*. Whatever argument there may be about the literary merit of these books, it is surely true that they succeed in describing Indians as recognizable human characters in exactly the same terms as the Europeans in them are recognizable human characters too. Considering that *Nightrunners of Bengal* is about the events of 1857, and *The Deceivers* about the thugs, this is particularly striking. The author, of course, like his heroes, comes from a family that has spent generations in India, and belongs to it more closely than to England in some ways. India has inspired love and reverence in many Englishmen, but these feelings have often been accompanied by the most fervent imperialism as they were in Kipling. In

Kim Kipling wrote a funny and touching passage whose depth of understanding and sensitivity would be hard to match in any story about the confrontation of different cultures: the meeting between the lama whom Kim served and the Anglican and Catholic chaplains of Kim's father's old regiment. The stereotype of the pretentious Bengali in the same book illustrates how many-sided racial attitudes can be, and how complicated was Kipling's personal vision of India.

But the message fiction conveys is partly in the mind of the beholder; perhaps there are many who have read *Kim* as a thriller about a boy and about beating the Russians in their imperialist machinations, who derive from it quite a different picture. It seems to me an almost impossible task to gauge the effect that fiction has upon attitudes, nor does it help us much to speculate how far the authors are merely reflecting the attitudes about them, rather than propagating their own. Even with the most popular and widely read of material, how can we be completely sure what are the characteristics and attitudes in the work itself that appeal to people? I do not see how it is possible to give any answers to these questions with certainty. Yet it remains important to consider, in all its variety and possibility of interpretation, the wealth of fictional material that is available to people now, whether as reading or as television, which ultimately depends on the written word, and does a lot of adaptation of established fiction. And perhaps the most striking thing about this is not so much the amount of material that depends on, or encourages, stereotyped attitudes about race, colour and nationality, but the *shortage* of material that does anything else. I am not advocating a flood of well-meaning books and programmes written to instil non-racist ideas into people; such self-conscious attempts are not notably successful in fictional form. Sometimes they defeat their own object by being too clumsy and earnest; sometimes they are too confused about what racism really is to do anything but harm. One can only hope that English work will appear which succeeds in describing human relationships, rather than race relations, in such a way that the message will get across:

Reading maketh a full man

Mankind is rich in unexpected resources, each of which, on first appearance, will always amaze men; ... progress is not a comfortable bettering of what we have, in which we might look for an indolent repose, but is a succession of adventures, partings of the way, and constant shocks ... it is not enough to nurture local traditions and to save the past for a short period longer. It is diversity itself which must be saved ... Tolerance is not a contemplative attitude, dispensing indulgence to what has been or what is still in being. It is a dynamic attitude, consisting in the anticipation, understanding and promotion of what is struggling into being.[1]

It is not by going over old ground that writers will succeed in transforming the way their public looks at life, not by basing a character drama upon a newspaper cutting about some 'race' incident, but by transforming through imagination the understanding of what human diversity in England is all about, and *will* be about in the future. And for such a gift we must wait and hope.

3. Newspapers: What I tell you three times is true

'All human life is here' stated a poster advertising the *News of the World* in 1970. A depressing thought. I never passed this poster without a prayer of thankfulness that there were more things in heaven and earth than were dreamt of by the editorial and reporting staff of the *News of the World*. In fairness, though, I must admit it would be just as depressing to reflect that *The Times* held a mirror up to the whole of human life in England: the picture is a less lurid one than the *News of the World*'s weekly fairground of adultery, theft, murder and sneaking buggery, but it is, in its own way, still limited.

The press does not attempt to tell us everything; it attempts to tell us what the people in charge of newspapers believe we shall be willing to pay good money to read. All papers, however, deal to some extent with political news. In those papers where this is a subordinate concern, it is still possible to find out something about strikes, wars, and new legislation, but the items will be small and haphazard. Major questions of national interest and policy do, however, rate feature articles given plenty of prominence in all kinds of newspapers. Devaluation, the Common Market, nationalization and de-nationalization, the traffic problem and so on have been discussed for every kind of reader. And the subjects chosen for prominent features by all kinds of newspaper become, in the minds of many millions of people, the most important of public and political issues. The actual importance to the country as a whole may be greater or lesser than the newspaper coverage suggests: river pollution was, for instance, the concern of only a tiny lobby for years until, very recently, the whole subject of pollution became news, yet our rivers were being polluted just as steadily during the decades when newspapers generally ignored the fact as they are now. The scandal of our housing situation was just as acute for ten years or more before the name of Rachman came into the news (quite fortuitously, because of his connection with the Christine Keeler affair) and people, began because of newspaper investigations, to wake up to the kind of ruthlessness, inefficiency and corruption that was depriving people of homes. Television's *Cathy Come Home* increased awareness and revived interest which, since then, 'Shelter' has kept alive. But what other scandals remain uncovered? and what achievements and contentedness go uncelebrated? We have usually no means of knowing unless journalists tell us.

I certainly do not want to blame journalists for failing to tell the whole truth about every event that occurs in this country daily; it is the job of newspapers to select and judge. Whether they attempt cynically to exploit the most sensational news or whether they try conscientiously to report on the most significant, they still have to select. What is published then serves to guide the newspaper-reading public towards regarding some issues as more important than others, for issues selected for *continuing* news reporting and discussion will obviously become more important in most readers' minds than the ones that are rarely touched upon. Whatever the editorial attitude to a particular topic may be, the selection of that topic for reporting and comment makes it an issue of public concern; while other issues of equal or greater importance are regarded as of minor interest if they are consistently given less space in the press.

Looking back over the past century to discern the biggest issues of political debate, affecting other countries as well as this one and having very great influence of the most practical life-and-death kind on millions of people, we can see conflicts between imperialism and insularity, between capitalism and socialism, between the policies of mass unemployment and

Keynesian economics, between Fascism and anti-Fascism, Liberalism and Communism. Nobody with any interest in world affairs can doubt that at present racism is a dominant issue in the world's political development. Other great issues are still with us, but the point around which the battle is joined has shifted, and the deployment of forces in the field has been rearranged.

Where foreign affairs are concerned the press in England is aware of the importance of racial issues. And the existence of a racial problem in this country is recognized, but it is seen as a problem created by the presence of black people. From no English newspaper except perhaps the *Sunday Times* do we get an inkling that *racism* is a factor of the first importance in our own national life. Whatever other passing excitements come and go, nudity and economics are the daily bread of popular communications. The really important divisions within our society, and the changes in our value-judgements these have created, are seldom mentioned: indeed, there seems to be a new Establishment prudery which will talk freely about sex and money, but not very loud about such embarrassing matters as justice and injustice.

What the eye doesn't see, the heart doesn't grieve over. Our eyes are offered a great deal to see: so much in the way of news of violence and misfortune that one might expect the sensibilities of all but the strongest to become blunted, and the reactions brutalized. The heart has ceased to grieve over a great deal that the eye does see: so any evils that are ignored by the press and television for most of the time can be sure of utter neglect by the general public, or else complete misunderstanding. For there simply is not time or opportunity to learn about issues which the press, radio and television do not choose to present at intervals frequent enough for us to understand the development of a situation. It is possible to find occasional feature programmes, or a ten-minute section of 'Twenty-four Hours', late at night on subjects that do not appear constantly in the main news broadcasts; it is possible to find feature articles on them occasionally in the more serious newspapers, but just because these items are occasional they have less impact than items which harp repetitively on one theme. The scandal of bad housing in England is now a familiar theme, and even people living in prosperous sections of prosperous towns in Southern England have become aware of it to some extent. In the 1950s and early 1960s hardly anybody except those suffering from the worst housing and a handful of people trying to help them were aware of the facts, and there was a comfortable assumption, widely held, that poverty and distress had been abolished by the Welfare State: the social problem was not material want, but the danger of people becoming soft through having too much done for them free of charge. Some people, indeed, still hold that view but they have to be wilfully blind to do so, whereas ten years earlier they would simply not have had information readily available to them about poverty, wretchedness and the breaking up of families because of housing shortage. Yet the evils of bad housing have not jumped in and out of people's lives at the same moments as they have moved in and out of the news; they have continued to be there all the time. The fact is an obvious one, but its implications are not adequately recognized. One implication is that the press has a very large part of the responsibility for the development of public policy: politicians, as well as the general public, rely heavily upon the press for their information and for their guesses about which way public opinion is moving (itself the function of what the press has emphasized as important by its selection of news). Another is that the public has little opportunity to understand and judge an issue unless the information on that issue is continually presented. It is easier to grasp the immediate effects of bad housing on one family in one reported crisis than to grasp the full effects on the entire society of whole lifetimes affected by bad housing; the effects of mental illness, bad physical health, children passed from one person to another and growing up isolated from a family bond.

Understanding of an issue must of course depend not only on the selection of information about it that we are given, but on the manner in which that information is presented, even before any overt comment has been made. The Frenchmen who dynamited German installations in occupied France during the war were referred to here as 'the Resistance'; Irish Republicans dynamiting buildings in Ulster are 'terrorists'. When you read about terrorists, you know these must be people on the wrong side. Other publications describing them as 'freedom fighters' reckon they are on the right side, and so will the readers. I remember reading in France in 1969 about riots in Belfast, both in *Le Monde* and in the *Daily Telegraph*. *Le Monde* devoted a great deal more space to the news than the *Telegraph* did, and reported a number of acts of violence, making it clear which participants were Catholic and which Protestant. The *Telegraph* report, by omitting reference to some participants being Protestant at crucial points immediately after attributing certain actions to Catholics, succeeded in implying that Catholics were responsible for some of the worst incidents which *Le Monde* had specifically attributed to Protestants. Which gave the correct impression I have no first-hand means of judging, but what is certain is that *Le Monde* left me with the strong impression of much greater responsibility for violence resting with the Protestants and the police, while the *Telegraph* left me with the impression that Catholic rebels had caused troubles which the forces of law and order had struggled to repress. Some reports from Rhodesia, received and republished in the terms of Rhodesian reporting, have described as 'terrorists' a number of Africans who have been killed fighting against the Smith regime. If these Africans had been reported as 'loyalist troops' fighting for the Queen, the reaction to their deaths might have been a different one. But only, of course, if reporting of events on Rhodesia had followed a consistent pattern, referring to the Smith government as the rebel government and providing frequent news of the effect upon the population at large in Rhodesia of illegal measures (not 'legislation') depriving the majority of the people of their right to trial when accused, and so on.

The information available on racial minorities in England

over the last twenty-five years has been of a nature to provide a hopelessly inadequate and seriously inaccurate picture of the truth. This is one very important reason why people of intelligence and goodwill so frequently respond inadequately or erroneously when racial issues are discussed, and have condoned disastrous mistakes in policy.

As with other kinds of news, the selection of what items are supposed to be newsworthy from the rest of the information available has been partly responsible for the impression we have of our racial situation; and the manner in which news has been presented, with particular words and phrases chosen and repeated, has had a strong effect on the way in which information is judged.

In the late forties and early fifties tiny paragraphs about numbers of West Indians arriving by ship to work here appeared at infrequent intervals in the national press. By the mid-fifties provincial newspapers were reporting such events as the refusal of white bus conductors in the Midlands to work with these West Indian immigrants. Conflict was resolved, however, and happy photographs of the first black conductor on a bus were published. On 16 March 1955 the *Western Morning News* reported:

'Taunton employers, generally speaking, have no objection to taking on Jamaicans if there are vacancies. This has been made apparent by answers to a questionnaire circulated from the local employment exchange.'

About the same time the hotel and catering industry arranged to recruit workers systematically from Barbados because of the acute shortage of labour here. The Barbadians were said to be honest, hard-working and cheerful.

Already, however, objections to this kind of immigration were being voiced, in terms that later became very familiar. A letter to the Editor of the *Hull Daily Mail* on 16 March 1955, commenting on a leading article that had cautiously suggested some restrictions on immigration, complained that the leader had not gone nearly far enough:

'Except for the genuine student, all further coloured immigration to this country should be halted before a colour problem is introduced into a country where one did not exist.'

Complaints that coloured people were suffering hostility and social discrimination were made by some white writers in newspapers. Every now and again reports in the local press mentioned instances of difficulties where black and white worked together.

To his great credit, Donald Wade, Liberal M.P. for Huddersfield, spoke firmly against racial discrimination and was reported not only in the provincial press but briefly in *The Times*, the *Daily Mail*, and the *Guardian*:

> Mr Donald Wade, M.P., said to a meeting of the Manchester University Liberal Society in Manchester yesterday that the West Bromwich bus workers' refusal to work with an Indian was an attitude which, if widely adopted, could have serious consequences. He suggested that an appeal to resist all colour prejudice should be made jointly by leading representatives of the Trade Unions, employers, all three political partics and the Churches.
>
> (*Manchester Guardian* 15 March 1955)

The Rev. William Neil, addressing the Nottingham and District Laymen's Association, was reported in the *Nottingham Evening Post* on 9 August 1955:

'The best way to deal with the problem,' he said, 'was to treat coloured people as though they were not coloured but as though they were ordinary Europeans – French or German – who needed to be considered a little more because they were strangers to the country!'

At first sight these reports are all unremarkable. But on consideration a number of characteristics that they demonstrate, and which would have seemed quite unimportant at the time, can be seen to have had a serious effect.

First, the sources from which newspaper material were gathered. There is news and comment about people of dark colour, voiced by white people. These few instances, of course, do no more than indicate this by omission, but let any newspaper reader reflect how often any items about dark-coloured people in England are written by them or quoted from them. In the last few years, the interested reader will have been able to find some examples but, overwhelmingly, news about dark-faced immigrants has been in terms of white reaction to them, or of reports about how white people are making arrangements to deal with them. Black people have been seen from the beginning as pieces to be moved around as in chess, not as fellow-players as in cricket. They are being sent for to do useful jobs. They are being considered for their acceptability in Taunton. They should be stopped from arriving, says a man in Hull. They should be allowed to work on the buses: they should not be allowed to work on the buses. They should be treated fairly. They should be treated as if they were European. The assumption behind discussion is that the white English have to decide what to do with the dark immigrants and how to treat *them*, but *their* views about what they want, how they wish to behave towards others and how they hope others will behave towards them are unimportant. When newspapers have referred to 'public opinion' on matters concerning race and immigration, it is white public opinion they are talking about. (Although we are sometimes given the impression that Wolverhampton is overwhelmingly black, which it is not, we are still given to assume that public opinion in Wolverhampton is the opinion of white residents and that black residents are somehow not members of the public.)

The press itself is only partly responsible for this kind of attitude. Newspapers picked it up inevitably, just by using their usual sources: reporters of proceedings at meetings; official handouts; quotations from trade journals; all sources controlled by white people. Finding out about immigrants' opinions in any systematic and reliable way would have meant a long and laborious search for new sources of information, the kind of search that can only happen when a reporter with a keen personal interest of his own finds time and opportunity to make it or when some particularly startling news item requires a special run-down of information of a kind that existing sources cannot supply. If there is a well-known individual or organization easily available on the telephone there is a source of news and opinion, but for a long time there was no such ready source to contact for the immigrants' point of view. When the Campaign Against Racial Discrimination came into existence early in 1965 it soon achieved a great deal of publicity, out of all proportion to its numerical support in the nation at large, simply because it provided one easy source of news at the end of a telephone line. CARD played a valuable role in many ways, and its effectiveness in lobbying for a Race Relations Act was in no small part due to the fact that the press found it newsworthy: politicians, reading frequently of its activities and demands in the press, believed it a strong force to be reckoned with and for a time it really succeeded in making black people's demands heard, though it was a multi-racial, not an all-black, organization.

Secondly, the extract from the letter to the *Hull Daily Mail* puts with marvellous brevity and clarity an opinion that has done more harm, perhaps, than any other to the cause of racial equality in England. 'Except for the genuine student, all further coloured immigration to this country should be halted before a colour problem is introduced into a country where one did not exist.' Here we have two very important assumptions. One is the combination of 'colour' with 'immigration'. The other is the assumption that 'a colour problem' is *created* by the presence of coloured people; get rid of the coloured people and you get rid of the problem.

The word 'immigrant' has lost its former meaning in the English language, while retaining some of its old associations. An immigrant is taken now to mean a person of dark colour. *The Times* had a headline in 1970 stating, 'Immigrant births on the increase', a nonsensical statement if we are to suppose that an immigrant is a person who has travelled from another country to this one; if you are born here, your only migration has been from your mother's womb to the outside world. The text below the headline, moreover, made it clear that the births referred to were of non-white children, and not of the children of Italian, Cypriot, Hungarian, Irish, Australian or other white immigrants to this country. Politicians and journalists refer quite often to 'second and third generation immigrants', a meaningless description, again, of people born here to ancestors who were not born here. Logically, we are all immigrants of one generation or another if such a way of describing people is accepted. The meaning intended is clear though; it is just a way of talking about non-white people in England. It is not taken to mean children of Austrian refugees from the Nazis, say, or children of Poles who settled here after the war. It has never occurred to anyone to describe either Disraeli or Bud Flanagan as a second-generation immigrant, or Handel as a first-generation immigrant: they are all famous Englishmen. Desirable categories of people are not described as immigrants; when you see the Irish referred to as immigrants you can be sure it will be in some disapproving context, unless in some scholarly work or little read compilation of statistics: such as the *Registrar-General's Quarterly Return on Population*. 'Immigrant children', even in official statistics, is a category which officially includes a number of non-white children born in this country. The meaning, a person arrived in this country for residence, has been lost but the association, a person strange to this society, has been retained. Immigrants do not really belong here: they are strangers from outside. Referring to non-white people as immigrants is a habit which emphasizes difference; it is then very easy for white people to make the transition to believing dark-coloured people, however many generations from now, to be 'aliens in our midst'. It is a less easy transition to think of the children of white immigrants in this way, just because they are so seldom described as 'immigrants' in general communication.

As a matter of fact, since 1945 two out of three immigrants (in the correct sense) to this country have been white people and only one third non-white. The largest single immigrant group is Irish and there have been substantial numbers of European and white Commonwealth arrivals. *All* these groups include substantial numbers who have left this country after a period of years. (This broad statement is based upon the Government's own Census figures, but allows for the under-enumeration of the Census by taking into consideration the Home Office's migration figures.) The way the word 'immigrant' has come to be used is particularly striking when we look at the fact that migration has been so mixed. Had all, or even almost all, the new arrivals in this country been non-white people over the last twenty-five years it would be a very natural thing for the word 'immigrant' to have become synonymous with 'non-white'. But this has not been the case. The immigration of non-white people to this country has been taken to be a threat (an 'unarmed invasion' as Lord Elton has pithily put it) while the immigration of white people in greater numbers has been on the whole accepted as a natural phenomenon.

It is my belief that this assumption, that 'coloured' people are immigrants and that 'immigrant' means 'coloured person', can be explained only by the fact that the *other* assumption in the letter quoted *comes first*: the presence of 'coloured' people creates a problem, and if you get rid of the coloured people you get rid of the problem. Most people have come to take it comfortably for granted that the reason there is prejudice against black people is because they are strangers to this country; but if that were really so we could expect prejudices to be just as great towards any new arrivals, and to be non-existent towards the English-born children of new arrivals. Obviously, this is not the case. Black people born in this country or entirely educated here often suffer much more discrimination against them than do newly-arrived immigrants, say from Pakistan, speaking hardly any English, and far greater discrimination than do white immigrants; both the P.E.P. report and the evidence to the Select Committee of the House of Commons on Race and Immigration confirm this, which can be observed any day of the week by anyone working in race relations. No, the reason why 'immigrant' has become a racial term is that racism has found it a very convenient one: its use succeeds in implying that all black people are strangers and that all strangers are black people, and the whole category is one that simply does not belong, and is no part of us. That this term has now become an everyday usage in the English language is an important factor in the formation of attitudes among people with little prejudice: these may have 'nothing against coloured people' and yet talking about coloured people as immigrants inevitably strengthens the feeling that here is a distinct category of people who do not quite belong to our society; they cannot just co-exist but must be *integrated*, worked in somehow, if not kept at arm's length.

Any word or term that can be used as a convenient short form in headlines is taken up readily and used frequently by the newspapers until, in many cases, it becomes common usage. 'Immigrant' has come in very handy for referring to West Indians, Indians, Pakistanis, together with a few Africans and Malaysians. 'Coloured' would equally well have provided a short term with a reference everyone would have understood, but if it had been used consistently, a number of news items would have *looked* as racist in presentation as they actually were, and until the beginning of 1968 this would have made a lot of people uncomfortable and might have violated the code of conduct expected by the Press Council. 'Coloured' has been used, notably in crime reporting, but 'immigrant' has been more popular, especially among those newspapers regarded as the most serious and responsible. Another *Times* headline, over a Law Report, which stated 'Immigrant Visitor Excluded', makes the point. Under the law in question, the Immigration Act 1962, immigrants and visitors were two separate categories, the former entering the country with a view to taking employment. The headline therefore made no sense at all in relation to the report, but it would have been most unlike *The Times* to put 'Coloured Visitor Excluded'. It might also have given the unfortunate impression that colour was the reason for the exclusion of the man in the case (which of course it was). But *The Times* readers would have no difficulty in understanding that an immigrant visitor was a non-white person trying to enter the country temporarily.

Thirdly, these brief extracts from 1955 newspapers indicate that while on the one hand there was some hostility to black immigration, the opposite of hostility was not always so much a complete freedom from racist attitudes as a willingness to concede that blackness was something that could be and should be put up with, a quality whose disadvantages could be overcome. The Rev. Mr Neil's address, reported in Nottingham, was in its entirety a very decent statement, but the particular sentence I have quoted from it is worth looking at because while it seems to express the perfection of an unprejudiced mind to most white people it would arouse immediate resentment in most black people. 'The best way to deal with the problem was to treat coloured people as though they were not coloured but as though they were ordinary Europeans – French or German – who needed to be considered a little more because they were strangers to the country.' You have to pretend that the dark colour is just not there: it is like an embarrassment or disability that nobody with any manners would dream of calling attention to. The assumption is the same as that which some kindly people make when they proclaim, 'they can't help their colour, can they?' – as though a dark skin was a liability, a disfigurement of the normal, or white, kind that all really proper human beings have. 'They should be treated as though they were ordinary Europeans' – that is, as if they were, again, the normal, acceptable kind of human beings and not the wrong kind of human beings; it would be tactless to remind them that they were in any way extraordinary or not quite normal. The enormous arrogance behind this way of talking cannot be blamed upon all the individuals who use it; it is an arrogance that is taught to us all throughout our education: Europe means civilization, Europe means our kind of people, Europe means knowing how to do things efficiently, Europe means beauty. Learning this attitude, what could be more natural than for us to assume that the greatest kindness to those who are unfortunate enough not to have been born of European ancestry must be to pretend that they are really Europeans?

But think for a moment how this looks to the black person. A white man greets him cordially and with a smile, saying, 'Let's pretend you look like me. Let's pretend you really are a normal kind of European, as I am. Then I shall be happy to know you.' Of course no one would ever use those exact words out loud, but many forms of words are used to express exactly this attitude, by English people who believe that they are being a hundred per cent unprejudiced towards 'immigrants'. And if the black person does not respond with warmth and gratitude to the invitation to forget who he really is, he is taken to be difficult.

In the context of the other reports Donald Wade's plain and straightforward condemnation of racial discrimination in employment strikes a note of relief. Between them, these few cuttings from many years ago give a fair picture of the range of attitudes existing, and reported in newspapers, both then and now; and those who like to argue that the passage of time will solve all our racial problems might well reflect that time has evidently not achieved any beneficial changes in attitudes so far.

Difficult though it now is to remember, or even to imagine, what such a state of affairs can have been like, it is broadly true that up to 1964 there was not much reporting in national newspapers about 'race' in an English context, and there was a general consensus that this was a matter which was outside politics and ought to remain so. In the 1964 General Election the racial propaganda used in the Smethwick constituency of Birmingham, reported on by *The Times* Midlands correspondent, Brian Priestley, without anyone taking much notice earlier in the year, suddenly attained national newsworthiness because of the electoral defeat of Patrick Gordon-Walker in that constituency. He was the sitting Labour member and had been for years past; 1964 saw the return of the Labour Party to power after thirteen years in opposition and Gordon-Walker was one of its leaders. Yet with Labour winning back seats all over the country Gordon-Walker, of all people, lost his – and in a campaign where his opponents had made use of crude and hate-making racist propaganda. Such a dramatic event was the stuff of which major news stories are made. It was easy to draw the conclusion that popular feeling among voters against black immigrants must be so hostile and powerful that it overrode all other considerations. Consider the facts. Against the national trend, and from what since 1945 had been a safe seat, Gordon-Walker had been ousted. There was just one factor to be observed in Smethwick that marked it out as different from other constituencies; the Conservative campaign had been openly and violently anti-immigrant.

But the conclusion was wrong; the facts were incomplete; and the results of both politicians and newspapers seizing upon these inadequate facts and drawing the wrong conclusions have been quite disastrous for this country. The description and analysis of the Smethwick election by Paul Foot in his 'Immigration and Race in British Politics' should be studied for the very full account they give of the whole episode. The sad part is that at the 1964 turning-point, after which both press and politicians were to become obsessed with the importance of 'the race issue' without even beginning to face up to what the real issue was, one journalist at least, Brian Priestley, was performing the responsible task of a journalist with real insight – but his lead was not followed. Instead, newspapers began seeking out and featuring prominently every kind of story where a sensational race angle could be introduced, taking for granted a popular, grass-roots racism that did not yet universally exist; when Gordon-Walker stood again a few months later at Leyton reporters kept putting into their reports of the by-election little queries about whether 'race' would be an issue in the campaign, and although there was no sign at all of any racial issues the repeated questions themselves probably helped both politicians and public conclude, after Gordon-Walker's second defeat, that it was again because of race that he had lost. It was necessary, the Labour Party clearly then believed, to ditch Gordon-Walker and along with him any reputation the party might have for being soft on immigrants, if it was to maintain electoral success. Within a few weeks of the Leyton by-election new and stringent controls on immigration were announced by the Home Secretary. Since that time 'race' has been firmly in the midst of politics and established in the news as a sensational factor, the assumptions being that the British masses are rabidly racist, that in comparison with the masses all political leaders and 'Establishment' people are more or less liberal and must bend their efforts to restraining or quietening down any popular signs of racism, brushing it under the carpet where they do not succeed in cleaning it away, and that any open opposition to racism will lose votes while any encouragement of it is in bad taste, a rather cheap and unsportsmanlike way of winning votes which the more respectable type of politician will not stoop to since to do so is a breach of the rules in the accepted political game. These assumptions have made possible the introduction of more and more racist measures, each one being explained as necessary in order to placate the thirst for blood of the British voter. They have also made it possible for newspapers to adopt positions defending racist measures while rebuking some people for being more racist yet, or for using intemperate language. They have also created the situation in which the two major parties have been competing for ten years to see who can be tougher on immigration and thereby win the votes of those racist masses.

How much of the responsibility for these assumptions lies with politicians themselves and how much with the press is not at all easy to assess. It is certainly true that both groups have perpetuated and strengthened these assumptions so that however many speeches and column inches are devoted to race, the amount of true information and enlightenment that results is very small, while the amount of propaganda in favour of a basically racist form of society is very considerable. But, however one wants to cut up and share out the responsibility for what has happened, it cannot be doubted that the press bears a heavy burden of responsibility for actually increasing popular support for racism among the general public during the middle and late sixties.

Paul Foot's account of Smethwick makes it clear that the local Labour Party there, far from being soft on immigration, had for a long time been effectively useless as a force against local racism. For three years before the 1964 election the Smethwick Labour Club had been operating a colour bar. Gordon-Walker himself, right back in the fifties, had supported control of immigration and although he followed his own party's official line opposing the Conservatives' 1962 Immigration Act he was reported in the local paper, the *Smethwick Telephone* as saying in August of that year, 'This is a British country with British standards of behaviour. The British must come first' – a statement whose full significance needs to be understood against the background of local affairs and reporting, in which it could be taken only as anti-black.

'Smethwick was unique for three closely interwoven reasons,' writes Paul Foot. 'First, a powerful and aggressive anti-immigrant organisation, independent of party and of extremist right-wing splinter groups, had been in the field some three years before the count, had built up a substantial membership and put out an enormous weight of propaganda. Secondly, the leaders of this group were assisted by the local paper ... Thirdly and most important, their policies and propaganda were absorbed by the local Conservative Association.'[1] In short, both press and politicians locally had been responsible for *emphasizing* anti-immigrant policies and sentiments over a considerable period. Neighbouring constituencies, with demonstrably worse housing and education difficulties than Smethwick, and with as high an immigrant population, did not share this vital element in local affairs of press and political emphasis and their election results were quite different from those in Smethwick. It was propaganda directed continually towards the public that built up racist feeling, not public feeling that forced a position upon press and politicians.

One of Brian Priestley's dispatches to *The Times* reported the *Smethwick Telephone* devoting in 1963 1,650 column inches to immigration, and described its role as 'unconstructive'. Another stated,

'Smethwick at last has come to this – that the great issues of the day are all twisted and perverted by the question of colour, and that slanders and verminous untruths which might be dismissed in a second elsewhere are here a considerable factor in the campaign ... In the creation of this electoral atmosphere, the Conservative Party at Smethwick has played a leading role.'

But how did *The Times*, the same newspaper that printed these dispatches, treat the matter in its comment from its parliamentary correspondent?

'The Smethwick Conservative Party and the electors were convinced that control of immigration was vital to racial harmony. Judge them, Mr Griffiths said, on first-hand knowledge, not on second-hand reporting.'

And the same correspondent then commended Mr Griffiths, who had condoned the slogan 'If you want a nigger neighbour, vote Labour' for his 'personal courage and integrity'. Clearly this correspondent had not studied the local campaign that preceded Griffiths's election, and the general policy of *The Times* since has not been to follow its Midland correspondent's line that deliberate propaganda encouraging prejudice was doing severe damage, but to accept at face value the argument that 'control' of immigration was vital to racial harmony.

This account points to three important features of the press where race is concerned: the enormously valuable role that an individual reporter can play, the way that a general editorial policy can frustrate or contradict the individual reporter's effort, and the effect that a sustained campaign of the kind the *Smethwick Telephone* undertook can have upon opinion, so long as it is constant and repetitive.

The individual reporter is ultimately dependent upon the general policy of his paper, not only for whether it publishes his reports fully and prominently, but for whether it backs him up with comment and with increased coverage for the issues to which he has drawn attention. Senior specialist correspondents can generally look for this kind of backing. But newspapers in England have not regarded race relations as important enough to warrant a race relations correspondent, with both title and responsibility to devote himself fully to the subject. It must be incredible to any American observer that even now *The Times*, with its particular brand of prestige and responsible reputation, has not a race relations correspondent; it had Peter Evans in this job for some months, but he was then re-named Home Affairs correspondent, and has had to deal with all matters that come under the Home Office empire – such as prisons, probation and national security – as well as race. The trouble with this is not only that obviously such a policy leaves utterly inadequate space for reporting on race relations; it is also that such a classification accepts the point of view that race is the concern of the Home Office, with its twin responsibilities for immigration and 'community relations', and does not establish a framework of reporting and comment where race relations can easily be seen to be the concern of black minorities, of politicians and officials concerned with education, housing, employment and economic affairs. The editorial assumption appears to be that race relations are just a part of Home Office affairs, whereas the fact is that the Home Office is one element, an extremely important and generally harmful one, in the race complex. Other newspapers, besides *The Times*, which take it for granted that specialist correspondents are necessary for industrial relations, education and even golf, manage without race relations correspondents, and assign different reporters to cover stories large and small, with the result that the reporters placed in this position often have no background of information at all against which to elicit and interpret a news story and can easily get things wrong, being uncertain of the differences between the Race Relations Board and the Community Relations Commission, for example. Though to understand what has been happening in race relations for the last decade it is essential not only to know which of these bodies is which, but also to know a good deal about their workings and their personnel, what effect these have had on the general situation, what are the relationships between their leading figures and the leaders of immigrant organizations, how much money they spend and on what, and so on: the equivalent of what, for instance, an industrial relations correspondent would know as a matter of course about the T.U.C. and the Confederation of Shipbuilding and Engineering Unions. It takes a specialist correspondent to know whether a news item that falls within his own specialized area is trivial or of great potential importance: a newspaper needs this kind of specialist judgement if it is to be able to report responsibly to its readers. The expert lobby correspondent can gauge from a chance remark in a corridor of the House of Commons a story important enough to rate a front-page headline, though the same remark, to the non-expert, would sound insignificant or meaningless. Without a specialized race relations correspondent to perform an equivalent service, a newspaper cannot hope to provide news coverage about race that adequately and accurately informs its readers. A knowledgeable and experienced journalist questioning a minister on some new policy or event can cut through the evasions, the half-truths, the verbal flannel and the false implications with which the minister tries to cover up what is going on, because such a journalist knows the field; he knows what to believe and what not to believe. But a reporter without extensive background knowledge can much more easily be fooled, and is often uncertain which are the crucial questions to ask.

Yet some individual reporters like Colin McGlashan in the late sixties on the *Observer*, Eric Silver and Martin Adeney on the *Guardian*, and Derek Humphry on the *Sunday Times* have made themselves specialists and have done great service. Their work, and the broadly anti-racist editorial approach of the *Sunday Times* and the *Guardian* have given some opportunity to a minority of readers of national newspapers to learn facts and opinions important for forming an accurate picture of what has been going on. The more popular national papers, however, have done enormously more harm than good, as much by ignoring facts of importance (the inevitable result of lacking, or neglecting, specialist correspondents) as by editorials acclaiming a tough line on immigration or opposing anti-discrimination laws. The tone and style of popular reporting have taken it for granted that 'immigrant' and 'colour' are words denoting 'problem', and whereas a white family under threat by black people is first-rate news, black people under threat from white are of very little importance – unless enough people are involved for an incident to be labelled a race riot. A white mother parted from her baby is worth months on end of lengthy reporting, while non-white mothers kept apart from their children by the immigration laws are simply not news.

The *Morning Star* deserves to be mentioned as a consistently anti-racist daily paper, but it reaches very few readers; it has sometimes given prominence to news items about race which other papers have ignored completely, but whereas other journals with a small circulation can achieve disproportionate influence because their limited readership is among the holders of power, the *Morning Star* quite evidently has no influence upon the shapers of government policy.

News reporting reaches the general public at least as much through television now as through newspapers. Comment and features are, however, separated from the news itself and presented in separate programmes at times spaced through the evening. Whereas most people watch the news because it is *there*, appearing between entertainment programmes when the TV set is switched on to run continuously, the debates and documentaries may be neglected, either because they compete with something lighter on another channel or because they simply appear too late for the large numbers of people who go to bed around ten o'clock, or even earlier. The reader of a newspaper can easily let his eye wander from football to a nude, to an item on rent racketeers and a photograph of 'illegal immigrants' being pushed into a police van in Kent; the television viewer, however, has to be more deliberate. Television items are presented for selection one after the other in time, not side by side in space. In many homes a television set is simply left switched on while people talk and eat and do odd jobs, so that counting the number of viewers for a particular programme cannot tell us for sure how much gets across in the kind of programme that requires some concentration. As far as the straight news broadcasts go, these follow very much the same rules in deciding what is and is not newsworthy as the papers, so that one gets the same repeated items about boat-loads of Pakistanis, reports of what politicians have said about immigration, and so on, again without matching comments, in the news itself, from immigrants themselves. Television, however, has produced in documentary features a great deal of material about race, some of it very good, giving black people the chance to speak for themselves in interviews. Discussion programmes, on the other hand, where it is often felt necessary to balance the presence of one Asian and one West Indian with one extreme right-wing M.P. and one 'moderate' (in favour of controlling immigration strictly but using conventional respectable language to say so) are usually fruitless. It is not possible to have a discussion that advances knowledge where the people involved are too far apart to agree on anything at all, and in particular where the time allowed for each speaker is perhaps a minute at a time and he is liable to be interrupted before reaching the point of his argument by a chairman with an eye on the next speaker. Informal conversation and formal debate both provide a chance for protagonists to present points of view and information; the television discussion, however, does little more than establish the names and faces of certain individuals taking part as authoritative spokesmen for particular groups and interests – which, in fact, they often are not.

What *is* the responsibility of the reporter, of the press or television? Obviously he has to present news by selecting from what actually happens. The Powell speeches of 1968 were news, they had to be reported, and it was not the fault of the media that the kind of response made to those speeches by leading politicians was so weak and inadequate; the reported responses had no obvious beneficial effect, but this was not the fault of the media. The media can, however, be challenged: why did you not take more initiative yourselves in exploding what Powell was doing, showing him up? why did you seize the chance to make him so big, when you had the power to make clear the kind of danger his propaganda really was? There were some such attempts. The BBC's *Twenty-four Hours* took the initiative in exploding the story in the first Powell speech about the little old lady terrified by grinning blacks who had taken over the entire street, and this piece of investigation was exactly in line with what I personally consider the responsibility of journalists to be: holding up public events and statements to examination so as to show up lies and inaccuracies and arrive at the truth. It may these days sound stuffy to say this; it may sound phoney, because so many people talk with reverence about the freedom of the press when in fact they are in favour of no such thing, but the fact remains that the job of newspapers and television is to find out the truth and report it without giving way to pressures whether they come from politicians, advertisers, or any other outside interests. The truth needs to be the whole truth and nothing but the truth. Reporting is often inaccurate, but it is far worse for reporting to be incomplete. The failure of the media to present the truth about race relations has not been so much a matter of getting the facts wrong here and there as of failing in the duty to see what the big issues are, and putting these in front of the public. It is racism that threatens our civil liberties, our peace of mind and our security, not the presence of black people in this country. There has been no lack of evidence that this is so, but the evidence has not been adequately presented, in spite of the efforts of some people working in the communications media. And this must surely be the responsibility not of the individual reporter but of those higher up who decide general editorial policy and who decide staff appointments. Where television has provided good journalism on race has been in programmes where particular teams or producers have had freedom within their own series to take a lot of time and trouble over looking at a particular issue; their work can be presented in ten, or thirty, or even fifty minutes, or in successive programmes. Someone writing about race for a newspaper has usually far less scope than this.

If the people in charge of newspapers would decide that race relations deserves the same kind of coverage and the same skilled continuity in reporting that foreign affairs and industrial relations receive, the public would have the chance of being sufficiently informed to use their own judgement. And if, even at this late date, we could see evidence of the courage of crusading newspapers, of the journalistic skill and bravery that, for instance, Ed Murrow used against the formidable power and prestige of Joe McCarthy in the United States, used to break down the lies of racism and the politics of exclusion in this country, the freedom of the press would be a means of liberation from fear for us all.

4. History

History has been called a lot of things, good and bad. It has been an art, presided over by its own Muse; a science, collecting evidence and propounding theories; an inexorable series of struggles to be interpreted by an understanding of economic laws; the manipulation of the masses by the force of superior individuals; to the Jews it has been the work of God upon earth and to Henry Ford it was bunk.

English historians in this century have mostly been very suspicious of interpreting the past as a creative design; historical method has been more revered than historical purpose, and much of the everyday business of studying history has been a painstaking labour of testing evidence by a variety of new scientific techniques. Historians have been more like bricklayers than architects; however, if one goes on laying bricks, a building rises, and those who look at it still search for a design.

Whether they want it to be so or not, academic historians have great practical influence upon their own society. Sooner or later, their work affects the teaching of history in schools. It may take ten or twenty years from the time that historians in universities decide it is all wrong to study kings and queens, and better to study the daily lives of ordinary people, before school text books jettison bad King John and merry King Charles and start bringing out illustrated stories about young Wat and Joan taking pigs to market, but eventually the change does occur. The reason that this is socially important is that history is an extension of our own personal experience: we use it to learn what we are like and what other people are like, and we reject any of it that seems to us irrelevant. But we can choose only from what is put before us, and from what the writer or historian tells us. When Henry Ford described history as bunk, he was saying something quite valid from his own point of view. To anyone whose whole life is making money out of the manufacture of motor cars, history has nothing to say. But it is very rare for anyone to lead such a limited life. At the opposite end of the scale from the Henry Ford life-picture is the history of the Jews, whose importance permeates the life of every Jewish child. You learn from Jewish history that God made a promise that He will not break to your ancestor Abraham, and that men must keep their promises to God. God delivered the Jews from captivity; He spared their first-born sons; He sent a leader to bring them to the land he had promised them and one day He will send a new chosen one to deliver them. He has given you a law, which you must keep, but you are among His chosen, and even if you break His law, history shows over and over again his mercy and forgiveness.

Every 'fact', every event, in Jewish history is an illustration of this great movement of God in human destiny. And the practical effects stare us in the face. There would be no modern state of Israel, of the kind we see, without Jewish history alive in the people who have made that state. The Jew in New York who sends money for the war is not only the son by blood but the same in spirit as the Jew who blew a trumpet outside the walls of Jericho nearly three thousand years ago; and Jewish pop groups sing songs about David and Goliath that mean just the same as the psalmist's exultation in defence of the promised land. Their history tells Jews what decisions they are to make in conducting their lives: Jewish historians have built out of the happenings of the past a temple that no invader can destroy.

In the case of the Jews, and also of the Marxists, the importance of what is held to be history has an obvious practical importance. It is less obvious, but just as true, that all of us are influenced in our decisions by what we think of as *our historical identity*. The reason that it is less obvious in us is that so many changes and inconsistencies occur in fashions of appraising history. The interpretation of Jewish history has remained consistent all through. But for English people, what can unite Bede's interpretation of Christianity working and growing through the history of the English, written down with great respect for the best evidence of events, with the romantic chronicles of King Arthur, where history is a tale of chivalry and courtly honour, with the Tudor protestant nationalists, Macaulay and his whiggery, Bishop Stubbs, the Father of Bureaucracy, and Tawney's indictment of protestant ethics? There is no connecting thread running through our understanding of our own history: each period has produced propagandists for its own understanding of life, selecting and interpreting known events of the past to support a thesis, and aptly illustrating Benedetto Croce's comment on historiography that 'All history is contemporary history.' What we lack is an understanding of history that is meaningful to us as English people now.

As fashions change, bits of past selections and interpretations are left over and included in newer versions. (The younger the age-group for whom a history book is intended, the more outdated are the selections and interpretations of the past provided.) The matter of selection is really the most important. Nobody ever writes down a word about history without emphasis resulting from selection, or without some distortion by omission; firstly, the writer cannot know all the knowledge from which historical accounts must be selected – there is too much of it – and secondly, he is picking out from what he *does* know the things that appear to him to be significant. Selection is itself an evaluation, before any argument at all is introduced into historical writing. If I wrote down, without comment, the most strictly factual account I could conscientiously produce of all the naval victories ever won by England, I should be producing a book which told the reader that England was a nation of victorious seamen, and if such a book were widely used in schools it might well produce an enthusiasm for a sailor's life and a militant determination to win battles that otherwise would not have been produced, especially if the parents had read books about naval victories when they were at school, and so were disposed to understand and be sympathetic with their children's reaction.

History teaches us about our destiny: military and cultural supremacy for the French; independence and poetic song for the Welsh. Those with no sense of their own history are without a sense of direction for the future. Generations of black American children have been cut off from awareness of their history; they have been taught a version of American history in which only white Americans took part; their only recorded role, a passive one, was to be enslaved and then set free. Only in very recent years has this state of affairs been changed at all. There is still a long way to go, and passionate debate is aroused on how best to teach the 'black studies' that will restore the black American his history.

In the British West Indies, history has customarily been taught by the simple transfer of English history syllabuses from England to schools in the Caribbean. Children of African descent and of Caribbean background have learnt not about Africa and the Caribbean so much as about the Norman Conquest, Queen Elizabeth and the Great Victorians. The values implicit in such teaching have been respect for the English legal system and the English way of life as Christian and freedom-loving. No wonder that so many adult West Indian immigrants to England can be called 'very English'. And no wonder that the shock of finding themselves not regarded as English has been so severe. They have been taught first that their destiny is an English one; and then that what they have been led to believe was their destiny is not theirs after all: Englishness was to be admired and embraced, but English people's Englishness rejects them as aliens. The situation of their children is different but just as wounding: it has strong similarities with the situation of black American children for a long time past. The children of West Indians in England learn about an English history in which they are not mentioned; the West Indies play no part except in an account of the abolition of the slave trade, attributed to Wilberforce. What they hear from their parents about the Caribbean means little to them, for they do not feel themselves a part of any society except England. Yet nothing they learn about England makes them feel they are regarded as belonging to it. To teachers and fellow pupils, they are 'immigrants'; to the authors of text-books they have no existence at all.

India and Pakistan are united, on the other hand, by the awareness of a long and proud history of rich civilization. Their sense of their own history was never expunged by British rule, and adult Indians and Pakistanis in England, whether they are aware of the greatness of Asoka and the Moghuls or whether they have an awareness of the past limited to one small rural locality into which a few heroic names have filtered, have all a sense of identity and a sense of pride rooted in their own history. Even the illiterate, who have had little education in school, know about themselves and their past from the Indian films which they attend every week at English cinemas, and which are fond of familiar historical stories and legends for their basic plots. The homes of Asian immigrants all over England contain as ornaments little models of the Taj Mahal. It is the finest building in the world, and it is theirs.

Again, however, the situation is different for the children. Obviously there is a great deal of individual variation in the degree to which the children of Indians and Pakistanis here identify themselves with their parents' heritage. But there are certainly many who have grown up only vaguely aware of the history of the Indian sub-continent and even less aware of an English historical identity. I remember helping a sixteen-year-old girl, who had come to England from the Punjab at the age of ten, prepare for an oral exam in English. She had chosen India as the subject to talk about in this exam, and so I asked her to name three Indian cities. After a lot of hesitation she said shyly, 'Ceylon?' She was not a stupid girl and she was a very hard worker. But she had left India at too early an age to have acquired, in a village, much formal knowledge and she had sat for years in an English school either not understanding the rapid-fire language of the teachers of history, geography and so on, or spending a few hours at remedial English classes which conveyed a practical everyday use of language concerned with television sets, buses and fountain pens – not King Alfred or Emperor Jehangir.

The children of non-white immigrants are being offered no frame of reference in our schools to illustrate the world they can take a creative part in. Information about those parts of the world with which they identify their parents' origins is unlikely to be helpful to them. English adventurers looting, burning and conquering in the Caribbean, Clive and Warren Hastings and the 'Indian Mutiny', are not topics to put these children at their ease. Information about the benefits taken overseas by white missionaries, white doctors, white railway-builders and governors is not very encouraging either, when it is not accompanied by any information concerning the achievements that these white people so often ignored or destroyed. They must feel sometimes like the people in the Congo, some centuries ago, who were vehemently harangued about the evils of idolatry by a Franciscan friar who held aloft a statue of Our Lady with a sword plunged into her heart. Talk about fetishes! Those Africans never succeeded in conveying to the missionary friar their belief in one God, nor did he succeed in persuading them that the statue he held was not an idol. The same total lack of communication must often characterize the teaching of the history of the British Empire to pupils from the Commonwealth.

And what of white English children? They are certainly learning a frame of reference for themselves, but it is an odd, lopsided one. Fifty years ago white English children learnt, according to their station of life, where they fitted in and what they were supposed to do. The children of the rich learnt that they had a destiny to govern lesser breeds, to guard the far-flung bounds of Empire, and to admire the discoverers, conquerors and governors of the past. The children of the poor assembled to sing 'All things bright and beautiful', in which the rich man was safe in his castle and the poor man immovable at his gate, and continued the day acquiring the three Rs and a smattering of information about English discovery, adventure and rugged independence, including respect for law and superiority to foreigners. For all these children, the superior power, wealth and law-abiding stability of England was a reality, and their destiny was, in one manner or another, to perpetuate that reality.

Now, however, confusion and uncertainty about the aims of the society we live in have affected the whole of education. It is possible for an English child to learn from his history text-book that there is a British Commonwealth of nations, embodying a great principle of co-operation between races and nations, and from his geography text-book that 'the only people who lived in East Africa before the white man explored it were dark-skinned African tribes like the Masai and the Kikuyu'. The *only* people – the implication is that not much was going on in East Africa until 'the white man' arrived there. The only people were 'dark-skinned' African tribes. I have never seen a book for young children which explained what the word tribe means, but there is really no need, for the meaning emerges clearly from the context. Tribes are non-European people who have to be put down. Whether they are hill tribesmen, or Arab tribesmen, or primitive tribesmen, or marauding tribesmen, their fate is to be tamed, or fought against and killed. There is an occasional mention of friendly tribes or peaceful tribes; but these are generally backward types who live in tents and eat with their fingers, a way of life which any English school finds deplorable, or naïve characters who offer presents of local bric-à-brac in exchange for valueless manufactures. They may present no threat, but they are not very bright. The same Hulton Educational textbook, *Africa and South Asia*, which puts tribesmen in East Africa, makes this clear in the part on Central Africa: 'A way has been found of inoculating cattle against disease, but to treat huge herds is expensive and the African tribesmen do not always agree to have it done.' Moving on to South Africa the book says, 'The first settlers in this country were from Holland ... However, there are many more Bantu than Europeans. Many of them moved into South Africa after the white men to work in the mines of the Rand district and Kimberley. They came from the north, bringing their cattle and families. Today there are also many Indians and people of mixed race living in the cities. So many different races living close together have created serious problems.'

What is the English child going to learn from this? Although the text-book is called a geography book, it is in fact teaching political history, in terms that were formulated at the height of Britain's imperial expansion. The text-book is new and glossy, but its sentiments are expressions of a firm belief in the superiority of the 'white man', so often explicitly mentioned as the bringer of good things, and the insignificance of the African. The statement that so many different races living close together have created serious problems is going to be connected by the child, less with apartheid in South Africa (of which it is, indeed, a curious explanation) than with the television programmes in England, and the conversation of his parents and their friends locally, which describes the presence of dark-skinned people in England as a problem.

This is not an exceptional text-book, and in quoting it I am not labelling it as the villain of the piece, but picking out one example among many of what even the most modern text-books convey, explicitly or implicitly, about different nations and races. In schools where older text-books are in use, the situation is often worse; and many of such schools are private, fee-paying institutions which are busily producing our future rulers – politicians, civil servants, judges and magistrates. The children most likely to benefit from new ideas and methods in education, and the newest text-books, are the children in the best of the comprehensives, secondary moderns and primaries in the state system. The grammar schools and direct grant schools often tend to conservative habits of mind and the private schools for the most part follow an ideal of education which is solid and consistent simply because it belongs to the past.

English children being reared on old-fashioned text-books are learning about a world that has vanished; those being reared on newer books are learning about a world that is rapidly changing and confused. Children who are lucky may be in schools where the advice is followed of the *Handbook for History Teachers*, published in 1962 by the University of London Institute of Education: 'The choice of stories is vast and should not be confined to British or even European history. Particularly with the older juniors, stories from China, India, the Americas, Africa and the lands of the Pacific should appear.' They may also hear some of the excellent world history broadcasts put out by the BBC. But many other children are still being taught little but English history, and that of a kind which regards the rest of the world as of importance only where English history, generally by means of conquest, touches upon it. R. J. Unstead, the author of many works on history for children, wrote, 'there is a liberal school of thought which deplores concentration upon British History alone ... [it] holds that we shall deprive children of their cultural heritage if we do not put before them the classical stories of the Ancient world and the great figures of European and World History.' But, he concludes, there simply isn't time to get all this in.

It is true, of course, that the school syllabus does not allow time to study the history of the whole world in depth. It does not even permit the history of England to be learnt in great detail. What matters is the framework of ideas in which the history of England or of any other country is taught. A year of study which dealt entirely in terms of white people's discovery of different parts of the African continent and its subsequent history from the European point of view would be worse than useless as African history. No ancient Ghana, no Zimbabwe, no Benin, nothing of African social organization, skilled tradition of metalwork, music, sculpture and dance. No great Islamic civilization of East Africa – no Ethiopia, for until Mussolini's attack this major African country had not been ruled from outside by Europeans, and, not being a colony, its centuries of history as a Christian state ruled by Emperors have been ignored by historians who devote long chapters to Mungo Park and David Livingstone. To present the history of the African continent as a history that began only with the arrival of white men was a distortion that was meaningful to English people at a time when their only contact with and interest in Africa lay in trade and colonial government. If colonial rule was to appear reasonable, it was natural to suppress information about African civilizations and to stress the benefits brought to the continent by white men. But to teach the history of Africa nowadays in this manner is to produce in the pupil a reaction of bewilderment and indignation that these Africans, who were nothing but a lot of ignorant tribesmen until white men came, are apparently ungrateful for what white men have done, and have insisted on governing themselves although they cannot do it as well as white people used to do it for them. There are plenty of mature English politicians, reared on African history of the white man variety, who reiterate these sentiments in speeches and in letters to *The Times*.

It is an odd quirk of the colonialist approach to history that Egypt, about whose past we have a great deal of information and whose achievements are tremendous enough to be included in books on our Western heritage that take in the Greeks and Romans, is seldom referred to as a part of Africa but as part of the Mediterranean world. Those who admit it to be part of Africa divide it off from the brutishness south of the Sahara, indicating that Egyptians were not Negroes, so it is less surprising that they achieved so much. I do not think anyone has gone so far, though, as to describe the ancient Egyptians as white men: they remain an oddly separate category of honorary Europeans, despite the importance in their history of other parts of Africa and of the Middle East, the Red Sea, the Persian Gulf and the Arabian peninsula, rather than of Europe.

If English people grew up knowing more about Africa, they

would be able to understand and support more realistic policies towards modern African countries, whether governed by black people or white. But this is only a small part of what is needed if we are to look at history in a way that is meaningful to us, and illustrative of our destiny now. First and foremost we have to understand English history in terms that make sense and show us a way forward. We do not require a vague internationalism in history, teaching us that all human beings are the same, and ironing out the differences to produce a neat and tidy picture. Human beings are extraordinarily varied; our need is to appreciate this variety; to understand what are the feelings and aspirations that unite them, and what are the fruits of achievement that differentiate them. And we have to understand our own history, not as something unitary, but as the story of different peoples and different cultures, a microcosm of the world which can help us to understand the rest of the world, as well as ourselves, a good deal better. As Claude Levi-Strauss says, in *Race and History*, 'There are many more human cultures than human races, since the first are to be counted in thousands and the second in single units; two cultures developed by men of the same race may differ as much as, or more than, two cultures associated with groups of entirely different racial origin.'[1] He also points out, 'Human societies are never alone; when they appear to be most divided, the division is always between groups or clusters of societies. . . . We should not, therefore, be tempted to a piece-meal study of the diversity of human cultures, for that diversity depends less on the isolation of the various groups than on the relations between them.'[2]

English history is the story of a diversity of cultures, often co-existing. And this diversity was greatly extended and enriched by the contacts which resulted from centuries of trading, exploration and conquest in recent centuries. The history of modern England does not make sense unless we understand what the expansion of trade, and imperialism, gave to us, as well as what they gave to other countries. We are used to seeing our gain described in purely economic terms, though even here we are often given an inadequate picture. The enormous wealth acquired from the slave trade and the sugar plantations of the West Indies had perhaps more to do with our Industrial Revolution than did our technological inventiveness, for the capital investment that made that revolution possible could never have occurred in a society without enormous spare sums of money in the hands of people whose interest was in commerce rather than in the land. The industrialization of England was a direct product of mercantile imperialism. From India, we obtained not only great wealth but technical expertise in the manufacture of cotton goods and in design; in some cases, a name like 'calico' reminds us of this; in others, the original provenance is forgotten, as with the design called Paisley, which is in fact of Indian not Scottish origin. At this very day two of England's most famous characteristic exports, cashmere (or Kashmir) knitted goods and pottery and porcelain, would never have existed without what we learnt from the Indians and the Chinese. And, of course, going further back, our technocrats would have no mathematics using the zero and a set of numerals based on the ten, without the Indian mathematicians whose work was brought to Europe by the Arabs.

We have invented, and others have taken from us; others have invented and we have taken from them. And in the process our own culture and those of others have developed and become diversified. If *this* can be put across in the teaching of history to classes of English children, of English descent, West Indian and African, Asian and Pakistani, Chinese and Arab and Cypriot descent, we shall be talking about a history that means something to *all* of them.

We must somehow get rid of the approach to history of which the ancient Greeks were guilty: calling everyone else barbarians. The Greeks were very far indeed from being the only civilized people of their time; and the Persian empire, for one, long outlasted them. English people have used words like 'savage' and 'native' instead of barbarian, but the meaning is much the same: it means 'not as civilized as us'. This attitude is a very common one, and gives rise to ludicrous misunderstandings between people. When white people first came to West Africa, they were frightened of being eaten by the Africans, but the Africans were equally frightened of being eaten by them. Levi-Strauss records that 'in the Greater Antilles, a few years after the discovery of America, while the Spaniards were sending out Commissions of investigation to discover whether or not the natives had a soul, the latter spent their time drowning white prisoners in order to ascertain, by long observation, whether or not their bodies would decompose.'[3]

We need to understand ourselves and our destiny as a system of relationships between people inside England, and between the English and the other peoples with whom they come into contact. Then we can formulate new aims for ourselves. The aims we are offered by the rulers of society are the aims of greater production and greater consumption of manufactured goods, and the trouble with this goal is that it represents a hope in life which not all can realize. The process is a competitive one in which some people never get beyond the middle range of achievement and others lose out altogether: being poor, they have failed not only materially but intellectually and morally, in the terms our society accepts. Many of our schools, to give them credit, do not share in these aspirations. They struggle to give their pupils a sense of values which will conflict with the values of society as a whole, to teach something beyond competition. Yet there is no agreement on just what or how to teach. No wonder there is confusion and alienation among young people, for education is generally a process of telling young people how to adapt themselves to, and live happily in, the total adult society, and our teachers, if they were really to do this, would have to concentrate on the pupils whose aptitudes were best fitted to getting rich in present-day England, and ignore the rest. Unhappily, there are some teachers who have, perhaps unconsciously, this attitude, and teach accordingly, and some quite distinguished people who actually propound it as a desirable approach to education. But children are not fools and many of them resent being manipulated, and many are eager to respond to teaching but often fail to find something they as individuals can care about.

The schools are only one educational force in a society, and if schools were to carry out the teaching of history, as a very few teachers have begun to try to do, as a means of respecting one another and of appreciating that English culture is a synthesis of cultures, like every other culture in the world, there would certainly be a conflict between the pupils that absorbed this message and the other people in the society who had learnt a destiny other than mutual respect and co-operation. Such a conflict is already obvious in the United States.

But what is the alternative to this conflict between different theories of what our destiny is, and the way our society ought to go? We can see in England the result of a situation in which English people have been, by and large, educated in a fitting manner for an imperialist destiny, only to find themselves citizens of a small country with very few overseas territories. Those few are certain to gain complete independence in the foreseeable future, and for England now to go out and annex a new piece of territory is absolutely unthinkable. The one obvious place for the imperialist destiny to find its expression is within England itself, towards those citizens of former Empire countries who have made their homes here. And that is what we now see happening. *This* is one of the deep and disturbing similarities between our race situation and that of the United States. The United States has indeed expanded overseas, into countries it then calls territories rather than colonies, and into small nations where it can effectively get its own way without formally appointing a Governor-General; the local government can be effectively subservient enough without the U.S.A. accepting responsibility for it. But within its own borders, the United States governments of the last two centuries have ruled over colonies of black people transported bodily into their midst, to create wealth without being offered a share in it, instead of being left to do so in their country of origin or transported to some other overseas possession. The similarity between England and America in this respect was well expressed, the other way round, by Roy Sawh: 'Never forget, you people in England, that the West Indies are your Southern States.' What has happened both to the United States and to England in recent decades is that the colonial black population has been leaving its agricultural homeland of poverty and coming to live in the cities. In the United States people from the South have spread out into every major city of the North. In England we have people from the Caribbean and from a few areas of India and Pakistan coming to London, Birmingham, Bradford and so on; to all the major cities of Britain. The process began in America some thirty years before it took place here. But the nature of the migration, which includes skilled and educated people as well as agricultural workers with little formal education, which includes bourgeois people with savings as well as the poor, is strikingly similar.

In the United States, in the last fifteen years, enormous changes have taken place. Black American people have been making themselves heard and have been asserting their own historical identity. Both black and white writers have produced an enormous amount of material, that has found its way on to the paperback racks in drug stores all over the place, about the Negro in American history. Civil Rights legislation may have disappointed the hopes placed in it; ghettoes remain as intractably deprived as ever; equality of educational opportunity is still a distant dream, and yet all the same one cannot ignore the transformation that has taken place between an America where even the sophisticated and educated saw the black man and woman as Jack Benny's Rochester and Aunt Jemima, of pancake fame, and an America that knows James Baldwin and Coretta King for who they are and for what they say and for all they represent. Racism is still enormously powerful in America, and yet in some ways things look more hopeful there than they do in England.

This difference in our future prospects is illustrated by the official report of the U.S. National Advisory Commission on Civil Disorders, which assembled after the summer of 1967 in which riots and burnings slashed open the faces of cities across the country. The Commission was appointed by President Johnson to investigate the causes of this enormously destructive violence, and Johnson was severely criticized for selecting as members of the Commission members of the moderate and responsible establishment. Many people complained that such an inquiry was doomed to failure unless it was conducted by a body which included Stokely Carmichael, Floyd McKissick, Martin Luther King and Tom Hayden. These original objections are in themselves striking; how many people in England would complain of an analogous inquiry that the body appointed by our Prime Minister did not include Jeff Crawford, Joe Hunte, Obi Egbuna, Roy Sawh, or representatives of the Marxist-orientated Indian Workers' Associations? President Johnson's Commission did include black people, but these were well-known as black moderates: Senator Edward Brooke of Massachusetts, and Roy Wilkins of the old-established NAACP. The white members who formed the majority of the commission of inquiry included a prosperous lawyer, a rural Senator, a Police Chief, a businessman, a Trade Union leader, and a woman – the whole following exactly the pattern of commissions of inquiry that we are used to in England. Yet what they produced was staggeringly different from anything one can conceive of an English commission of inquiry producing in the same circumstances. The Commission wrote in its report:

> Certain fundamental matters are clear. Of these, the most fundamental is the racial attitude and behaviour of white Americans towards black Americans.
>
> Race prejudice has shaped our history decisively; it now threatens to affect our future.
>
> White racism is essentially responsible for the explosive mixture which has been accumulating in our cities since the end of World War II. Among the ingredients of this mixture are:
>
> Pervasive discrimination and segregation in employment, education and housing, which have resulted in the continuing exclusion of great numbers of Negroes from the benefits of economic progress.

Black in-migration and white exodus, which have produced the massive and growing concentration of impoverished Negroes in our major cities, creating a growing crisis of deteriorating facilities and services and unmet human needs.

The black ghettoes where segregation and poverty converge on the young to destroy opportunity and enforce failure. Crime, drug addiction, dependency on welfare, and bitterness and resentment against society in general and white society in particular are the result.

At the same time most whites and some Negroes outside the ghetto have prospered to a degree unparalleled in the history of civilization. Through television and other media, this affluence has been flaunted before the eyes of the Negro poor and the jobless ghetto youth.

Yet these facts alone cannot be said to have caused the disorders. Recently, other powerful ingredients have begun to catalyse the mixture:

Frustrated hopes are the residue of the unfulfilled expectations aroused by the great judicial and legislative victories of the Civil Rights movement and the dramatic struggle for equal rights in the South.

A climate that tends towards approval and encouragement of violence as a form of protest has been created by white terrorism directed against non-violent protest; by the open defiance of law and federal authority by state and local officials resisting desegregation; and by some protest groups engaging in civil disobedience who turn their back on non-violence, go beyond the constitutionally protected rights of petition and free assembly, and resort to violence to compel alteration of laws and policies with which they disagree.

The frustrations of powerlessness have led some Negroes to the conviction that there is no effective alternative to violence as a means of achieving redress of grievances and of 'moving the system'. These frustrations are reflected in alienation and hostility towards the institutions of law and government and the white society which controls them, and in the reach towards racial consciousness and solidarity reflected in the slogan 'Black Power'.

A new mood has sprung up among Negroes, particularly among the young, in which self-esteem and enhanced racial pride are replacing apathy and submission to the 'system'.

The police are not merely a 'spark' factor. To some Negroes police have come to symbolize white power, white racism and white repression. And the fact is that many police do reflect and express these attitudes. The atmosphere of hostility and cynicism is reinforced by a widespread belief among Negroes in the existence of police brutality and in a 'double standard' of justice and protection – one for Negroes and one for whites.[4]

This analysis, squarely laying the blame for the summer riots on white American society was, it is worth repeating, the work of moderate, establishment white Americans – the opposite number of Conservative M.P.s from the rural West Country, secretaries of the Transport and General or the Woodworkers' Union, chairmen of Chambers of Commerce in Halifax or Birmingham, Labour party lawyers, all presided over by a distinguished and totally upper-middle-class barrister. The difference between what the U.S. Commission produced and what we can imagine an analogous English body producing, represents the gap between the hope of realistic policies in their country and in ours. At least, there are people in the top levels of white American society who understand what racism is and what are its effects, and who have explicitly identified America's race problem as a problem created by white people and not by the presence of black ones. The opposite is the case in England. 'Middle' educated and informed opinion is convinced that the presence of black people constitutes our problem, and it is the liberally-minded moderates in both Labour and Conservative parties who claim that the more we reduce black immigration the better our prospects for racial harmony. These moderates are shocked at the extremists who want to ban all immigration and deport all black people but they are shocked at an argument that is only a logical extension of their own. They are a thousand miles away from grasping what the members of President Johnson's Commission learnt and understood.

Not only the big gap in understanding but the closeness in the kind of facts reported are disturbing for us. Of course, England is different from America, but in what ways is it different and in what ways is it the same? The alienation and hostility, the employment difficulties, the deep distrust of the police, the discrimination in housing, the gaps between the affluent and the poor, are all present here. The example of white violence is less obvious but it is still present. The Commission actually endorsed the aims of the Black Power movement in its final recommendations as a necessary preliminary to any meaningful attempt at integration, and its understanding is again far removed from the level of understanding in England; an article in *The Times* can describe black people as taking a *perverse* pride in being black! And as to any responsible English politician upholding the Black Power movement, this cannot possibly, at the time of writing, be imagined.

But then the educational forces in the United States schools, newspapers, churches, black and white authors, have been hammering home to America for some years now what racism is all about. The same kind of education is completely missing here. A few things have been written, a few things said, but the weight of social urgency has not been thrown behind the discussion of race

This situation may change quite rapidly as far as the churches and the newspapers and the trade union leaders are concerned. It may or may not happen in the seventies that urgent debate about racism backed by solid information and charged with the zeal to change things will take a central place in public discussion among the leaders of opinion. But what happens in the more formal process of education in our schools is certain to involve a slower change, if any change at all. New text-books have to be written, new approaches to teacher training introduced, and the new teachers have to be hired and the new books bought. The open timetable method of project work in schools is of course the cheapest as well as the most rapid way of introducing new methods and approaches in the classroom, but the encouragement of pupils to find out facts for themselves in this project method of teaching is again dependent upon the teacher's own background and training. All the processes of education are interdependent, and whether a new understanding of racism in our own society is pioneered by the schools or by the churches or by students or politicians or immigrant organizations, little headway will be made until one group has succeeded enough in influencing another for influences to satrt cross-fertilizing each other and growing through a vitality generated in themselves.

To see what can be done, it is well worth looking at educational programmes in the United States. But the difference is that whereas American schools need to teach about the American Indian, the English schools need to teach about the Indian Indian, for each nation to understand its own culture the better. The similarity is that we both have to reinterpret our history, not as the history of the white man, but as the history of *man*, in a particular country.

When I wrote to the Department of Health, Education and Welfare in Washington for detailed information about new syllabuses, they sent me a publication from Oakland, California, which is entitled *Resource Guide for Teaching about Contributions of Minorities to American Culture* (1966). It is intended for use in secondary schools, and is issued by the Superintendent of Oakland Public Schools, the equivalent, that is, of an English Chief Education Officer with a local education authority, and it states in the foreword that 'Respect, appreciation and understanding of people from various ethnic groups, faiths and cultures derive from recognizing and honoring the contributions of all people.' It is firmly stated that education must 'do more than develop the powers of the intellect. Education should infuse youngsters with a commitment to the brotherhood of man, and provide them with an appreciation of the multitudes of people of all colours and ethnic derivation who have helped to shape American society.' This is a mere preamble, and the practical way of doing what the Guide proposes is set out in a long list of teaching strategies, which emphasize, at every point, the need to use primary sources, such as diaries and eye-witness accounts, literary materials and personal contacts, and to use one's critical faculties in evaluating all these materials. Geography, History and American Government are the three formal subjects covered in the guide, and it lists three main types of resources on which the teacher can draw: audio-visual material, bibliographies, and 'community resources concerned with minorities'. This last is a list of organizations in San Francisco and the Bay Area, that is in Oakland's own neighbourhood, providing their own written publications and their own speakers. As well as religious and multi-racial organizations, there are included CORE (Congress of Racial Equality), famous for its non-violent direct action tactics in American politics and run entirely by black Americans, the Mexican-American Political Association, the NAACP, Jewish, Chinese-American and Japanese-American community organizations, side by side with the official department of Social Planning, the Lowie Museum, the Oakland Public Library and, significantly, three agencies directly concerned with employment opportunities for minorities.

The geography section is a striking contrast to the material so commonly used for geography teaching in English schools. Five of the films listed for classroom use are directly on group differences and prejudice about race and colour. The other films are concerned with the separate contributions to American culture of the French, the English, the Negroes, the Mexicans. A film about the Bay area is described in the Guide as 'an excellent concise history of the Bay Area. Examines objectively and frankly the history of racism in San Francisco. Deals specifically with the contributions and problems of Latin Americans, Indians, Chinese, Italians, Germans, French and Spanish.' The tape recordings listed describe law among the Eskimos and the Yurok Indians, village government in Bali, religion and ritual among the Arunta of Central Australia and much more of the same kind. All this is for children in Grade seven, around the age of thirteen; in Grade eight they proceed to learn in far more detail about American history, using films, tapes and text-books to study the Indians of California and the South West, their arts, customs and dwellings, and the Negro in American history under such headings as 'The Glory of Negro History' and 'We are Americans with a heritage from Africa'. There are records of Negro poetry and of Negro songs sung by Negroes, and there is also ceremonial music from the Far East on records, to be used with other material on the background culture of Chinese-Americans and Japanese-Americans. The parts played by minorities in the revolution, in invention, music and literature and in battle, is described in the context of American history as a whole.

The section on American government, for the most senior grade, provides material for a history of the American Constitution, and again the material illustrates that America has been built by a great variety of people, of all colours and nations. It also includes sociology; a tape recording about the West Side in New York describes the troubles and disillusions shared by Negro, Puerto Rican and white inhabitants. A substantial number of the tape recordings available are by well-known black Americans: James Baldwin, Whitney Young, Louis Lomax and Robert Weaver.

The whole Guide is a hundred and twenty-one pages long, and the bibliographies list over three hundred books about minorities and about prejudice, not text-books (which are listed in the main body of the Guide) but books for general reading, for different age-groups.

This inadequate summary of a single public-schools programme in the United States may serve to give some idea of what *can* be done and what is already being done across the Atlantic to revitalize the approach to history and geography in schools. It does not represent an isolated and eccentric effort: I doubt if there is any sense in which Oakland could be called a show-place untypical of the United States. It had severe riots in 1967, but less severe than those of Detroit and Newark. It should be noted that Oakland already has more Negro children than any other group in its schools, and the city is expected to be over half Negro by 1983, but it is not unique in this respect; the flight of white people to the suburbs has already created Negro majorities among the inhabitants of several cities, including Washington itself.

To propose a revision of the history and geography syllabuses in England would require a book by itself, but at least it is not difficult to see how we could follow the guidelines already laid down in the United States. Most important of these guidelines, however, which should be the first we attempt to follow, is the path of learning from and using the speech and writings of the minority groups themselves. It would be a terrible mistake for us to try to extend the limits of our understanding of history, when we ourselves are so bounded by the limitations in which we learnt that we could only succeed in reshuffling the cards we hold; we need to accept new cards from the pack to make up our hand.

It would not, however, be necessary to commission new books from scratch: West Indian writers like C. L. R. James and Eric Williams, to name but two, have produced material which could be used with profit in English schools. North London already has a West Indian bookshop; West London has a Free University of Black Studies, and these are signs already of what may become a movement for change.

It is not the availability of good books and educational films nor even the voice of black American intellectuals and political leaders that has produced a new educational approach in the United States. It is a change that has occurred in the white American establishment, a desire and a strong motivation for finding some means to unify a country that risks being torn apart. I fear that we shall not get a renewal of teaching here, of a kind that will break down racism, until teachers and educationists themselves feel a similar motivation. At present there is an awareness in many schools and teacher training colleges that something needs to be done in schools to help good race relations, but most of the concern is directed towards the 'immigrant child' who is seen as an unfortunate with an educational and social handicap. The teaching of white English children about race is seldom discussed; it is regarded as quite a liberal triumph if a college of education has one or two day conferences, during its whole course for teachers in training, on 'race relations' and if the teaching in civics lessons in senior forms is recommended to include a few sessions on what is wrong with racial prejudice. There is no incentive for the student to take the question seriously. The educational problem of race is identified as a problem of 'immigrant' children, not as a problem of black and white children in one society learning to live and work together with mutual respect and understanding.

Yet there are many teachers in England who are uneasy and unhappy about the present state of education, because of the confusion and uncertainty about what its aims are meant to be. These teachers might feel hesitant about a new syllabus that was frankly geared to overcoming racism, because racism is something English people are nervous of talking about and anxious to explain away; teachers are generally convinced that it does not exist in their own schools and very unwilling even to discuss the possibility that it does. Whereas American teachers are all too aware of it, English teachers are frequently grateful to follow the lead of the spokesman for the Department of Education and Science, giving evidence to the Parliamentary Select Committee on Race Relations, who described children of Indian origin in English schools as suffering from the *cultural handicap* of an Indian background.

But after all what *is* overcoming racism in education? It is to present new and exciting information in a new approach to tired old subjects, to make information relevant to the lives of the children in the class, to stimulate them to curiosity about finding out the truth about other people, to get rid of fallacies. It is educationally valid just because racism itself is invalid, just because racism is something which distorts and misinforms. There are three ways in which racism manifests itself in education. One is by the provision of false information, for example, H. A. L. Fisher's statement in his *History of Europe* that, 'To the conquest of nature through knowledge the contributions made by Asiatics have been negligible and by Africans (Egyptians excluded) non-existent.' One is by a description of events that gives false explanations or values to them, and which amounts to giving false information if its tendentious character is not recognized. This is where the description of Asians and Africans as 'savages' or 'tribesmen' or 'natives' comes in. Also, the following bit of information from the Jackdaw Folder on *The Indian Mutiny*, a supposedly up-to-date history teaching method in the form of authentic documents copied on to separate sheets of paper, together with commentary also printed on separate sheets of paper, so that it gives the impression of sharing some of the authenticity:

> Today we can understand that people do not wish their countries to be colonized or parts of other people's empires; they would rather make their own decisions, even if wrong ones, than receive benefits from a foreign ruling race. It is part of human nature to resent other people's interference, even though it is intended to be for one's own good.

And the third is to give a definite and false impression by selecting some pieces of factual information and suppressing others. Here belong all those books which teach the history of the world in terms of European discovery and conquest, but which say nothing of the achievements of any of the other countries concerned.

Not all distortions are concerned with race and nationality; some are to do with religion. This too, of course, can have a bad influence on racial attitudes, when racial minorities in England practise religions other than Christianity, as many do.

A text-book for quite young children which must, judging by the large number of reprints since it first appeared in 1933, have influenced many children and which is still in print, deserves to be contrasted with the material suggested for the Oakland High Schools in the United States. This book, *Life in Later Days*, part of a series on 'Life in Past Ages' published by Nisbet, contains the following passage on Islam:

'Mohammed taught his followers that it was not wrong to fight and make war, and he even said that it was good to kill people who did not believe the things that Mohammed taught.

'But Jesus had taught men peace, kindness and gentleness.'

No mention of any of the teachings of Mohammed about prayer, giving one fortieth of one's goods to charity, caring for strangers, duty to the family or anything. What is more, the bit about Jesus's message of peace, kindness and gentleness, which is frequently reiterated during the book, goes oddly with 'Charlemagne and all the people that he ruled were Christians, and they fought bravely and well against the enemies of Christianity.' Later we hear that the Moors 'were good fighters and they won many battles, but they were very cruel to the people whom they beat'. No mention of cruelty, however, with the Northmen who 'were very brave and warlike. They believed that fighting was the finest thing a man could do. They were afraid of nothing, and they sailed bravely to seek great adventures.' The chapter on the Arabs, by the way, is headed 'The Dark-skinned Peoples'. The chapter headed 'The Northmen' begins in contrast by telling us that the Northmen 'were tall and fair-haired. Their eyes were blue and they were brave and strong.'

The Red Indians, the same book tells us, 'were not clever like the Incas. They lived in tents on the open lands and in the woods, and spent their time in hunting for their food.

'They loved fighting, and when they killed an enemy in battle they used to cut off the skin, or scalp, from the top of his head and carry it tied to their belt.'

So much for the 'Red Indians'; really, so much; for this is all the information, or rather misinformation, that the book provides. All the peoples of North America, an extremely varied set of nations, are grouped together as 'Red Indians'. They are described as living in tents, which is true only of some of them; no mention is made of the Pueblo Indians, for instance. They are described as hunters, although many of them practised agriculture. They are called 'not clever', a value judgement which nothing except the small amount of untrue information provided supports, and they are described, universally, as fighters and scalpers of their enemies. There is no mention of their arts, religion, social organization, languages, laws and technology. Nor is it mentioned that they were systematically annihilated as far as possible, and that those who fought against the European invaders successfully enough to bring about negotiations for peace treaties were tricked and murdered in many instances.

The section on India, *in the 1953 edition* of this book, which I have, says, 'the white people in India have many servants. Most of them are merchants, or engineers, or people in charge of large works. Some are there to help and advise the people of India.

'All the other work is done by the brown-skinned people of the country.'

I must emphasize again that this text-book is not a wild exception, unfairly picked out; anyone who cares to look at history and geography text-books currently in use, which will include some recent publications and some copies of books first written as long ago as this one or even before, can find examples of an approach to education that, while it may not make a child racist by itself, makes racism readily acceptable and convincing. It is also an approach that makes it very difficult for those educated by it to shift their own ground in looking at the world and to recognize what they themselves, and other people, are really like. Education has two functions, to impart information and to inculcate values; one cannot, in fact, do one of these things without the other, for the provision of information, being selective, itself suggests values of what is good and desirable and what is not, and the inculcation of values can only proceed by the giving of examples. It is easy for anyone to see that the provision of inaccurate information to children is a wrong way of going about education. It may be less easy to see that all teaching of history, geography, civics and even of literature and the fine arts is a teaching of value judgements. We often fail to recognize that ideas we have acquired are value judgements open to question. I expect some people will want to object to what I am saying, protesting that I want to brainwash or propagandize children, or turn education upside down with a lot of political gimmicks. On the contrary, I am suggesting that this is what has already been done, and that we need to reverse the process by making more accurate information available and by encouraging children to evaluate this information for themselves. This applies to classes of entirely white English children, to racially mixed classes, and to classes almost entirely composed of the children of West Indian and Asian parents. It is possible to construct a syllabus meaningful and exciting for all of them, to which all of them can contribute and from which all can derive a sense of pride in the various sources of their heritage. If we do not succeed in producing such a situation in our schools, but continue instead to educate the white children to a sense of national pride that is all bound up with being white and having an imperial past, and to educate the other children to believe they are natural victims, we shall be busily laying a long fuse leading to explosion. And even worse, we shall be destroying the intellectual potential of many children, both black and white, who deserve better than the warmed-over myths of imperialism when they look for knowledge.

Part Four

But what does it mean?
What are we going to do?
– W. H. AUDEN

1. William's Mother
2. But now, face to face

1. William's Mother

You couldn't have called her pretty. Perhaps she never had been. Sometimes you can see the ghost of good looks glimmering behind the middle-aged face of a woman who has known trouble, but this woman had features that could never have been handsome. Her figure was shapeless, wrapped in a brown tweed coat that had taken on the dispirited lines of her own experience; a ragged thread hung where the middle button should have been. How could anyone feel sorry for a woman like that? She was the sort of woman you wouldn't notice; if you did, you'd be impatient to get away as soon as possible.

Her husband was not there to help her the day she sat in the magistrate's court. He was at work. It was a nice, new courtroom with cream paint and big airy windows, presided over by a woman chairman, her jersey suit impeccably buttoned, her hat large and assertive. On either side of her sat a male magistrate, two local shopkeepers whose view of human nature had been formed by years of watching for petty pilfering, and arguing with customers who pretended they had given a five-pound note and not a pound. Before them sat a clerk, droning out the routine prose that assured people of their rights. There were social workers and a uniformed policeman, and the little boy, William, whose fate was to be decided that morning, and the woman in the tweed coat, who was his mother, and me.

William was twelve. When he was a baby, he had been left in St Vincent with his grandmother, while his father and mother came to England to find a good job and a home. They had eventually sent for William some years later, when they had a small, cheap house on a mortgage provided by the local council; he had arrived, after the usual administrative delays and difficulties over the fare with the travel agency, when he was seven. The first sight of England had been terrifying for him. It was cold and grey; there were houses, houses, houses everywhere, and people hurrying by in the street who didn't know him and didn't say hallo to him, and here were two people, called his father and mother, whom he couldn't remember seeing ever before in his life. He was taken into the small house and told not to wander outside. The children he saw in the street took no notice of him. There was nothing to do in the house. He felt suffocated and shut in, and the second night he ran away from the house and wandered about until he fell asleep in the porch of a church. A policeman found him and brought him back.

Next day he started school. More new people that he had never seen before. There was a schoolmaster who spoke kindly to him, but the other children paid him little attention. His loneliness grew. The other children rushed out at break, in groups of two or three friends together, and shouted and played, and gave each other sweets and potato crisps. Perhaps if he gave them sweets and potato crisps they would talk to him and play with him too. He asked his mother for money to buy some, but he picked a bad moment when she was tired and worried about the payments on the three-piece suite and the television; the man at the shop was trying to say she hadn't paid last week, and she had; it wasn't her fault that her book hadn't been properly marked. She told William sharply she hadn't money to throw around on sweets that day, and anyway they were bad for his teeth. He couldn't explain. He went down to the corner shop and loitered about, trying to think what to do. And then he thought of going to Woolworth's, where anyone could walk in and the sweets were all laid out on the counter. He stole some jelly babies, some sweet cigarettes and some dolly mixtures. He got away with it. Next day he tried giving the sweets to the other children, but he was shy and awkward. One of them laughed at him. One girl said 'Thank you', but then didn't know quite what to say next. A big boy from the next class shouted 'Sambo's got some sweets' and grabbed a packet from him.

He would have to do better. He went back to Woolworth's with a carrier bag and lifted a handsome pencil-case for the little girl, and pencils and elastic bands and a beautiful box of crayons. This time he was caught. The vast machinery of the law creaked into action to deal with William's thieving. He appeared in court. His mother was deeply upset and ashamed, but most of all amazed at the weightiness of the whole procedure. He was only a little boy. Why couldn't they just have told his father? Why all this fuss with the police and the courts, and social workers coming round, and cross-questioning her about the time William had run away and fallen asleep in the church porch? She didn't like the police coming. What were the neighbours going to think about them?

But that was only the beginning. A few weeks later, the same policeman was back. Mrs Heather at number twenty-nine had lost her purse. He had reason to believe that William had taken it. There was a furious scene. William cried and swore he hadn't taken it. When, an hour later, Mrs Heather's purse was returned by the assistant from the corner shop, where she had left it on the counter while buying a loaf of bread, the matter was quickly dropped. But William's mother was afraid now. Everything that disappeared was going to be blamed on her son. She no longer felt ashamed. She was angry. When she saw a policeman her heart beat faster with fear and anger; this was the enemy who was trying to harm her son.

Soon, however, she had different things to worry about. William's father began to have weeks on end of short time at the factory where he worked, due to a strike in a different firm fifty miles away. Week after week there was only three pounds left over each Friday once the mortgage, the hire purchase and the gas and electricity had been allowed for. Food was short, and both parents became bad-tempered. William was quiet and gave no trouble; he spent hours out on his own. He had made a rare discovery: the English countryside. It was nothing like St Vincent but there were birds to watch and listen to; there were favourite places he felt were his own, little hiding places in the overgrown tangle of bracken and bushes where, he told himself, nobody but himself ever came. He made some crude furniture; a shelter and wooden seat, camouflaged with an overhanging arch of brambles; he crept in and watched the sunlight through the crossed stems and leaves. His parents knew nothing of the small world he had found. They were worried about making ends meet, and had loud, angry, futile quarrels. One of the neighbours reported to the police on the noise from next door. A policeman came round, and was not too unpleasant, not particularly interested. It was a different one from the man who had called about the purse.

William's mother tried to get a job to help out with the shortage of money. She went to the employment exchange; she answered advertisements, but over and over again she was turned down, once with the remark, 'We don't want coloureds'. At last she was taken on for the evening shift of housekeeping staff at the hospital, which was so desperate for help, two women having left simultaneously and unexpectedly, that it accepted her. Ironically, the factory where her husband was employed went back to full-time working the very next week. But she decided to carry on at the hospital; it would be a help and a security to have a little extra. It meant that she saw little of William; he came home from school just as she was going out.

For some months life went by fairly smoothly and uneventfully. But then, suddenly, the world fell apart. William came home from school, took some bread and some milk from the new bottle and went out to his favourite place, the shelter under the brambles. When he arrived at the waste piece of land he had made his own, he could not at first believe his eyes. It was as though an earthquake had shaken the foundations on which he walked. Instead of the loneliness and quiet there were men and machines and a big builder's lorry. The earth was being torn apart, and his home, his own home, had been destroyed, the wooden furniture thrown on to a pile of rubbish. He did not know the land had been bought long ago by the city for development, that it was to be the site of a dozen new streets of municipal housing. What he saw was his own piece of ground being forcibly taken away from him.

He went on an orgy of destruction. He smashed up two telephone boxes. He threw stones at the builder's lorry. It was a clear case of wanton vandalism. He was taken to court again.

The damning evidence was reported quietly and dispassionately by the policeman and the social workers. It was clear that the home was a bad one for William; he was not adequately cared for and the marital relationship between the parents was most unsatisfactory. William had run away, all those years ago. No wonder: his parents quarrelled violently and a neighbour had overheard his mother threaten to kill his father. The mother went out to work leaving the child unattended until his father got home, though there was no financial need for this since the father was in steady employment. The thefts were brought up again. When, eventually, after hearing repeated condemnations of the private lives and characters of the parents, the magistrates withdrew, William and his mother sat quiet and humiliated. William's mother was, for a moment, too bruised and unhappy to take it in when the magistrates returned to announce their decision: William should be taken into care of the local authority until he was eighteen years old. When she understood, William's mother uttered a great cry like a howl of acute physical pain, and began to shout, 'No, no. You can't take him away from me. Oh God, don't let them take him away from me.' It was the kind of hysterical behaviour you expect from a West Indian woman. Her agony made her grotesque. Nobody looked at her; the chairman began to tell her loudly that her son would be well looked after and she would be allowed to visit him at the approved hours. But she heard nothing; and went on calling out, 'Oh God, oh God', and one of the children's officers, embarrassed but professionally bright, tried to cheer her up. 'You mustn't say that.' She clung to my hand with a tight grip, and shouted at her son, 'Do you know why they're doing this to you? It's because you are black. You're black. That's why they're doing this to you.' And William sat quiet as a stone, not crying, not speaking.

She held on to my hand, and asked me not to leave her, so I went with her and William and the children's officer to the children's department, to deal with the formalities, and then on to the children's home, where William was instantly to be installed. As we walked along the street, through lunch-time crowds jostling outside the shops, William's mother cried out again very loud, 'Oh God, I must be a wicked woman. Why have you done this to me?'

'She seems to have a religious mania,' whispered the children's officer to me. And she began to tell William's mother that she had better bring his clothes up to the home next day, and a brush and comb please, properly marked.

All the time William did not cry or speak or change expression. He was like a dead child walking. He remained utterly calm until the moment of saying goodbye to his mother; awkwardly he tried to comfort her, to tell her to look after herself, and two tears ran down his face. His strength and his concern for her calmed his mother at last.

*

Extract from the report of the Government-sponsored National Committee for Commonwealth Immigrants 1967:

> ... a conference under the title 'The Social Services and a Multi-Racial Society'. The programme was structured to give both social workers and representatives of the immigrant communities an opportunity to share their difficulties and needs in relation to the operation of the social services. It is hoped that these conferences will provide greater understanding of the implications of different cultural patterns on the work of local authority welfare departments.[1]

What was William's cultural pattern? And what, in Heaven's name, is this English one?

2. But now, face to face

If you find you have a social or political problem on your hands, this is how to deal with it. If you are in politics, you set up a commission of inquiry. You tell this commission to find out facts, but before they begin their work you give them what are called 'terms of reference'. That is, you tell them what kind of facts to look for and what they are not allowed to look for, and you prevent them considering and evaluating the problem itself that is the cause of their being brought into existence. They can work on the problem only as you define it, not as they may determine it is. Deciding what is to be done is a political matter; the commission just has to get at the facts. The utter uselessness of this process has been demonstrated again and again. For whatever commissions find out, and recommend within their limits, their findings are either ignored completely, or else used for random selections of clauses here and there, having nothing to do with the policy as a whole that the inquiry put together; or else sometimes, the findings are flouted by those in power putting into operation exactly the opposite of what the commission of inquiry has proposed. The point of setting up such commissions is, of course, not to find out the truth or to get anything done, but to stave off criticism and to ensure delay, while pretending to be responsible and responsive to the general public.

If you are not a politician, and you find a social problem, you can hold a conference. To this you invite a large number of people of opposed interests, some of whom come and some of whom don't. They are addressed by a few speakers; they split up into discussion groups, and at the end of the day they return to pursue their own interests in the same way, with everyone agreeing what a good conference it has been.

Or of course you can go out on to the streets and march. This ensures a few seconds on television, more if there happens to be violence, and some press coverage; as there will certainly be reported at the same time several other marches, riots and protests, the public at large will get you inextricably mixed up with Japanese students, striking Ford workers, and Irish housewives: a mish-mash of vocal 'troublemakers', with the issues themselves in the background unobserved.

Or you can despair. Or emigrate. Or decide that the answer to the whole thing is education.

Surely if only people knew the real facts they would understand what should be done, and see that it was done?

The trouble is, of course, that most people in England today are completely powerless to see that anything gets done, in the face of the Government and its immense bureaucratic empire. And the people in power are not really bothered about truth or about what is the right thing to do; the only thing that bothers them badly is the thought of losing the next election, or failing to get promotion. Even decent individuals who would like to care, and who decide to work their way up in the power system so as to do something good and useful, find the machine too strong and inflexible; either they become converted to the ruling ideology of staying in power, or they find themselves thwarted by their own colleagues and by the structure of the machine; they can either get out of the whole business or decide to struggle on, working quietly from within; and once they *are* within the power structure, they find forced upon them over and over again the necessity to condone policies they cannot agree with in conscience, but have to co-operate with in public and in fact.

Enormous changes have been wrought in England in the last twenty-five years, but these have mainly been changes initiated by the ruling Government, or depending upon the policies of those with great wealth; large corporations, local authorities and the Government itself again. As small newspapers and magazines die, as units of local government become ever larger and more remote, as people's identity is reduced, over and over again, to different sets of numbers on gas bills and university entrance forms and National Insurance cards and examination results, so the opportunities for individual expression and initiative have decreased. There have been a few changes in the opposite direction: local radio stations, local community associations joining to get themselves better street lighting or a zebra crossing, but many attempts at change or independence have failed: the police move people on and the houses come down and the motorway goes up; the school closes; the farmland is turned into a runway – the ordinary person finds it hard to oppose the forces of money and power.

And, as we have seen, the forces of money and power are tied up with institutions whose clumsy workings perpetuate racial inequality and injustice. Getting rid of racism is going to be a much more difficult and complicated matter than getting rid of individual misinformation and prejudice. If tomorrow every English man and woman were to put on a magic pair of spectacles through which he could see fellow human beings *as* human beings, then life would be warmer and happier, and misfortunes far more bearable – but there would still be unavoidable difficulties in the way of people getting homes and jobs and decent education; all kinds of rules and regulations and ways of spending money would have to be changed.

However, one has to start somewhere. And if only those magic spectacles existed, it would become a great deal easier to bring about change. If people saw others as human beings like themselves, with the same needs, magistrates might become a little more like Solomon and a little less like Herod. And nobody would say, 'We don't want coloureds.' For nobody wishes for himself that he should be unwanted. People would not be punished for the sin of being homeless by having their children taken from them; the rules about 'care' and homeless families' units and so on would be ignored and new institutions would develop. Of course it would not all go smoothly, but there would be something very important about life that many people now lack – a feeling of hope.

So, faced with the problem of a deeply racist society in England and a power structure unwilling to change it, I believe that what is needed is not the collection of large numbers of facts about the subjects called 'race relations' or 'community relations'; what we need is not to garner information, but to learn how to *think* and how to *feel*. The only way to solve a problem is to understand it, and that understanding does not depend on just *getting* the facts; it depends on *evaluating* them. Information, the truth about the situation, is essential to begin with, but you have to be able to discern which facts are important and which are not, and you cannot do this if you think like a computer, a busy administrative brain without a conscience or a heart.

There is a sense, then, in which 'education' is the beginning of an answer. Provided education is taken to mean the humility to learn, an honest search after truth and goodness, rather than a new subject shoved into the O-level syllabus or a day conference into a teacher training course. The education that children and young people are offered is, in any society, an expression of the aspirations of that society. If we want to aspire to be a country free from racism, we have to look at the values influencing the kind of knowledge that is now handed out, and consider whether there may not be a better way of learning about the world around us than how to turn living things into gold and people into different currencies, stamped with a mark to show one is worth more than another. And whether there are not better aspirations for our country than bigger airports, bigger prisons and a balance of payments, the proud marks of a White Man's country. There may be a better kind of society to live in than a white man's country, and a more humane kind of civilization than what is called Western. And I hope that English people will begin to think out what such a country might be, before it is too late and they have lost the chance of survival as a racially mixed, racially equal society, where Englishness connotes not your looks but your sense of decency, humour and independence, into the new kind of world that is surely coming, in which white supremacy will be as dead as Babylon.

Notes

The full titles and publishing details of the books referred to in these notes are given in the Bibliography.

Part One What's in an Attitude?

1. The P.E.P. Report, pp. 31–2.
2. ibid., pp. 41–2.
3. ibid., p. 34.
4. ibid., p. 37.
5. ibid., p. 35.
6. ibid., pp. 29–30.
7. ibid., pp. 23a–25.
8. The Rose Report, pp. 551–88.
9. ibid., Appendix VII, 3, p. 790.
10. ibid., p. 597.
11. ibid., p. 599.

Part Two Institutional Racism

1. Rex and Moore, p. 2.
2. Marina Maxwell: 'Violence in the Toilets', an article in *Race Today*, September 1969.
3. Judy Bainbridge: *Race Relations and Racial Fiction: some observations of the Liverpool scene*, unpublished dissertation, 1969.

Part Three For the Good of the People

1. The Street Report, p. 134.

Part Four Fiction: Words and Pictures

1. Lévi-Strauss, p. 46.

Newspapers: What I tell you three times is true

1. Paul Foot, p. 134.

History

1. Lévi-Strauss, p. 8.
2. ibid., p. 11.
3. ibid., p. 13.
4. The Kerner Report, pp. 10–11.

Part Five William's Mother

1. N.C.C.I. Report, p. 40.

Bibliography

This bibliography is intended for those who, after reading this book, wish to find out more about racism in England, and perhaps also to read something about other countries whose racial situation is either directly influential upon ours or analogous to it. The list of books below is, I must emphasize, a brief personal selection, and I have deliberately chosen, where possible, titles easily available in paperback.

By far the best way to be well-informed about the racial situation here is to take out a subscription to *Race Today*, the monthly periodical of the Institute of Race Relations. It has articles from a remarkably wide variety of contributors of all points of view and deals with the race situation in many other countries as well as with the problems of such minorities as the gipsies and European migrant workers in E.E.C. countries. Its coverage of race in Britain is unique. The Institute also publishes an academic quarterly, *Race*, with longer specialist articles. The Institute library and information service are indispensable to anyone concerned with contemporary race issues, and advice on further reading in any particular branch of the subject can be obtained from the library service at 36 Jermyn Street, London, SW1.

The New Beacon Bookshop, 2 Albert Road, N4, is a West Indian bookshop with a wide selection of history, literature and comment from Caribbean and African authors in particular, and will send book-lists on any particular topic on request. Like the I.R.R. library, it has many periodicals published by black organizations, and it stocks major works like *The Black Jacobins* (see below), not otherwise readily obtainable in England.

Anyone browsing in a public library among books on race in Britain is likely to find a very small selection, variable in quality and in some cases already out of date though only a few years old. It is important to be aware of how to read such books with a critical eye, and this is where *Race Today* is so helpful.

The English Scene

E. J. B. Rose and associates: *Colour and Citizenship* (the 'Rose Report'), an encyclopedic reference work published for the Institute of Race Relations by Oxford University Press, 1969.

N. Deakin: *Colour, citizenship and British Society* (a shortened edition of the Rose Report), Panther, 1970.

Political and Economic Planning: *Racial Discrimination in Britain* (the 'P.E.P. Report'), made and published by P.E.P. for the National Committee for Commonwealth Immigrants and the Race Relations Board, 1967. Obtainable from P.E.P., 12 Upper Belgrave Street, London SW1.

W. W. Daniel: *Racial Discrimination in England* (a shortened edition of the P.E.P. Report), Penguin Books, 1968.

Michael Banton: *White and Coloured*, Jonathan Cape, 1959.

John Rex and Robert Moore: *Race, Community and Conflict: a Study of Sparkbrook*, published by O.U.P. for I.R.R., 1967.

Wilfred Wood and John Downing: *Vicious Circle*, S.P.C.K., 1968.

Gus John and Derek Humphry: *Because They're Black*, Penguin Books, 1971. *Police Power and Black People*, Panther, 1972.

Lewis Donnelly, Ed.: *Justice First*, Sheed and Ward, 1969.

Harry Street, Geoffrey Howe and Geoffrey Bindman: *Anti-Discrimination Legislation* (the 'Street Report'), published by P.E.P. for N.C.C.I. and R.R.B., 1967.

Race Relations Board: Annual Reports. These, and other informative literature on the Race Relations Acts, can be obtained from the Board at 5 Lower Belgrave Street, London SW1.

Reports of the Parliamentary Select Committee on Race Relations and Immigration, H.M.S.O. These voluminous reports, so far covering coloured school-leavers, control of immigration, housing, and relations with the police, are too detailed and expensive to buy, but very illuminating and may be studied in libraries.

New Perspectives on Britain and the Commonwealth

V. G. Kiernan: *The Lords of Human Kind*, Penguin Books, 1972.

Eric Williams: *British Historians and the West Indians*, André Deutsch, 1966. *Capitalism and Slavery*, André Deutsch, 1964.

C. L. R. James: *The Black Jacobins*, Vintage Books, New York, 1963. *A History of the Pan-African Revolt*, Drum and Spear, Washington, 1969.

Basil Davidson: *Black Mother*, Gollancz, 1961.

Adu Boahen: *Topics in West African History*, Longmans, 1966.

Racism in Contemporary Africa

Cosmas Desmond: *The Discarded People*, Penguin Books, 1971. (On South Africa.)

Frantz Fanon: *The Wretched of the Earth*, Penguin Books, 1967. (On North Africa.)

Eshmael Mlambo: *The Struggle for a Birthright*, C. Hurst & Co., 1972. (On Rhodesia.)

Patrick van Rensburg: *Guilty Land*, Penguin Books, 1962. (On South Africa.)

Judith Todd: *Rhodesia*, Macgibbon & Kee, 1966.

Racism in the United States

(I have not here included any of the copious recent literature on Amerindians or on other minorities such as Mexican-Americans.)

J. W. Schulte Nordholt: *The People that Walk in Darkness: A History of the Negro People in America*, Ballantine Books, New York, 1970.

Louis E. Lomax: *The Negro Revolt*, Harper-Row, New York, 1970.

Martin Luther King: *Stride Towards Freedom: the Montgomery Story*, Hodder & Stoughton, 1959.

Otto Kerner and others: Report of the National Advisory Commission on Civil Disorders (the 'Kerner Report'), Bantam Books, New York, 1968.

Charles E. Silberman: *Crisis in Black and White*, Jonathan Cape, 1965.

Kenneth B. Clark: *Dark Ghetto*, Gollancz, 1965.

Malcolm X: *The Autobiography of Malcolm X*, Penguin Books, 1968.

Stokeley Carmichael and Charles V. Hamilton: *Black Power*, Penguin Books, 1969.

James Baldwin: *The Fire Next Time*, Penguin Books, 1964.

Eldridge Cleaver: *Soul on Ice*, Jonathan Cape, 1969.

Bobby Seale: *Seize the Time*, Hutchinson, 1970.

George Jackson: *Soledad Brother*, Penguin Books, 1971.

Race and Education

Jonathan Kozol: *Death at an Early Age*, Penguin Books, 1968.

Herbert Kohl: *36 Children*, Penguin Books, 1972.

Bernard Coard: *How West Indian Children are made educationally subnormal in the British School System*, New Beacon, 1971. Published for the Caribbean Education and Community Workers' Association. Obtainable from New Beacon, 2 Albert Road, N4.

The English and Immigration

National Committee for Commonwealth Immigrants: Report of N.C.C.I. for 1967, published 1968 and now available from N.C.C.I.'s successor, the Community Relations Commission, Russell Square House, London WC1.

Paul Foot: *Immigration and Race in British Politics*, Penguin Books, 1965.

Facts Papers on the U.K., Institute of Race Relations, 1970 and 1971–2, available from the Institute, 36 Jermyn Street, London SW1.

Geoffrey Bindman and Roger Warren-Evans: *The Immigration Bill 1971*, a pamphlet published by the Runnymede Trust, Stuart House, 1 Tudor Street, London EC4.

W. R. Böhning and David Stephen: *The E.E.C. and the Migration of Workers: the E.E.C.'s system of free movement of labour and the implications of U.K. entry*, a Runnymede Trust pamphlet, 1971.

Ian A. MacDonald: *Race Relations and Immigration Law*, Butterworth, 1969. (A book for lawyers.)

Joint Council for Welfare of Immigrants: *Return to Sender*, *The Unemployed, Homeless and Destitute*, *A People Without Hope*, pamphlets obtainable from J.C.W.I. at Toynbee Hall, Commercial Street, London E1.

Report of the Committee on Immigration Appeals (Wilson Committee), Cmnd 3387, H.M.S.O., 1967.

Michael and Ann Dummett: 'The Role of Government in Britain's Racial Crisis', a chapter on immigration policy from *Justice First*, ed. Donnelly (see above).

Race and History

Claude Lévi-Strauss: *Race and History*, UNESCO, Paris, 1958 (obtainable from H.M.S.O.).

Juan Comas: *Racial Myths*, UNESCO, Paris, 1958 (obtainable from H.M.S.O.).

Geoffrey Bibby: *The Testimony of the Spade*, Fontana, 1962. *Four Thousand Years Ago*, Penguin Books, 1965. These are not ostensibly about race, but are excellent in creating a sense of proportion about the achievements of undervalued cultures.

L. Stavrianos: *The World before 1500*, and *The World since 1500*, Prentice-Hall, New York, 1966. Written for American teachers; to reinterpret the place of Western culture in the world.

Philip Mason: *Patterns of Dominance*, O.U.P., 1970. A study of racial dominance in very widely varying cultures.

A. L. Basham: *Aspects of Ancient Indian Culture*, Asia Publishing House, 1967.

Basil Davidson: *Old Africa Rediscovered*, Gollancz, 1959.

Eduardo Mondlane: *Struggle for Mozambique*, Penguin Books, 1969.

Victor Wolfgang von Hagen: *The Ancient Sun Kingdoms of the Americas*, Panther, 1967.

Penguinews *and* **Penguins in Print**

Every month we issue an illustrated magazine, *Penguinews*. It's a lively guide to all the latest Penguins, Pelicans and Puffins, and always contains an article on a major Penguin author, plus other features of contemporary interest.

Penguinews is supplemented by *Penguins in Print*, a complete list of all the available Penguin titles – there are now over four thousand!

The cost is no more than the postage; so why not write for a free copy of this month's *Penguinews*? And if you'd like both publications sent for a year, just send us a cheque or a postal order for 30p (if you live in the United Kingdom) or 60p (if you live elsewhere) and we'll put you on our mailing list.

Dept EP, Penguin Books Ltd,
Harmondsworth, Middlesex

Note: *Penguinews* and *Penguins in Print* are not available in the U.S.A. or Canada

Because They're Black

Derek Humphry and Gus John

Because They're Black, first published as a Penguin Special, is the winner of the 1972 Martin Luther King Memorial Prize. Its two authors (one of them is a black social worker and the author of the Handsworth report) have managed to get black people in England to 'tell it like it is'. The major part of their book, which the *Tribune* called 'admirable', describes in detail, through individual case histories, what it feels like to be on the receiving end of discrimination in our society.

The authors then examine the way out. Integration is discussed and shown for what it is: the desire to convert black men into white men. Black power, different in kind from its U.S. counterpart but equally strong, is seen as a humanizing necessity for black and white alike; and political conflict and struggle are essential if we are to change ourselves and our society. As the *Guardian* wrote: 'It is an exhilarating development, and this pugnacious little book will speed it along.'

Racial Discrimination in England

W. W. Daniel

This book is based on an authoritative report which assessed the extent of discrimination against Commonwealth immigrants in Britain and was published by PEP in 1967. The report received enormous and controversial press coverage, both because of the subject matter and because of the thoroughness and objectivity of the survey.

As written up by W. W. Daniel, the contents of the report make an important, readable, and (in the post-Powell era) timely book on a subject which is of concern to everyone.

'The report topples myth after popular myth on colour and immigration like a fast bowl hitting ten-pins . . . A coloured man will need this book to use as a scourge for the white liberal conscience. And a white man will need it to immunize himself from the virus of discrimination which is now more widespread than most Britons would dare to admit publicly.' – Dilip Hiro in *The Times*

a Pelican Original